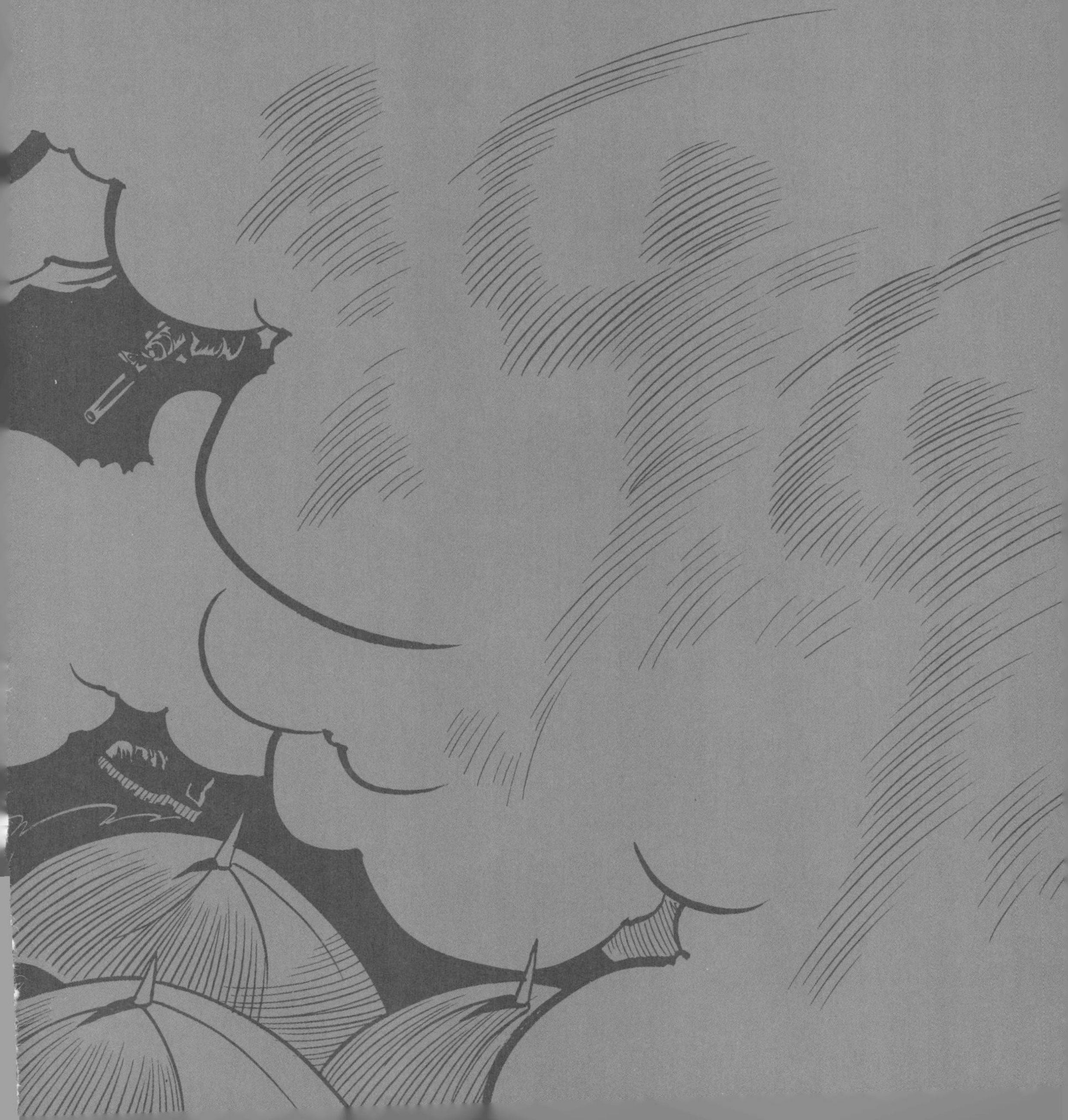

SAVE IT FOR LATER

PROMISES, PARENTHOOD, AND THE URGENCY OF PROTEST

by NATE POWELL

ABRAMS COMICARTS, NEW YORK

Editor: Charlotte Greenbaum
Designer: Charice Silverman
Managing Editor: Mary O'Mara
Production Manager: Alison Gervais

Cataloging-in-Publication Data has been applied for and may be obtained from the Library of Congress.

ISBN 978-1-4197-4912-4

Copyright © 2021 Nate Powell
Excerpt from "Tornado Children" © 2005 Art Middleton and Gus Martin

Published in 2021 by Abrams ComicArts®, an imprint of ABRAMS. All rights reserved. No portion of this book may be reproduced, stored in a retrieval system, or transmitted in any form or by any means, mechanical, electronic, photocopying, recording, or otherwise, without written permission from the publisher.

Printed and bound in the United States
10 9 8 7 6 5 4 3 2 1

Abrams ComicArts books are available at special discounts when purchased in quantity for premiums and promotions as well as fundraising or educational use. Special editions can also be created to specification. For details, contact specialsales@abramsbooks.com or the address below.

Abrams ComicArts® is a registered trademark of Harry N. Abrams, Inc.

ABRAMS The Art of Books
195 Broadway, New York, NY 10007
abramsbooks.com

"Grown to be tornado children
  beating thunder drums
to fill the air with their sound
  in the concave of the room
and the echoes of young storms
  bearing tornado shoulders—

No longer sons and daughters,
but weathered by their fight—

Thrown from anger tornadoes
  into the strong suns
   after storms."

—Tiny Hawks, "Tornado Children"
   from PEOPLE WITHOUT END LP, 2005

DEDICATED TO

JOHN LEWIS
(1940-2020)

AND TO REVOLUTIONS
STILL INCOMPLETE
♡

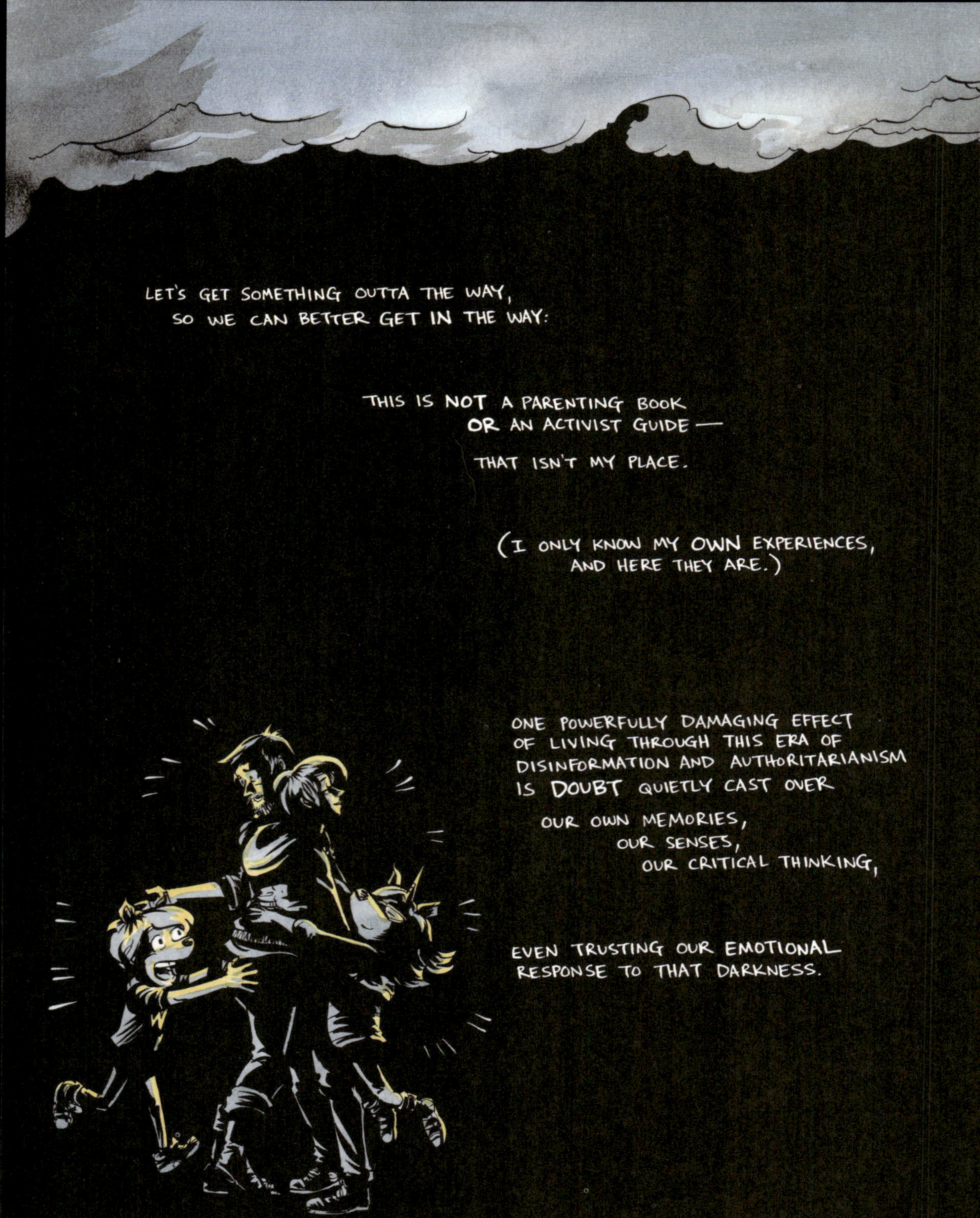
LET'S GET SOMETHING OUTTA THE WAY, SO WE CAN BETTER GET IN THE WAY:
THIS IS NOT A PARENTING BOOK OR AN ACTIVIST GUIDE—
THAT ISN'T MY PLACE.
(I ONLY KNOW MY OWN EXPERIENCES, AND HERE THEY ARE.)
ONE POWERFULLY DAMAGING EFFECT OF LIVING THROUGH THIS ERA OF DISINFORMATION AND AUTHORITARIANISM IS DOUBT QUIETLY CAST OVER
OUR OWN MEMORIES,
OUR SENSES,
OUR CRITICAL THINKING,
EVEN TRUSTING OUR EMOTIONAL RESPONSE TO THAT DARKNESS.

YOU'RE NOT ALONE.

NONE OF US ARE.

MY FAMILY'S EXPERIENCE LIKELY ECHOES SOME OF YOURS.

HERE'S TO LOOKING OUT FOR EACH OTHER,
TO STAYING LOUD,

TO THE PROMISE OF A FUTURE IN WHICH WE STILL POSSESS

OUR VOICES,
OUR VOTE,
OUR SELF-DETERMINATION.

THAT'S WHY WE'RE STILL HERE,
SAVING IT ALL FOR LATER.

(REMEMBER?)

REMEMBER.

♡ N.P.

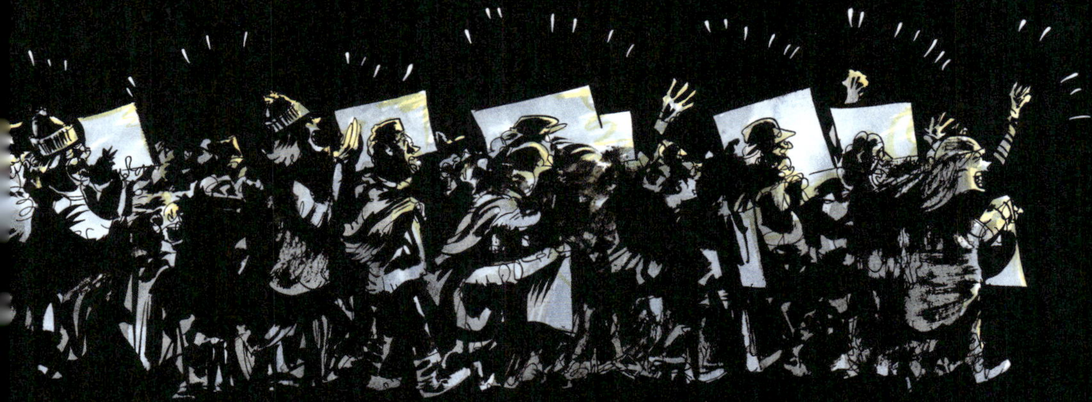

1
BUTTERED NOODLES

NOVEMBER 9, 2016

THE DAY AFTER

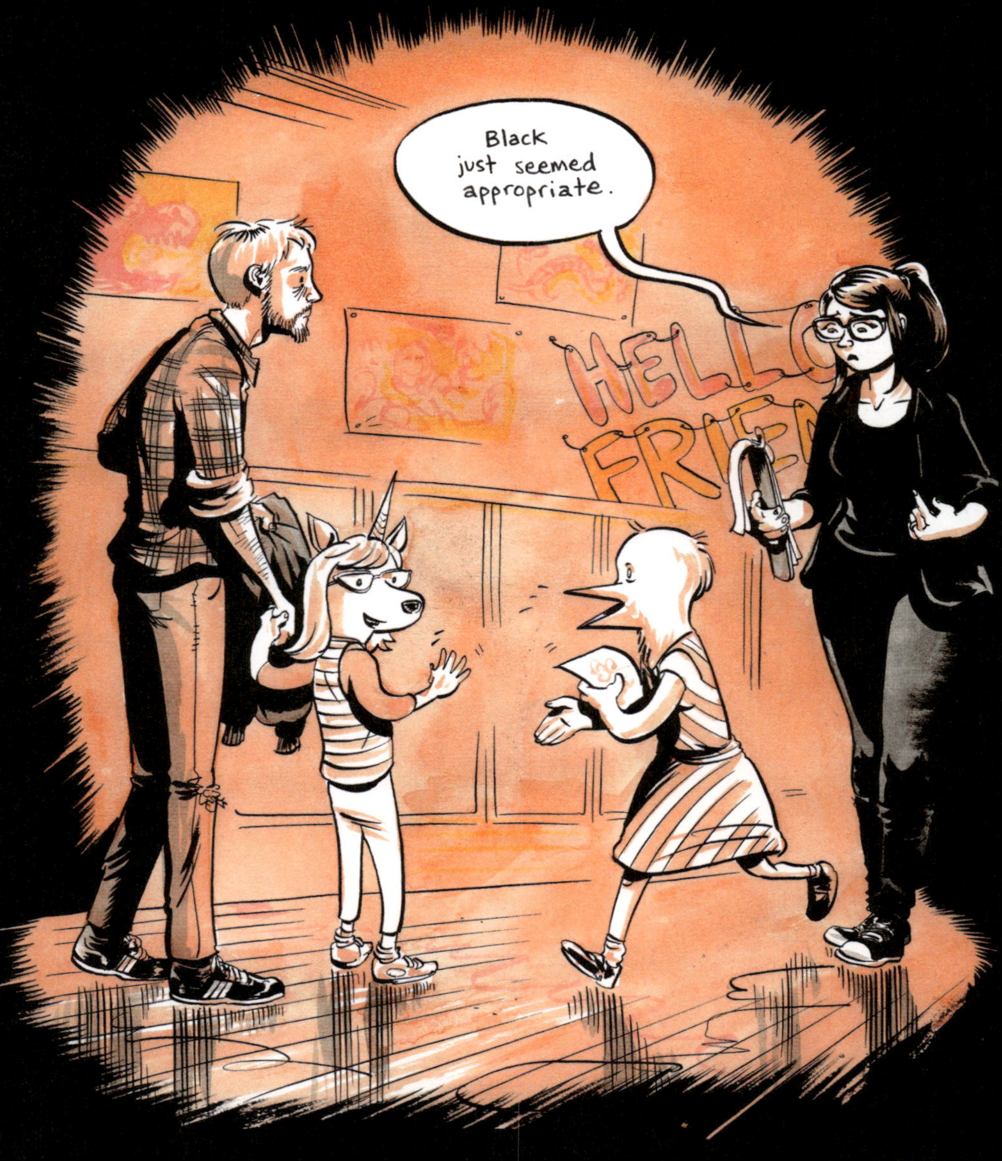
Black just seemed appropriate.

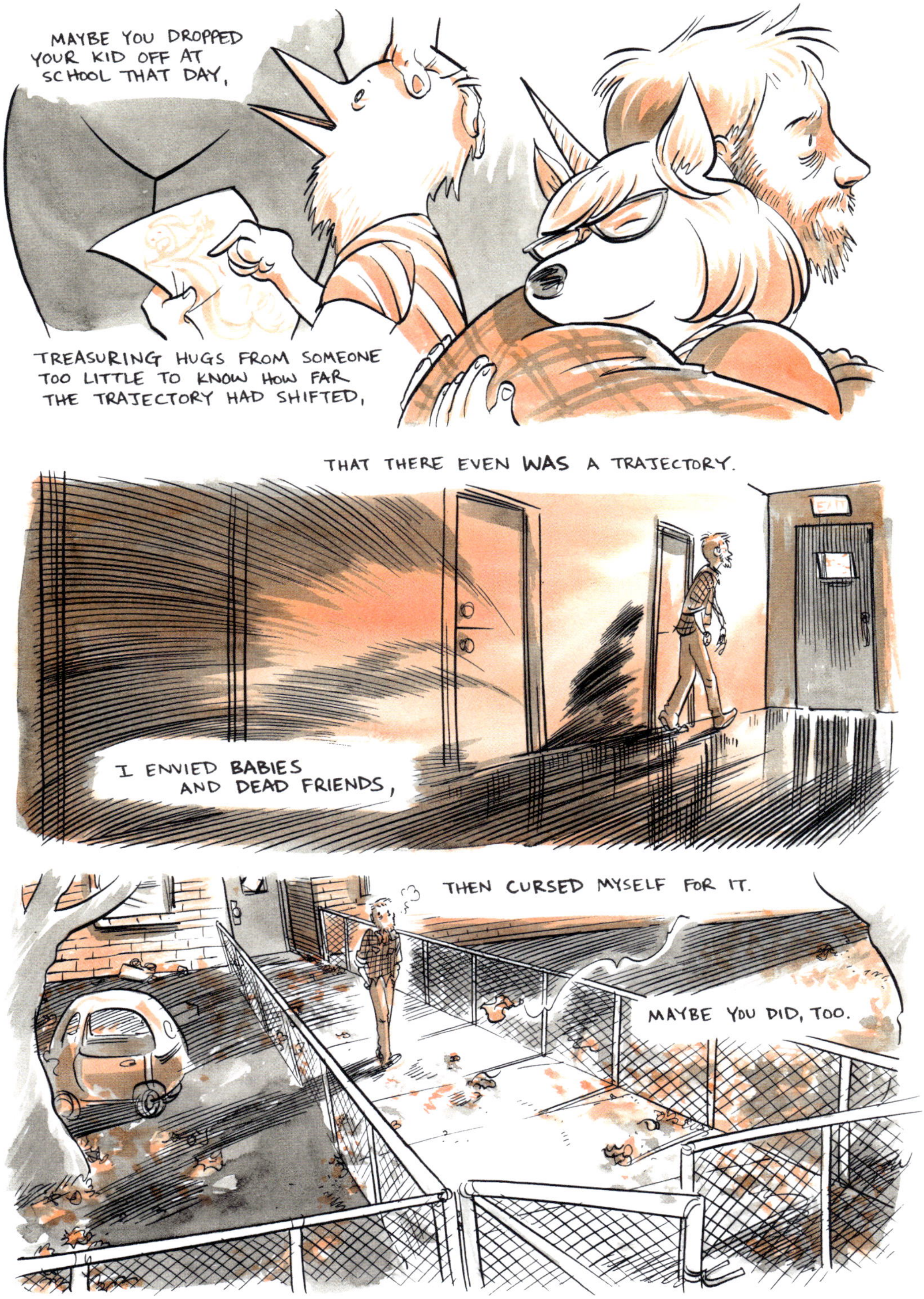
MAYBE YOU DROPPED YOUR KID OFF AT SCHOOL THAT DAY,
TREASURING HUGS FROM SOMEONE TOO LITTLE TO KNOW HOW FAR THE TRAJECTORY HAD SHIFTED,
THAT THERE EVEN WAS A TRAJECTORY.
I ENVIED BABIES AND DEAD FRIENDS,
THEN CURSED MYSELF FOR IT.
MAYBE YOU DID, TOO.

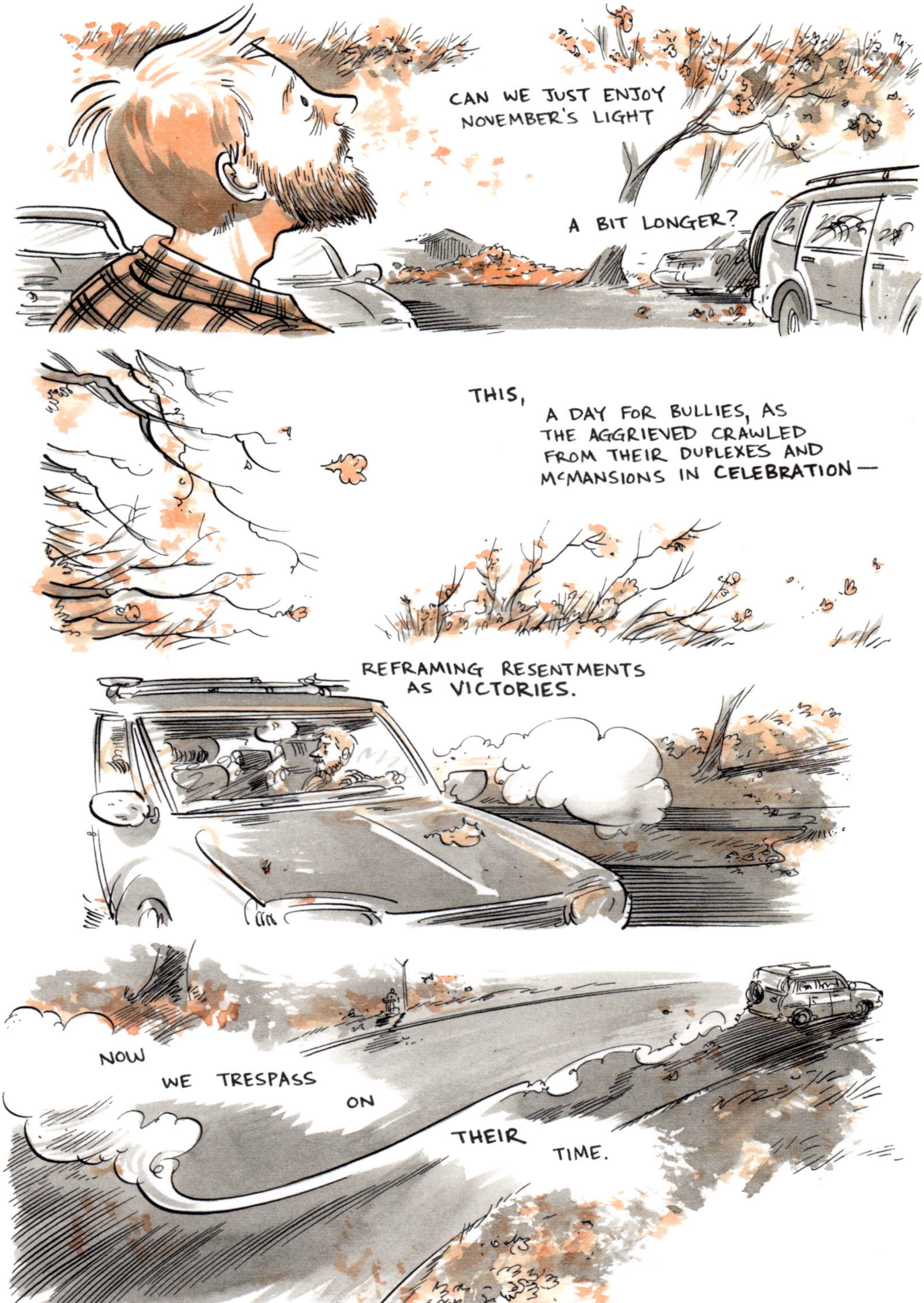
CAN WE JUST ENJOY NOVEMBER'S LIGHT
A BIT LONGER?
THIS,
A DAY FOR BULLIES, AS THE AGGRIEVED CRAWLED FROM THEIR DUPLEXES AND McMANSIONS IN CELEBRATION—
REFRAMING RESENTMENTS AS VICTORIES.
NOW
WE TRESPASS
ON
THEIR
TIME.

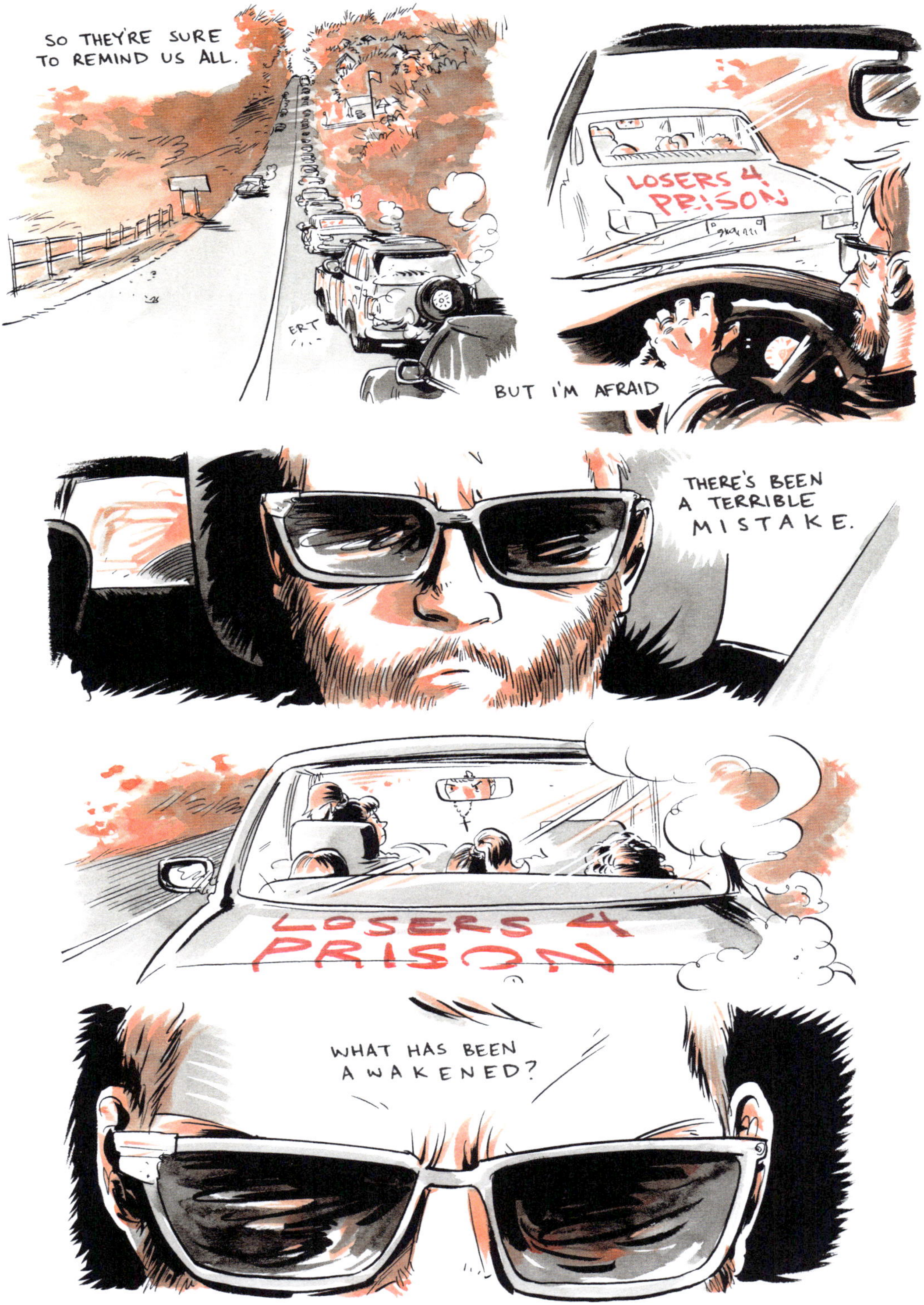
SO THEY'RE SURE TO REMIND US ALL.
ERT
LOSERS 4 PRISON
BUT I'M AFRAID
THERE'S BEEN A TERRIBLE MISTAKE.
LOSERS 4 PRISON
WHAT HAS BEEN AWAKENED?

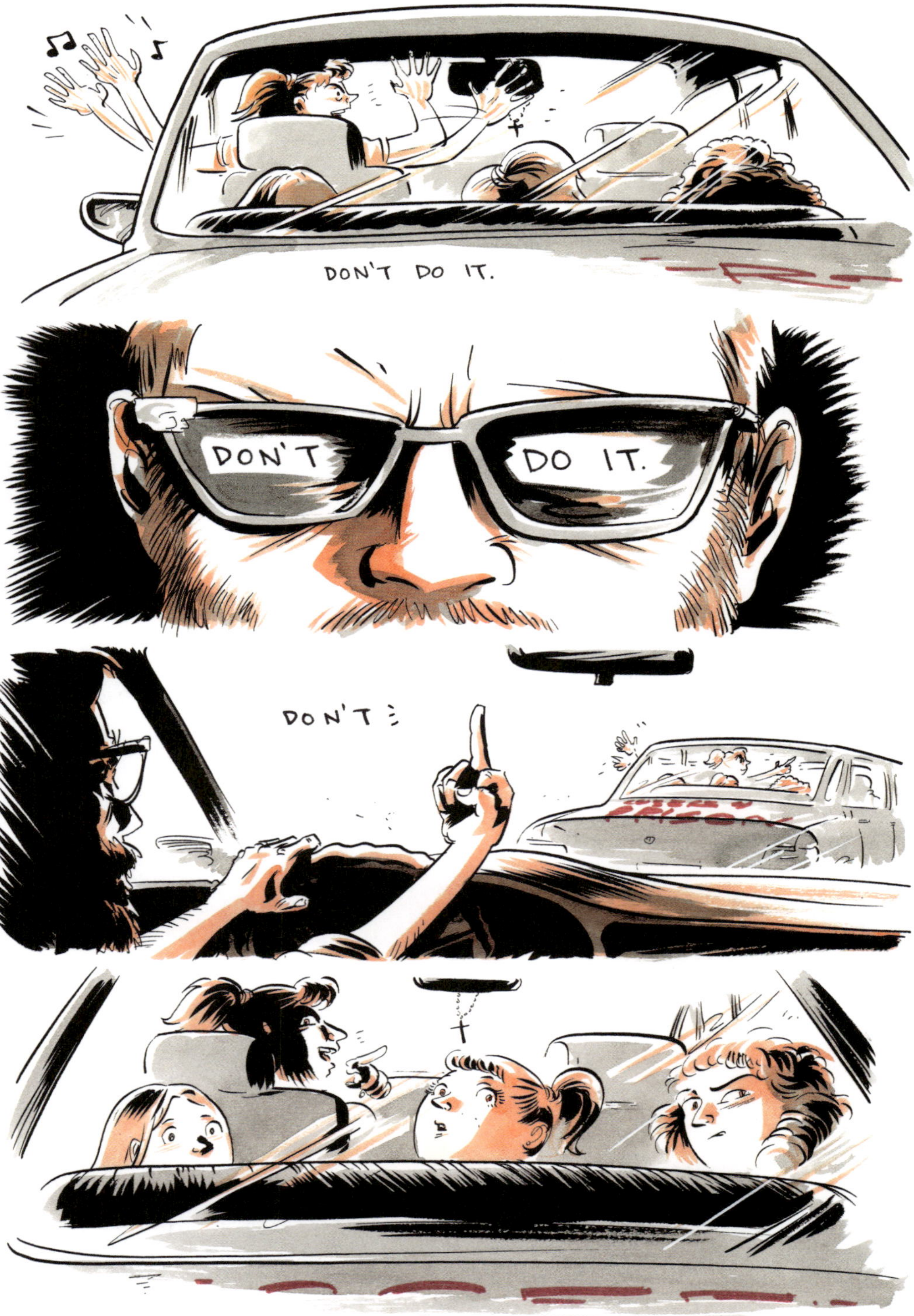
DON'T DO IT.
DON'T
DO IT.
DON'T

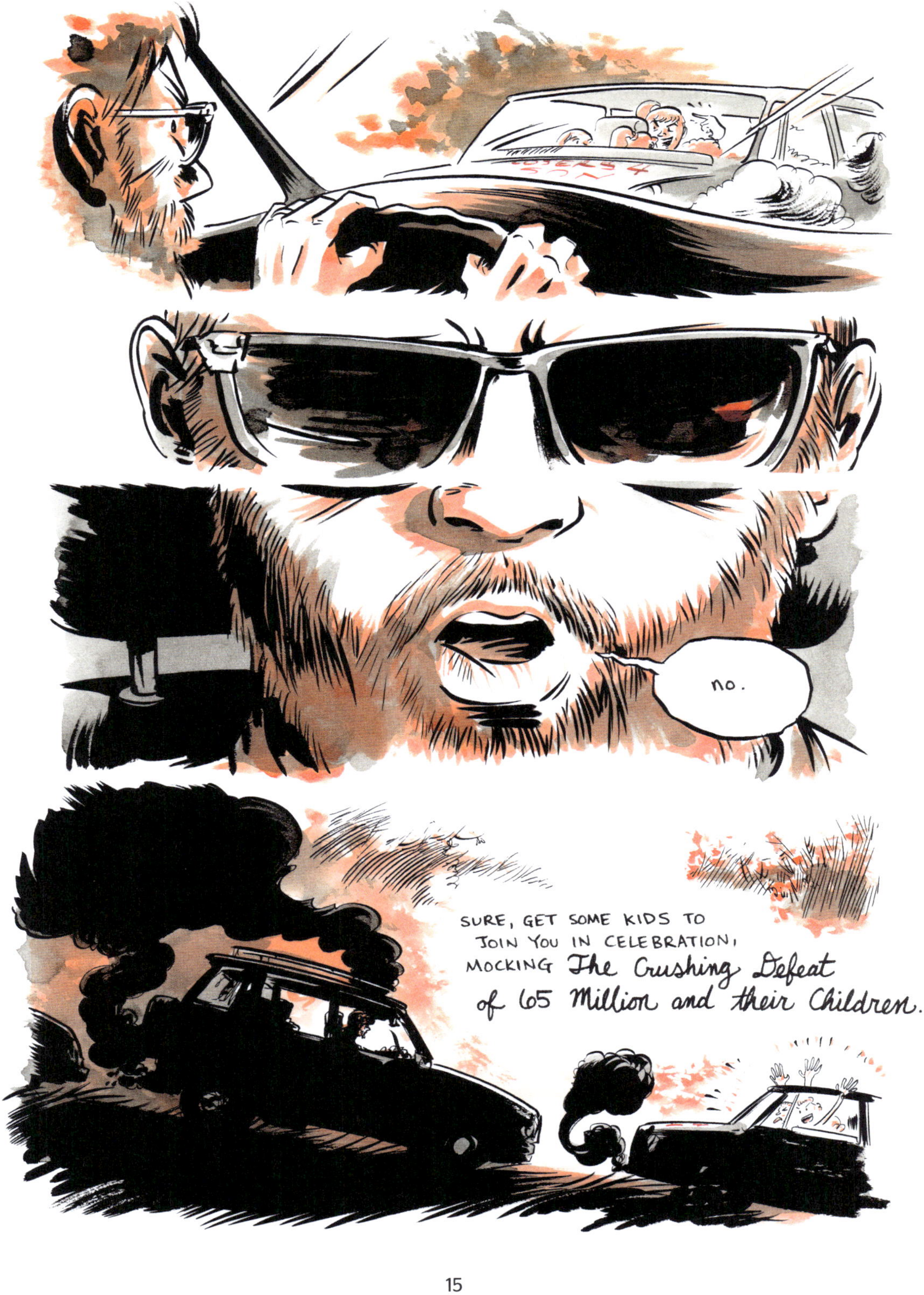
no.
SURE, GET SOME KIDS TO JOIN YOU IN CELEBRATION, MOCKING The Crushing Defeat of 65 Million and their Children.

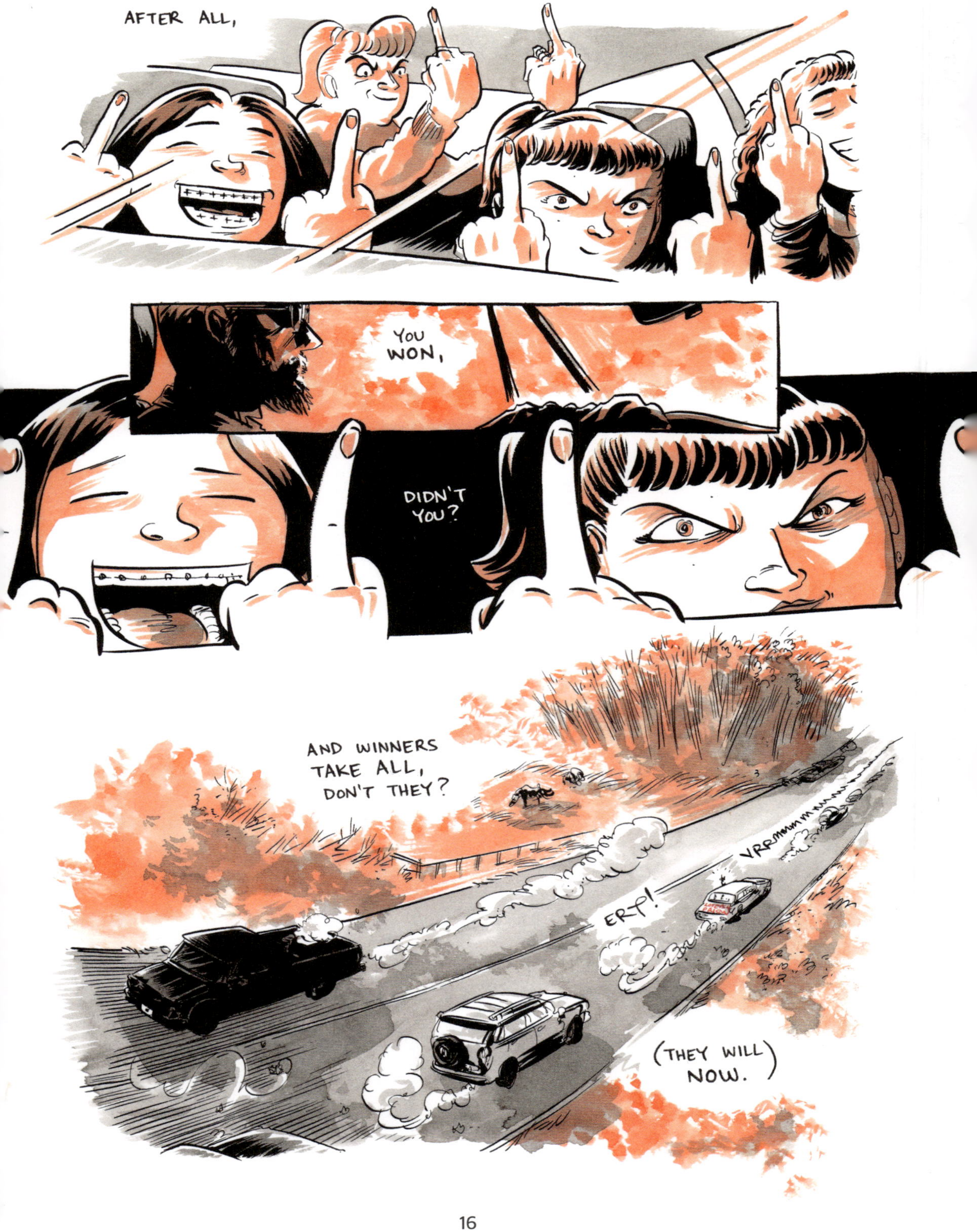
AFTER ALL,
YOU WON,
DIDN'T YOU?
AND WINNERS TAKE ALL, DON'T THEY?
ERT!
(THEY WILL NOW.)

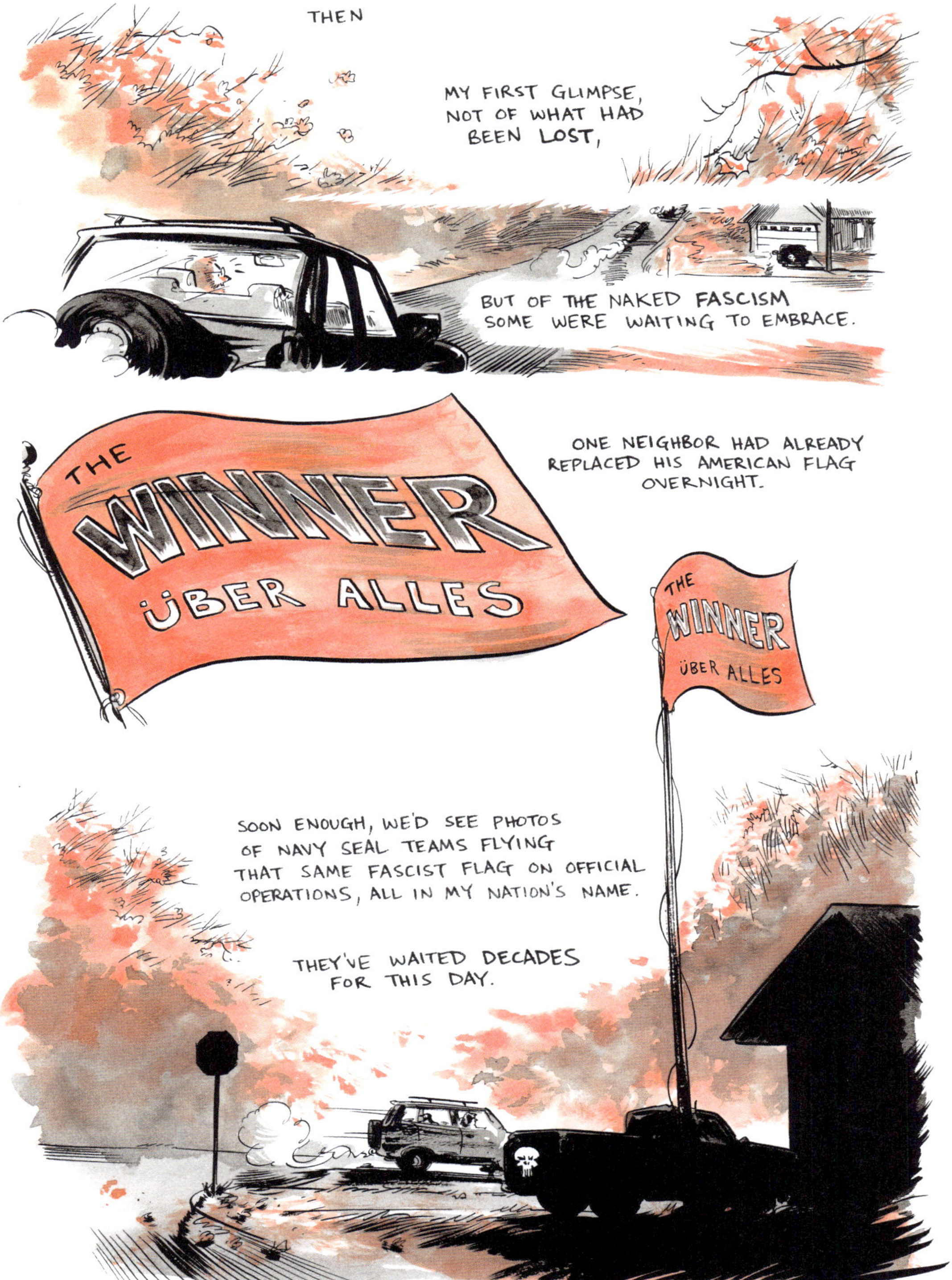
THEN
MY FIRST GLIMPSE, NOT OF WHAT HAD BEEN LOST,
BUT OF THE NAKED FASCISM SOME WERE WAITING TO EMBRACE.
THE WINNER ÜBER ALLES
ONE NEIGHBOR HAD ALREADY REPLACED HIS AMERICAN FLAG OVERNIGHT.
THE WINNER ÜBER ALLES
SOON ENOUGH, WE'D SEE PHOTOS OF NAVY SEAL TEAMS FLYING THAT SAME FASCIST FLAG ON OFFICIAL OPERATIONS, ALL IN MY NATION'S NAME.
THEY'VE WAITED DECADES FOR THIS DAY.

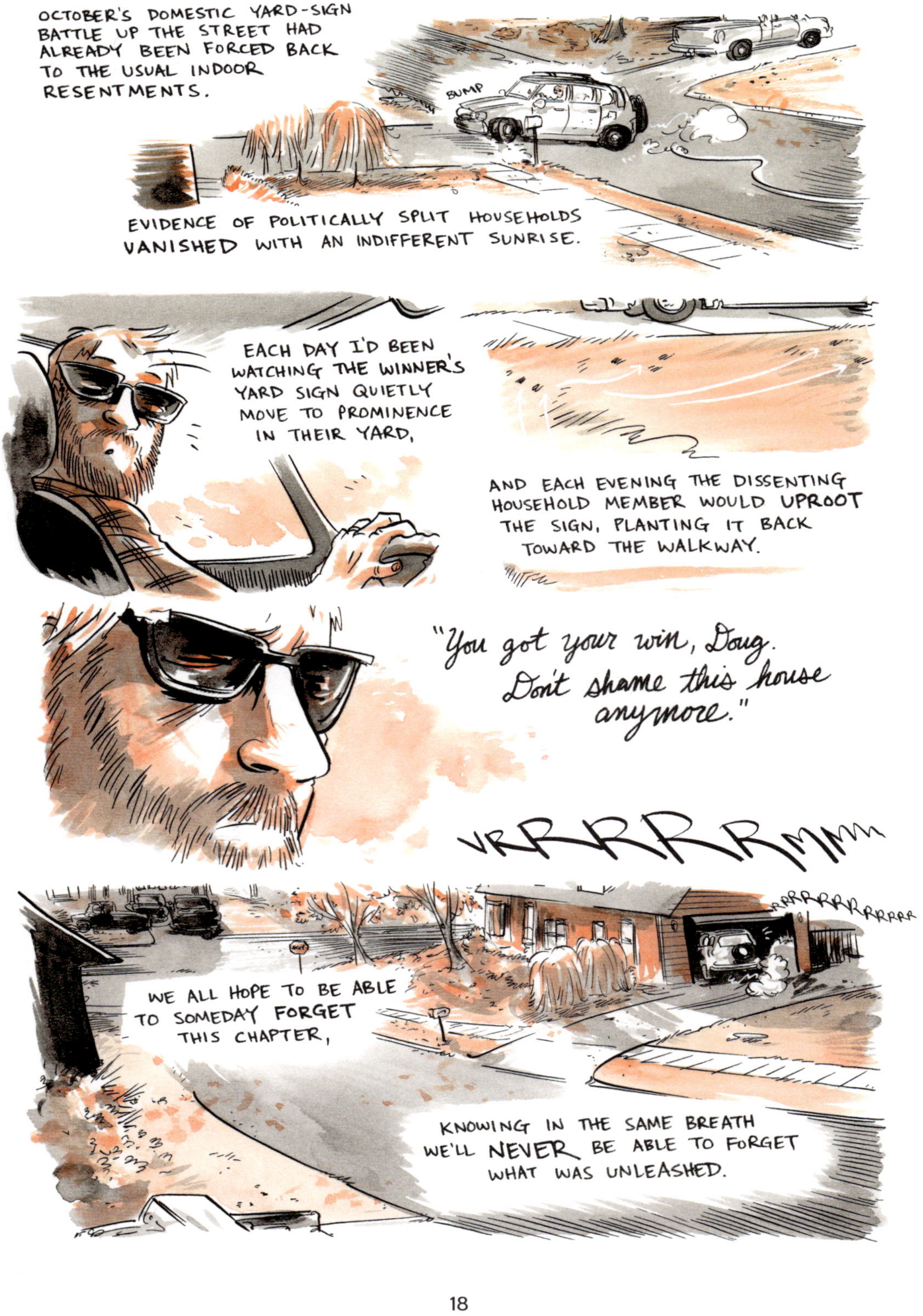
OCTOBER'S DOMESTIC YARD-SIGN BATTLE UP THE STREET HAD ALREADY BEEN FORCED BACK TO THE USUAL INDOOR RESENTMENTS.
BUMP
EVIDENCE OF POLITICALLY SPLIT HOUSEHOLDS VANISHED WITH AN INDIFFERENT SUNRISE.
EACH DAY I'D BEEN WATCHING THE WINNER'S YARD SIGN QUIETLY MOVE TO PROMINENCE IN THEIR YARD,
AND EACH EVENING THE DISSENTING HOUSEHOLD MEMBER WOULD UPROOT THE SIGN, PLANTING IT BACK TOWARD THE WALKWAY.
"You got your win, Doug. Don't shame this house anymore."
VRRRRRRMMM
RRRRRRRRrrrrr
WE ALL HOPE TO BE ABLE TO SOMEDAY FORGET THIS CHAPTER,
KNOWING IN THE SAME BREATH WE'LL NEVER BE ABLE TO FORGET WHAT WAS UNLEASHED.

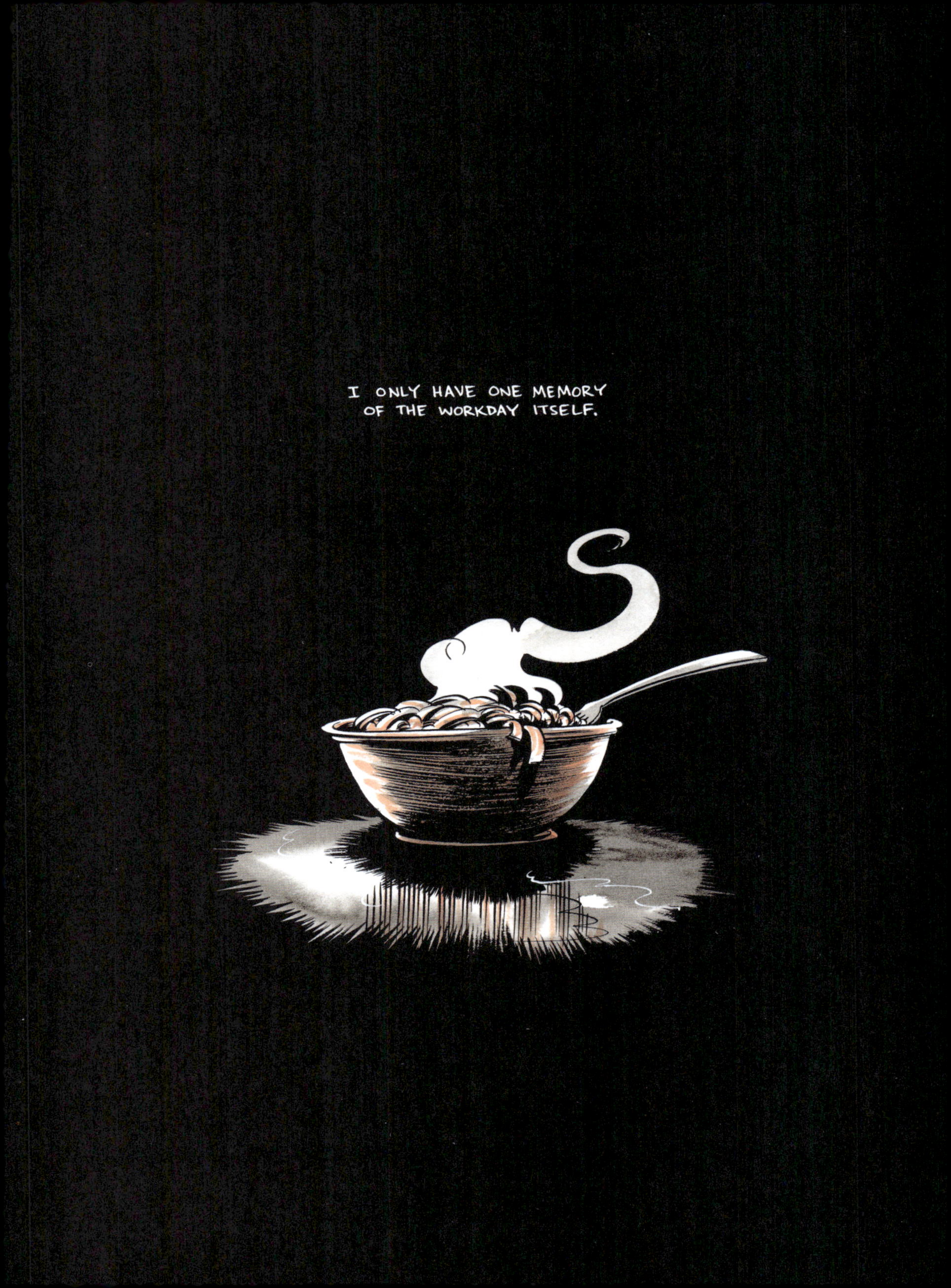
I ONLY HAVE ONE MEMORY
OF THE WORKDAY ITSELF.

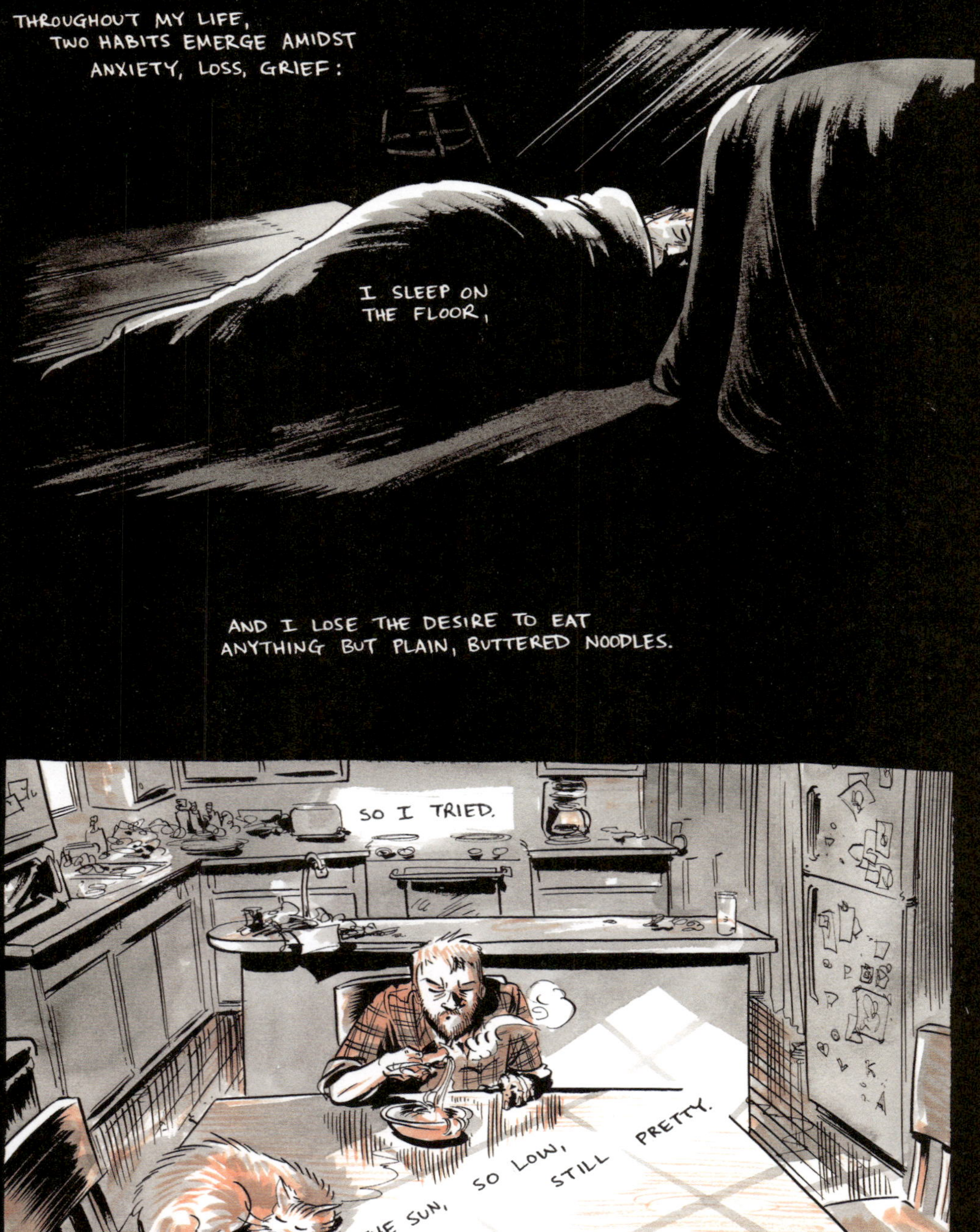
THROUGHOUT MY LIFE,
TWO HABITS EMERGE AMIDST
ANXIETY, LOSS, GRIEF:
I SLEEP ON THE FLOOR,
AND I LOSE THE DESIRE TO EAT
ANYTHING BUT PLAIN, BUTTERED NOODLES.
SO I TRIED.
THE SUN, SO LOW, STILL PRETTY.

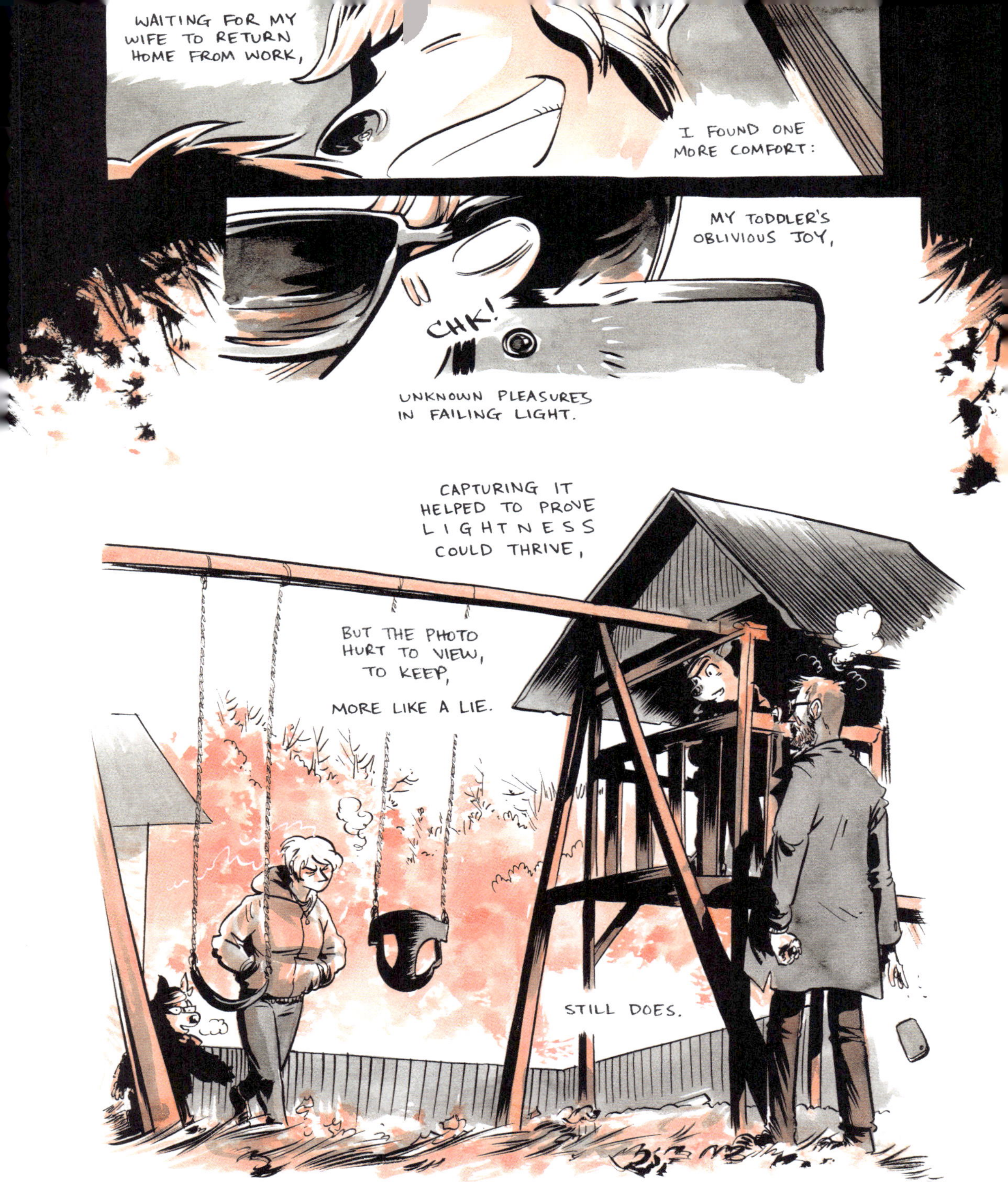
WAITING FOR MY WIFE TO RETURN HOME FROM WORK,
I FOUND ONE MORE COMFORT:
MY TODDLER'S OBLIVIOUS JOY,
CHK!
UNKNOWN PLEASURES IN FAILING LIGHT.
CAPTURING IT HELPED TO PROVE LIGHTNESS COULD THRIVE,
BUT THE PHOTO HURT TO VIEW, TO KEEP,
MORE LIKE A LIE.
STILL DOES.

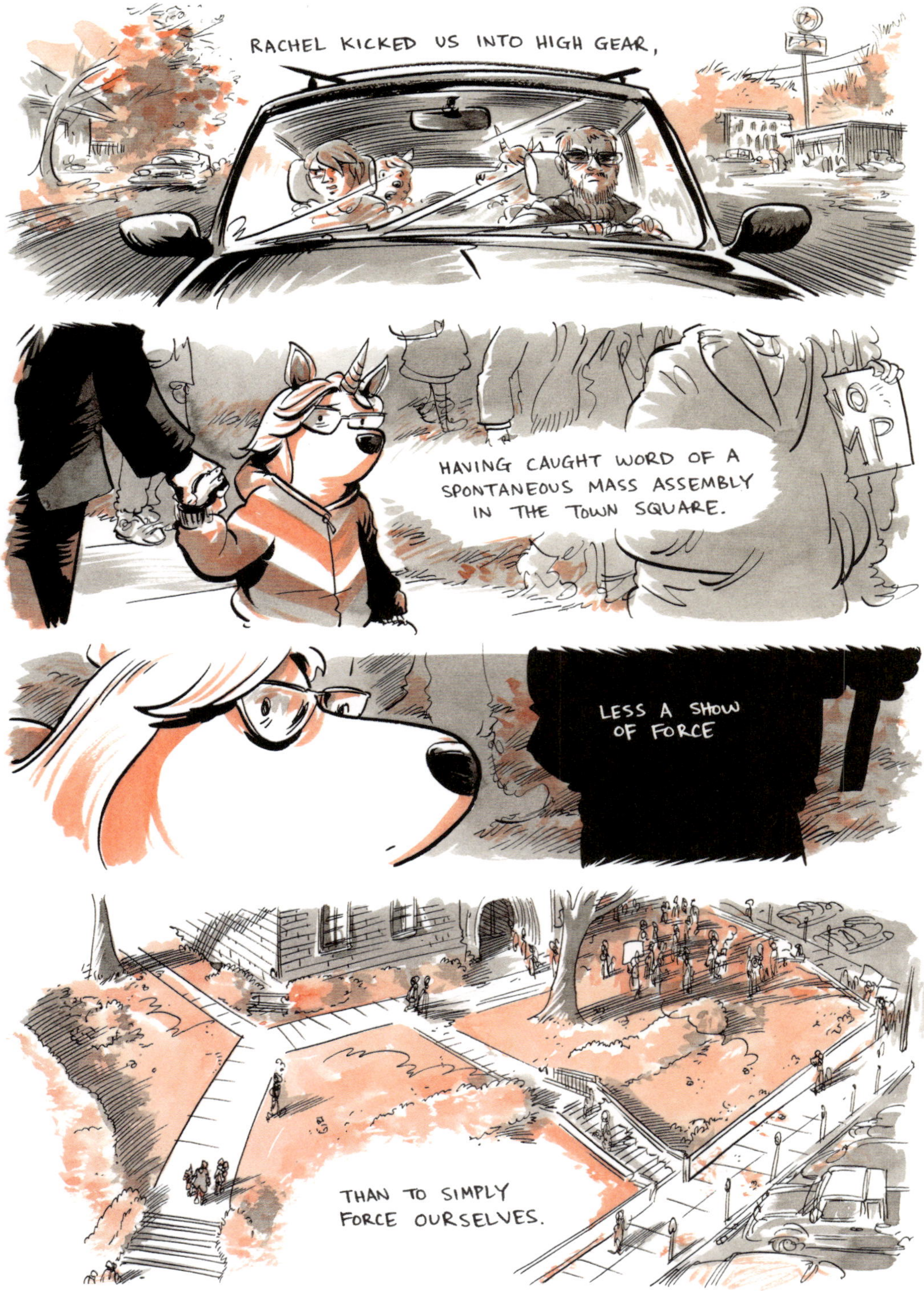
RACHEL KICKED US INTO HIGH GEAR,
HAVING CAUGHT WORD OF A SPONTANEOUS MASS ASSEMBLY IN THE TOWN SQUARE.
LESS A SHOW OF FORCE
THAN TO SIMPLY FORCE OURSELVES.

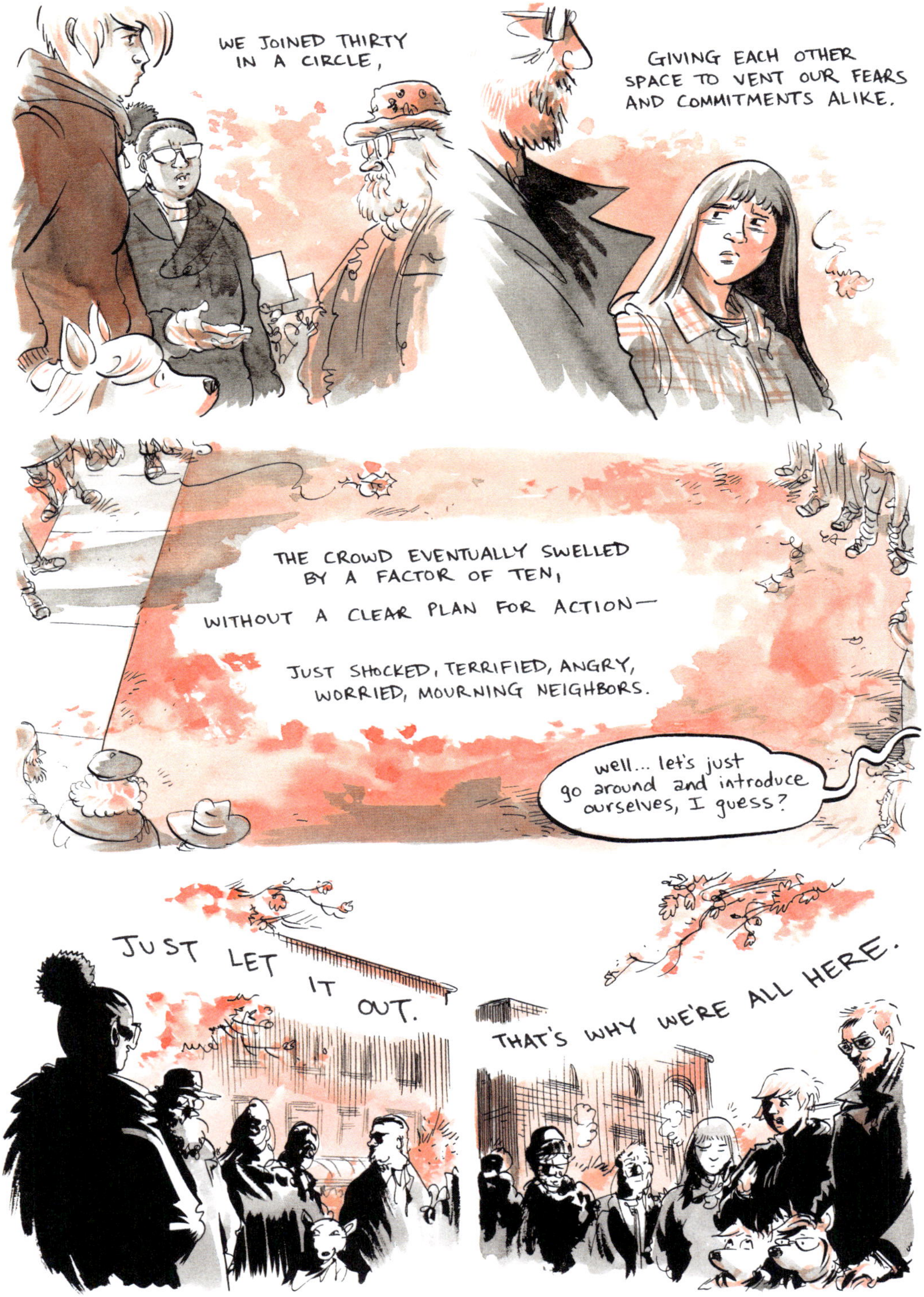
WE JOINED THIRTY IN A CIRCLE,
GIVING EACH OTHER SPACE TO VENT OUR FEARS AND COMMITMENTS ALIKE.
THE CROWD EVENTUALLY SWELLED BY A FACTOR OF TEN,
WITHOUT A CLEAR PLAN FOR ACTION—
JUST SHOCKED, TERRIFIED, ANGRY, WORRIED, MOURNING NEIGHBORS.
well... let's just go around and introduce ourselves, I guess?
JUST LET IT OUT.
THAT'S WHY WE'RE ALL HERE.

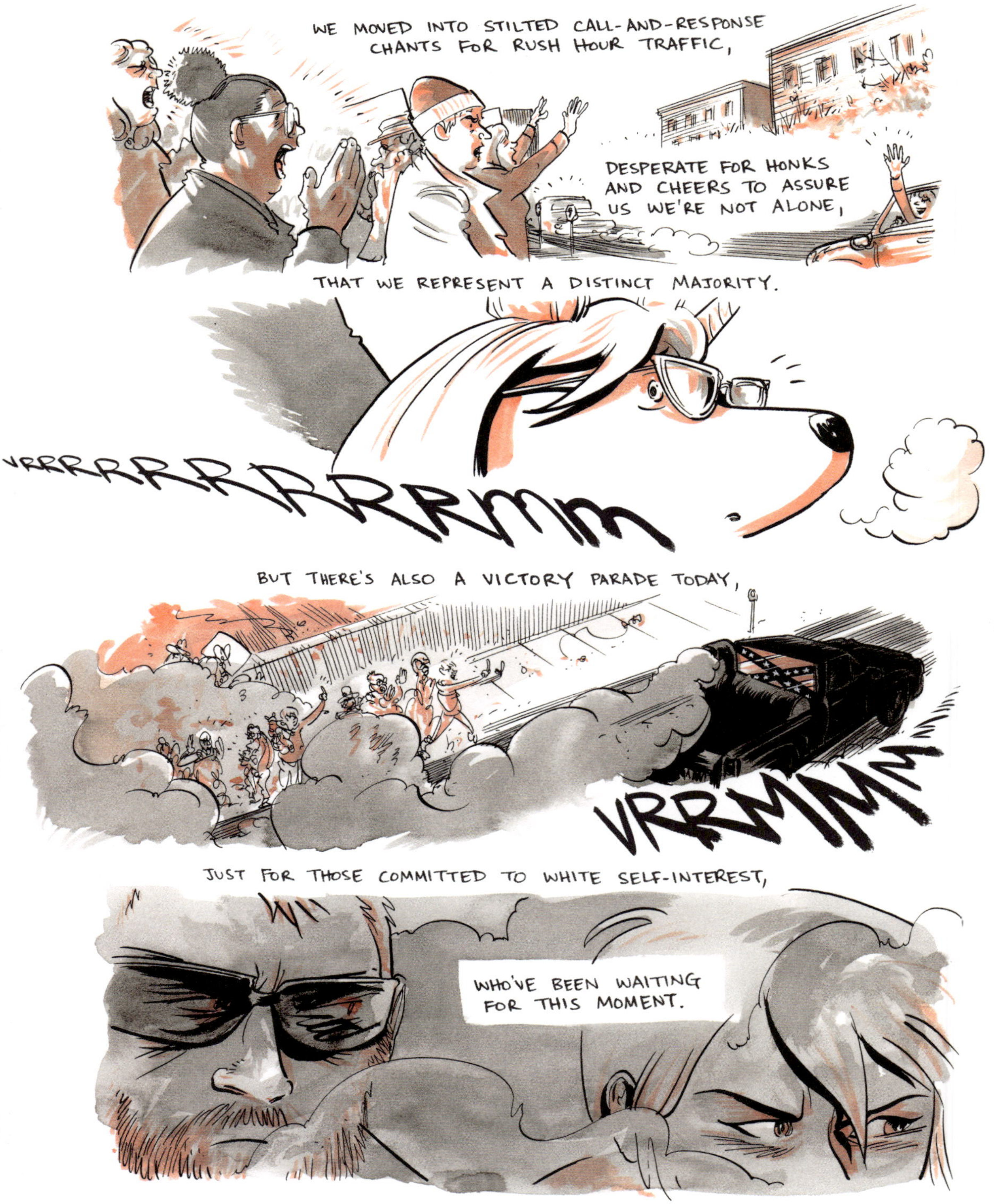
WE MOVED INTO STILTED CALL-AND-RESPONSE CHANTS FOR RUSH HOUR TRAFFIC,
DESPERATE FOR HONKS AND CHEERS TO ASSURE US WE'RE NOT ALONE,
THAT WE REPRESENT A DISTINCT MAJORITY.
VRRRRRRRRRRRMM
BUT THERE'S ALSO A VICTORY PARADE TODAY,
VRRMMM
JUST FOR THOSE COMMITTED TO WHITE SELF-INTEREST,
WHO'VE BEEN WAITING FOR THIS MOMENT.

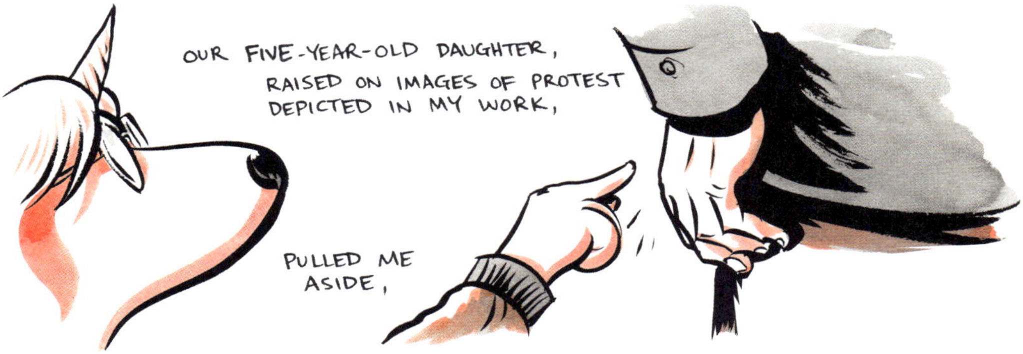
OUR FIVE-YEAR-OLD DAUGHTER,
RAISED ON IMAGES OF PROTEST DEPICTED IN MY WORK,
PULLED ME ASIDE,

DISAPPOINTED THAT NO ONE WAS MARCHING.

I EXPLAIN THAT SOMETIMES IT'S IMPORTANT TO BE AROUND OTHER PEOPLE WHO FEEL THE SAME WAY, EVEN WHEN THEY'RE STRANGERS.

ESPECIALLY WHEN THEY ARE.

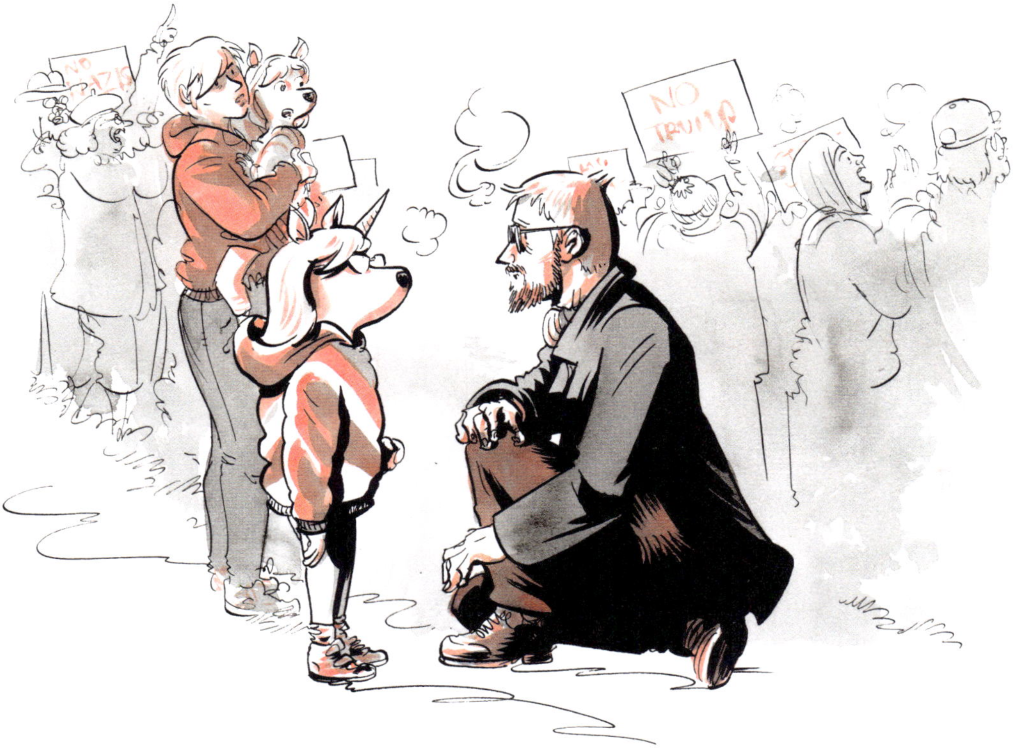
NO TRUMP

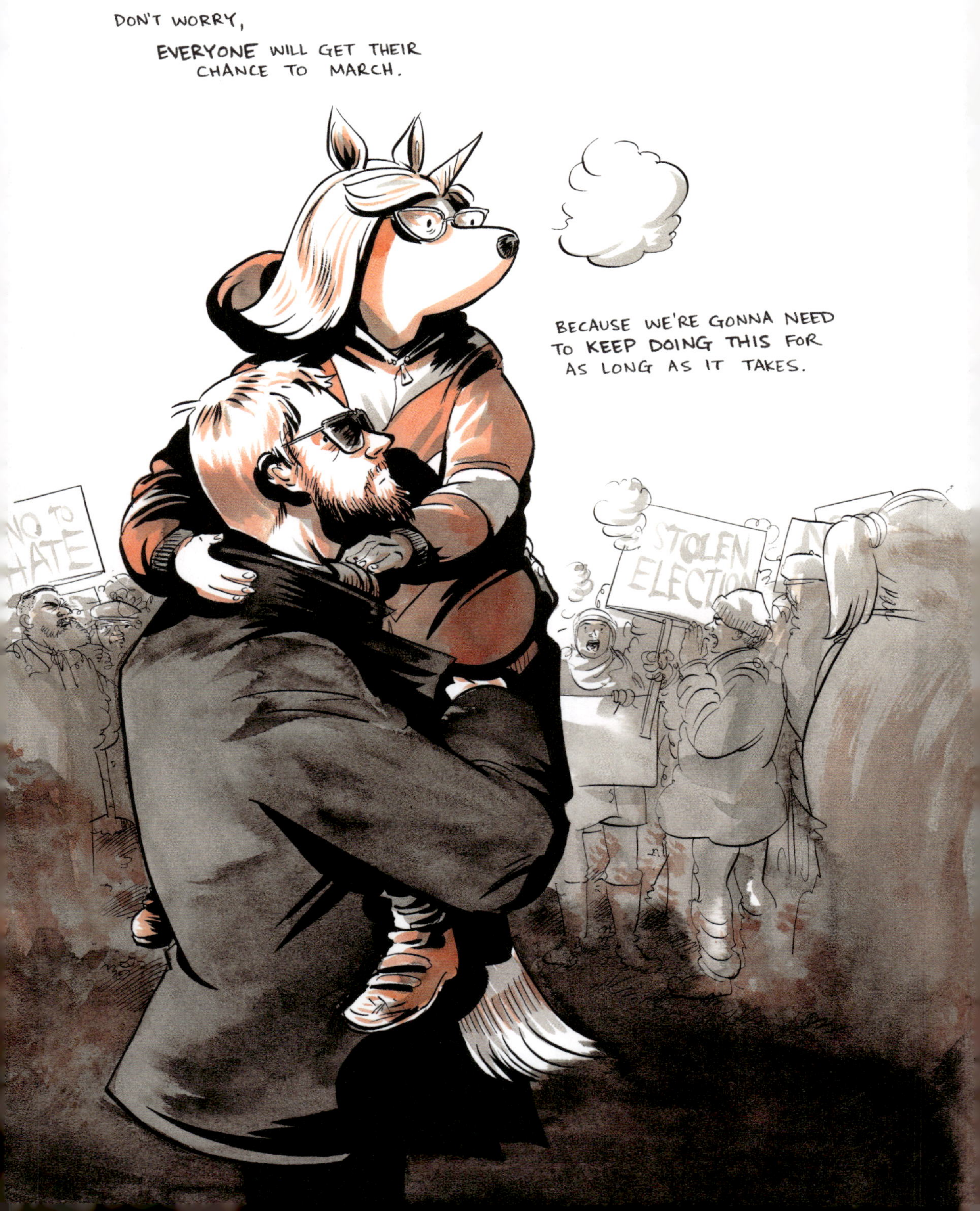
DON'T WORRY,
EVERYONE WILL GET THEIR CHANCE TO MARCH.
BECAUSE WE'RE GONNA NEED TO KEEP DOING THIS FOR AS LONG AS IT TAKES.
NO TO HATE
STOLEN ELECTION

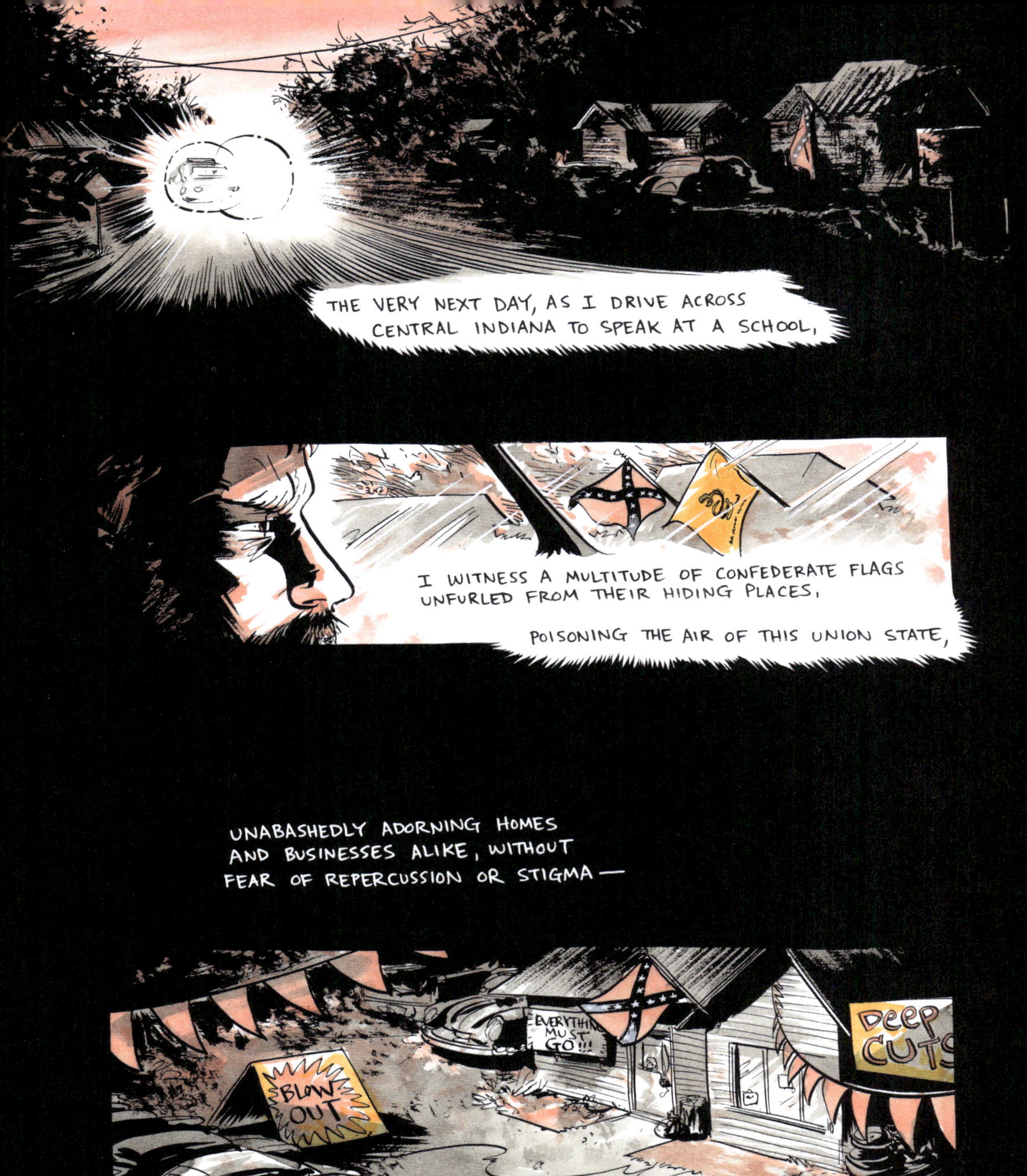
THE VERY NEXT DAY, AS I DRIVE ACROSS CENTRAL INDIANA TO SPEAK AT A SCHOOL,
I WITNESS A MULTITUDE OF CONFEDERATE FLAGS UNFURLED FROM THEIR HIDING PLACES,
POISONING THE AIR OF THIS UNION STATE,
UNABASHEDLY ADORNING HOMES AND BUSINESSES ALIKE, WITHOUT FEAR OF REPERCUSSION OR STIGMA—
MUST GO!!!
DEEP CUTS
BLOW OUT

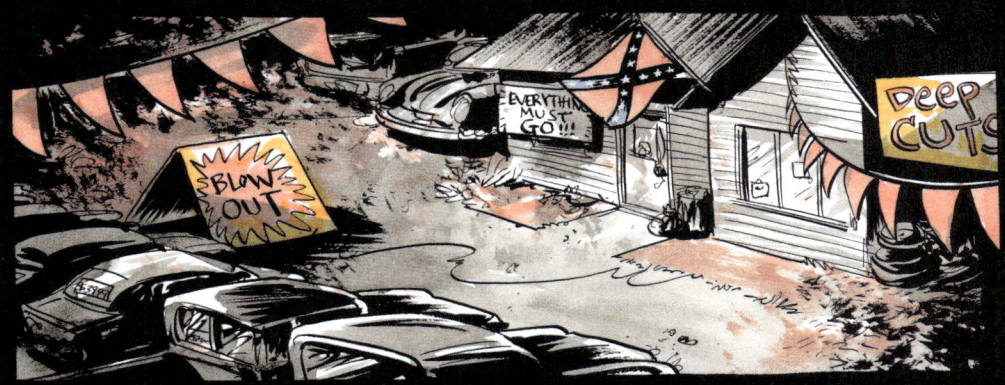

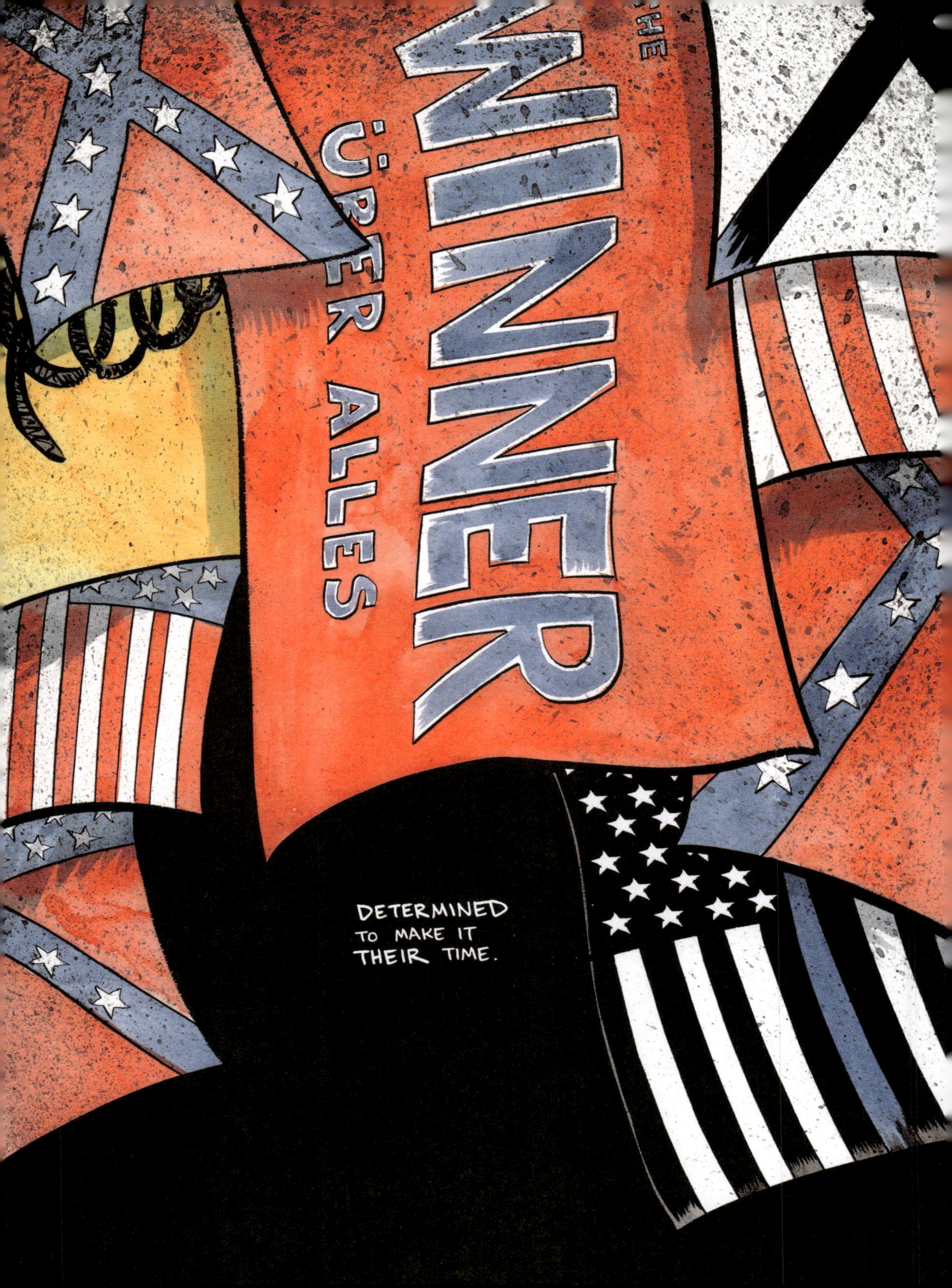
WINNER
ALLES
DETERMINED TO MAKE IT THEIR TIME.

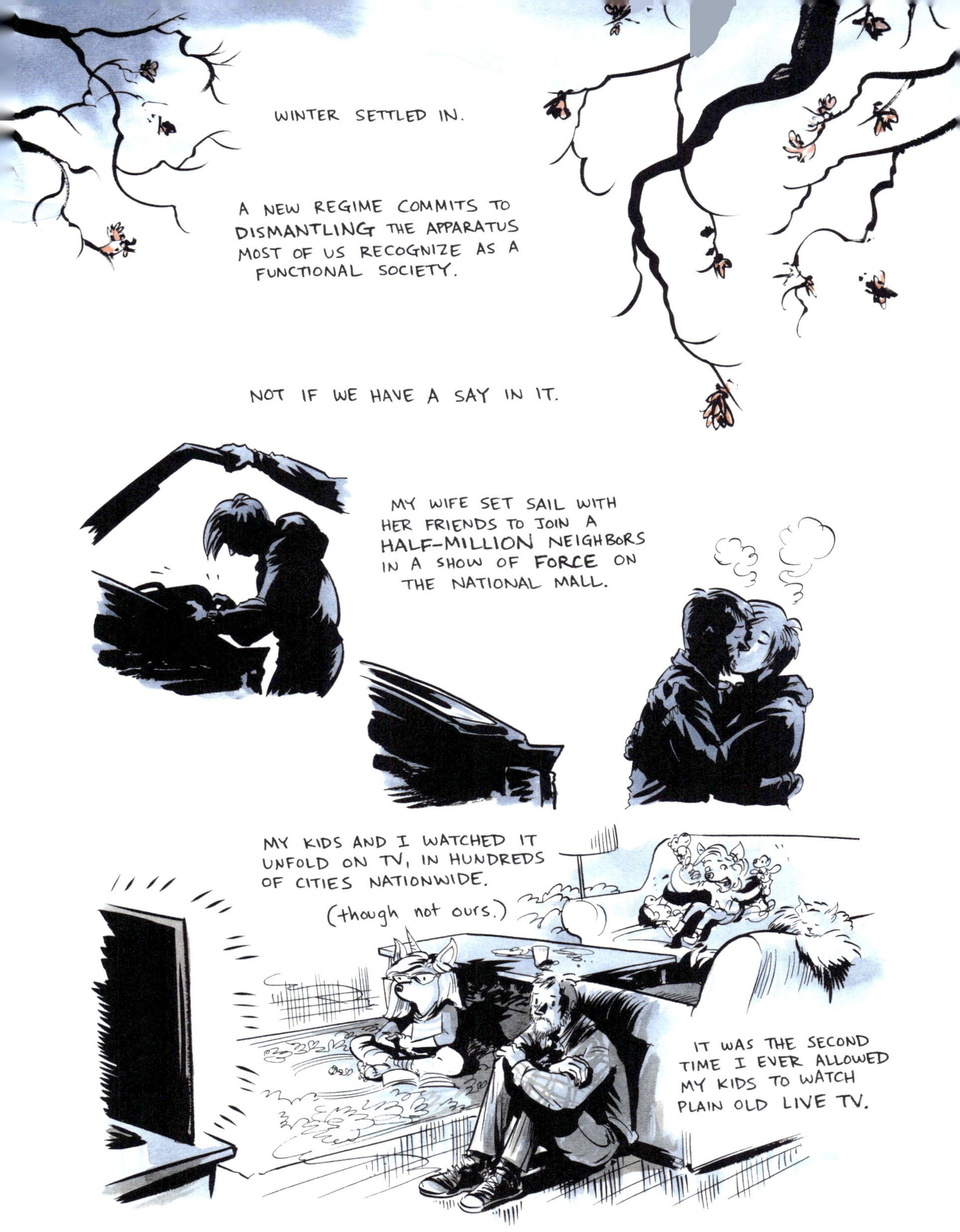
WINTER SETTLED IN.
A NEW REGIME COMMITS TO DISMANTLING THE APPARATUS MOST OF US RECOGNIZE AS A FUNCTIONAL SOCIETY.
NOT IF WE HAVE A SAY IN IT.
MY WIFE SET SAIL WITH HER FRIENDS TO JOIN A HALF-MILLION NEIGHBORS IN A SHOW OF FORCE ON THE NATIONAL MALL.
MY KIDS AND I WATCHED IT UNFOLD ON TV, IN HUNDREDS OF CITIES NATIONWIDE.
(though not ours.)
IT WAS THE SECOND TIME I EVER ALLOWED MY KIDS TO WATCH PLAIN OLD LIVE TV.

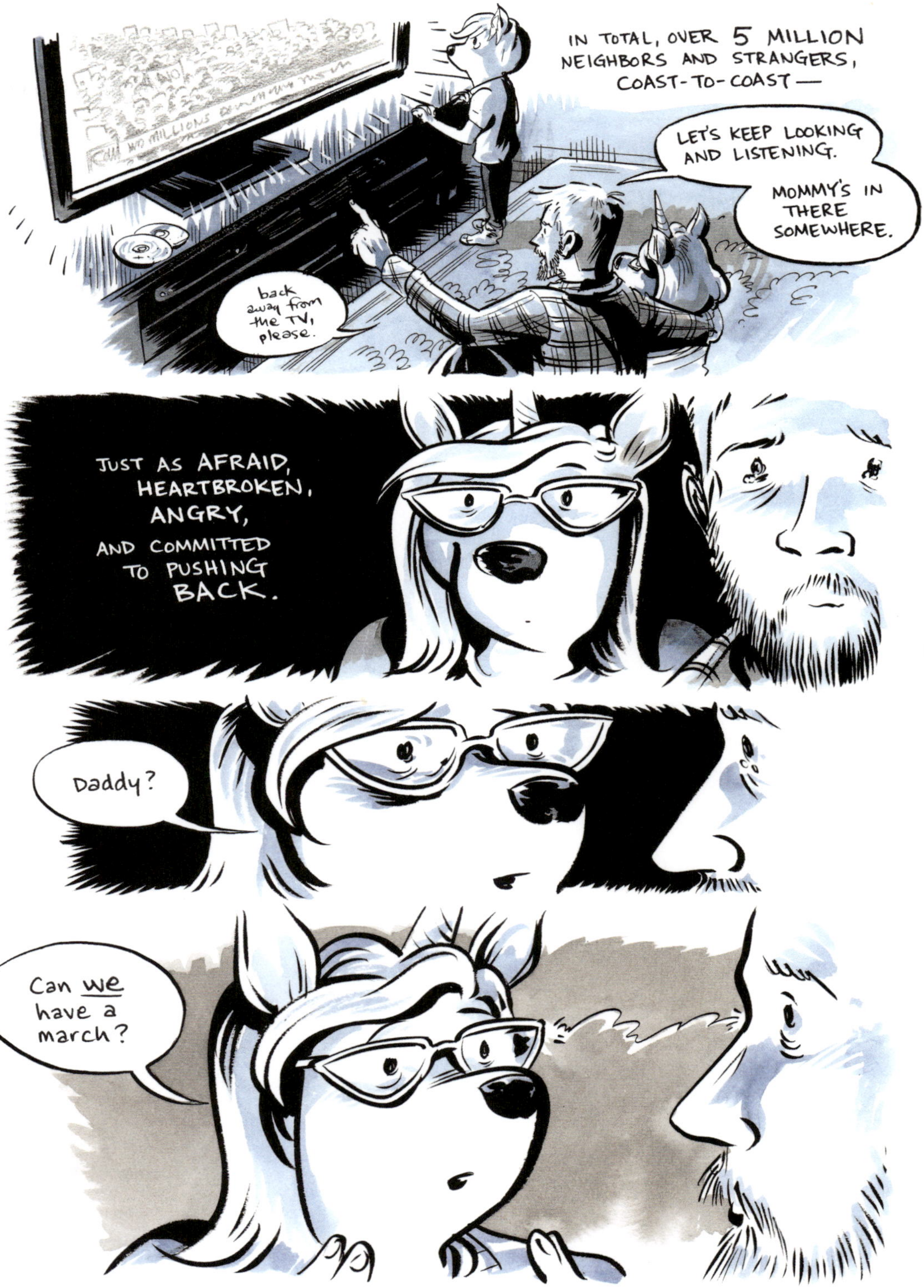

IN TOTAL, OVER 5 MILLION NEIGHBORS AND STRANGERS, COAST-TO-COAST—
LET'S KEEP LOOKING AND LISTENING.
MOMMY'S IN THERE SOMEWHERE.
back away from the TV, please.
JUST AS AFRAID, HEARTBROKEN, ANGRY, AND COMMITTED TO PUSHING BACK.
Daddy?
Can we have a march?

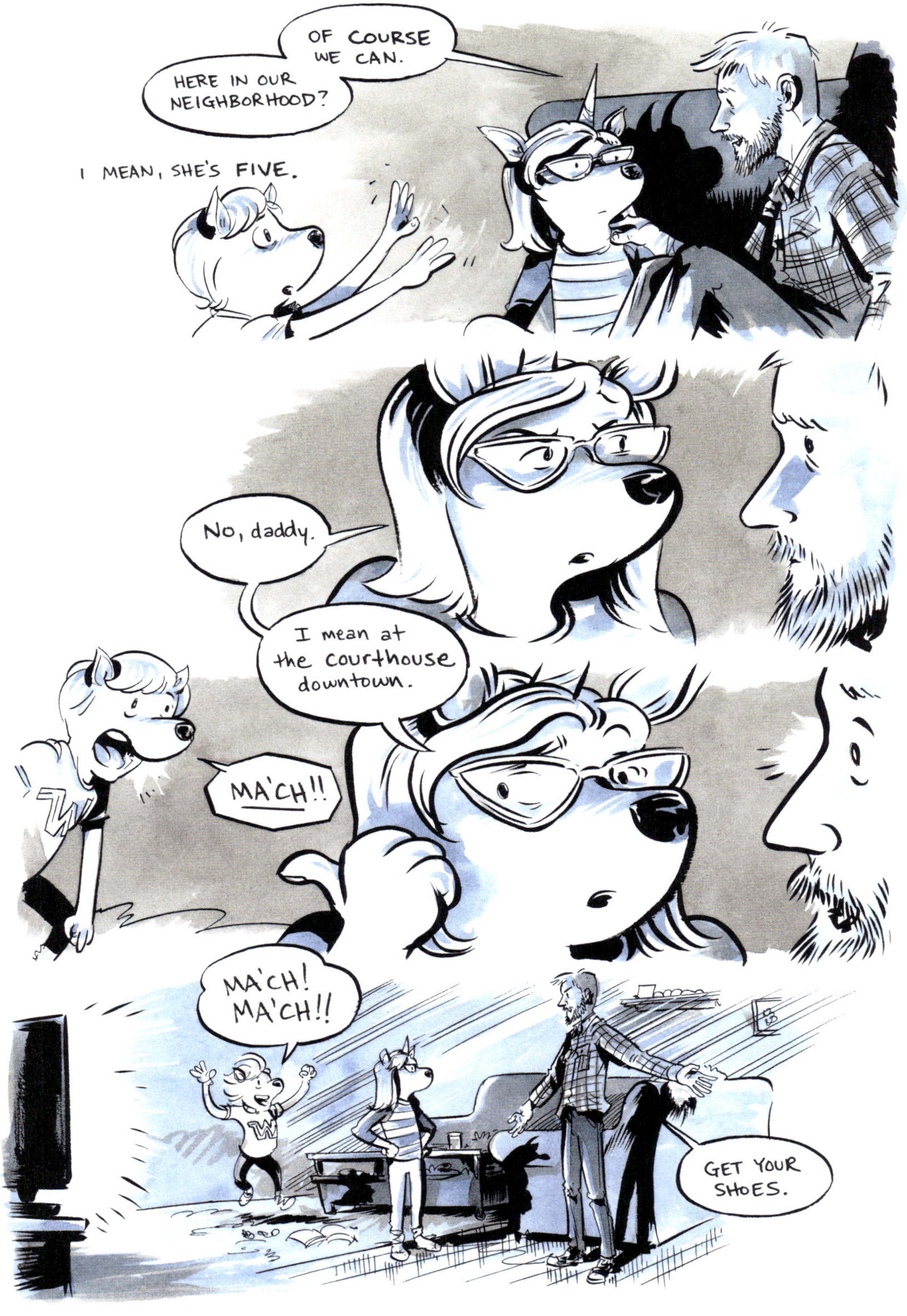
HERE IN OUR NEIGHBORHOOD?
OF COURSE WE CAN.
I MEAN, SHE'S FIVE.
No, daddy.
I mean at the courthouse downtown.
MA'CH!!
MA'CH! MA'CH!!
GET YOUR SHOES.

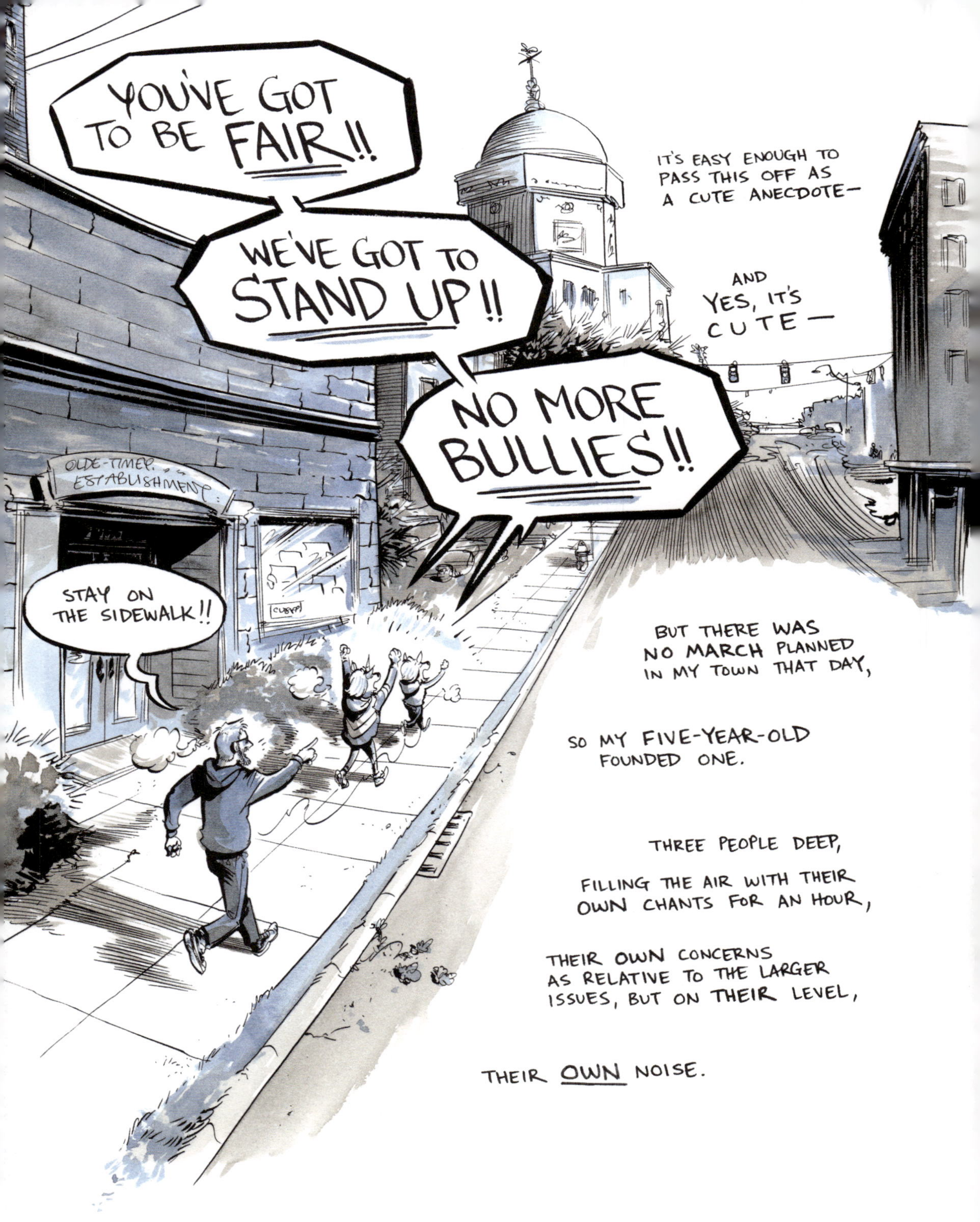
YOU'VE GOT TO BE FAIR!!
WE'VE GOT TO STAND UP!!
NO MORE BULLIES!!
OLDE-TIMER ESTABLISHMENT
STAY ON THE SIDEWALK!!
IT'S EASY ENOUGH TO PASS THIS OFF AS A CUTE ANECDOTE—
AND YES, IT'S CUTE—
BUT THERE WAS NO MARCH PLANNED IN MY TOWN THAT DAY,
SO MY FIVE-YEAR-OLD FOUNDED ONE.
THREE PEOPLE DEEP,
FILLING THE AIR WITH THEIR OWN CHANTS FOR AN HOUR,
THEIR OWN CONCERNS AS RELATIVE TO THE LARGER ISSUES, BUT ON THEIR LEVEL,
THEIR OWN NOISE.

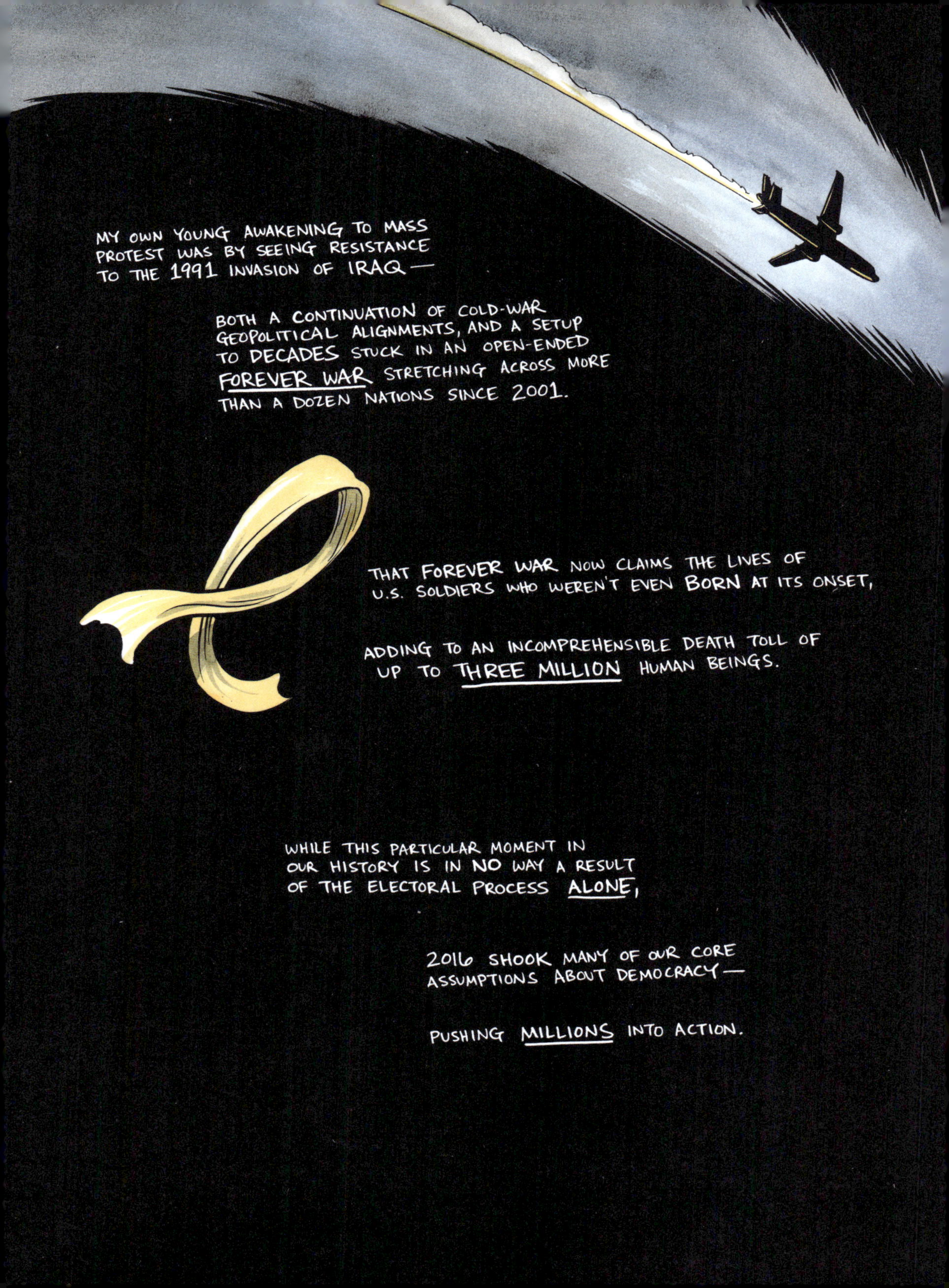
MY OWN YOUNG AWAKENING TO MASS PROTEST WAS BY SEEING RESISTANCE TO THE 1991 INVASION OF IRAQ—
BOTH A CONTINUATION OF COLD-WAR GEOPOLITICAL ALIGNMENTS, AND A SETUP TO DECADES STUCK IN AN OPEN-ENDED FOREVER WAR STRETCHING ACROSS MORE THAN A DOZEN NATIONS SINCE 2001.
THAT FOREVER WAR NOW CLAIMS THE LIVES OF U.S. SOLDIERS WHO WEREN'T EVEN BORN AT ITS ONSET,
ADDING TO AN INCOMPREHENSIBLE DEATH TOLL OF UP TO THREE MILLION HUMAN BEINGS.
WHILE THIS PARTICULAR MOMENT IN OUR HISTORY IS IN NO WAY A RESULT OF THE ELECTORAL PROCESS ALONE,
2016 SHOOK MANY OF OUR CORE ASSUMPTIONS ABOUT DEMOCRACY—
PUSHING MILLIONS INTO ACTION.

SO A MERE WEEK AFTER THE FIRST WOMEN'S MARCH, THOSE MILLIONS OF CONCERNED NEIGHBORS GOT **ANOTHER** CALL TO ACTION.

THE NEW AMERICAN REGIME, AMIDST A BARRAGE OF EXECUTIVE ORDERS AND DECLARATIONS INTENDED TO DIFFUSE ANY SINGLE AVENUE OF RESISTANCE — TO "FLOOD THE ZONE WITH SHIT," IN THE WORDS OF ITS PRINCIPAL ARCHITECT —

BANS ALL TRAVEL TO OUR NATION FROM SEVEN **MUSLIM-MAJORITY** COUNTRIES.

BUT **NOT** CERTAIN NATIONS WITH HISTORIES OF FUNDING OR SUPPORTING ACTS OF TERRORISM ON OUR SOIL **IF** THOSE EXEMPTED NATIONS ALSO HAPPENED TO HARBOR **BUSINESS DEALINGS** WITH OUR NEW RULER'S PRIVATE CORPORATION.

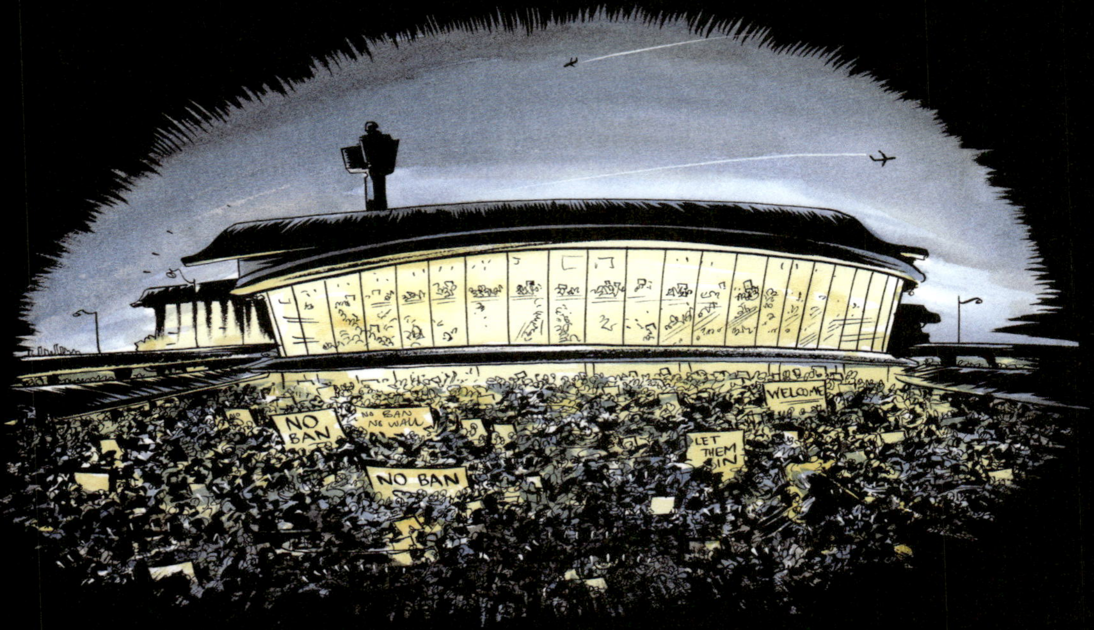
NO BAN
NO BAN NO WALL
WELCOME
LET THEM IN
NO BAN

(BUT YOU REMEMBER THAT, DON'T YOU?)

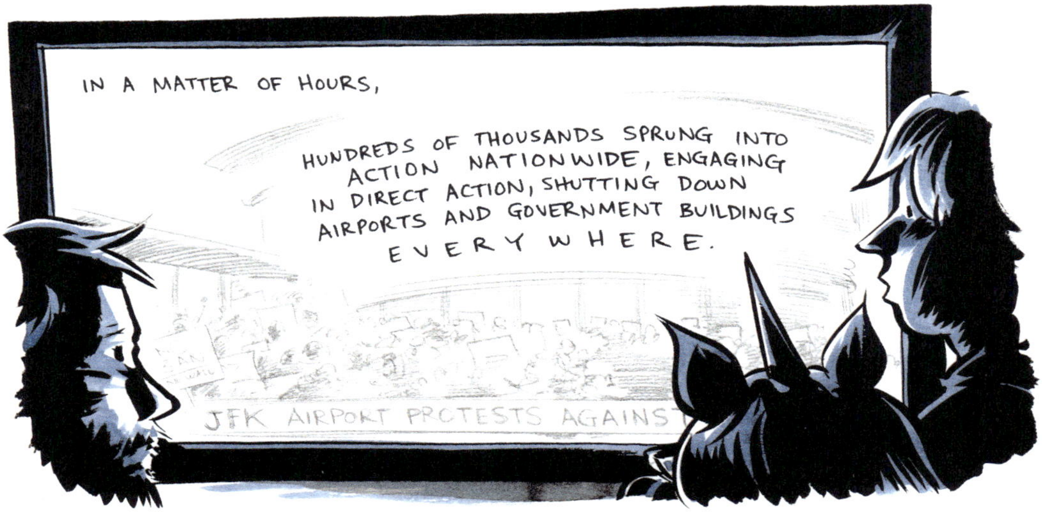
IN A MATTER OF HOURS,
HUNDREDS OF THOUSANDS SPRUNG INTO ACTION NATIONWIDE, ENGAGING IN DIRECT ACTION, SHUTTING DOWN AIRPORTS AND GOVERNMENT BUILDINGS EVERYWHERE.
JFK AIRPORT PROTESTS AGAINST

WE CAUGHT WORD THAT FOLKS IN OUR TOWN WERE CONVERGING ON THE COURTHOUSE SQUARE.

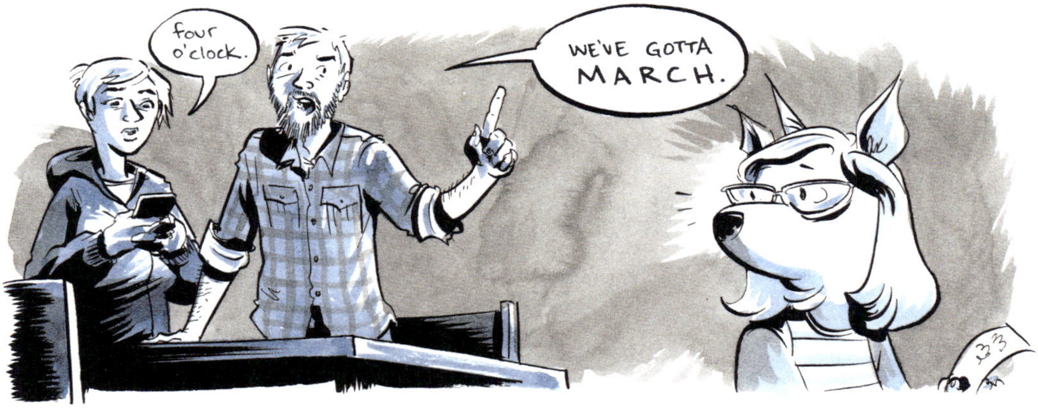
four o'clock.
WE'VE GOTTA MARCH.

TWO HOURS TO PREPARE.

AVENGERS ASSEMBLE.

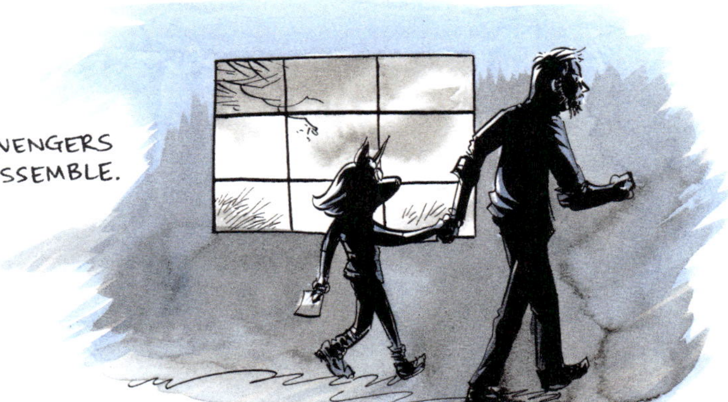

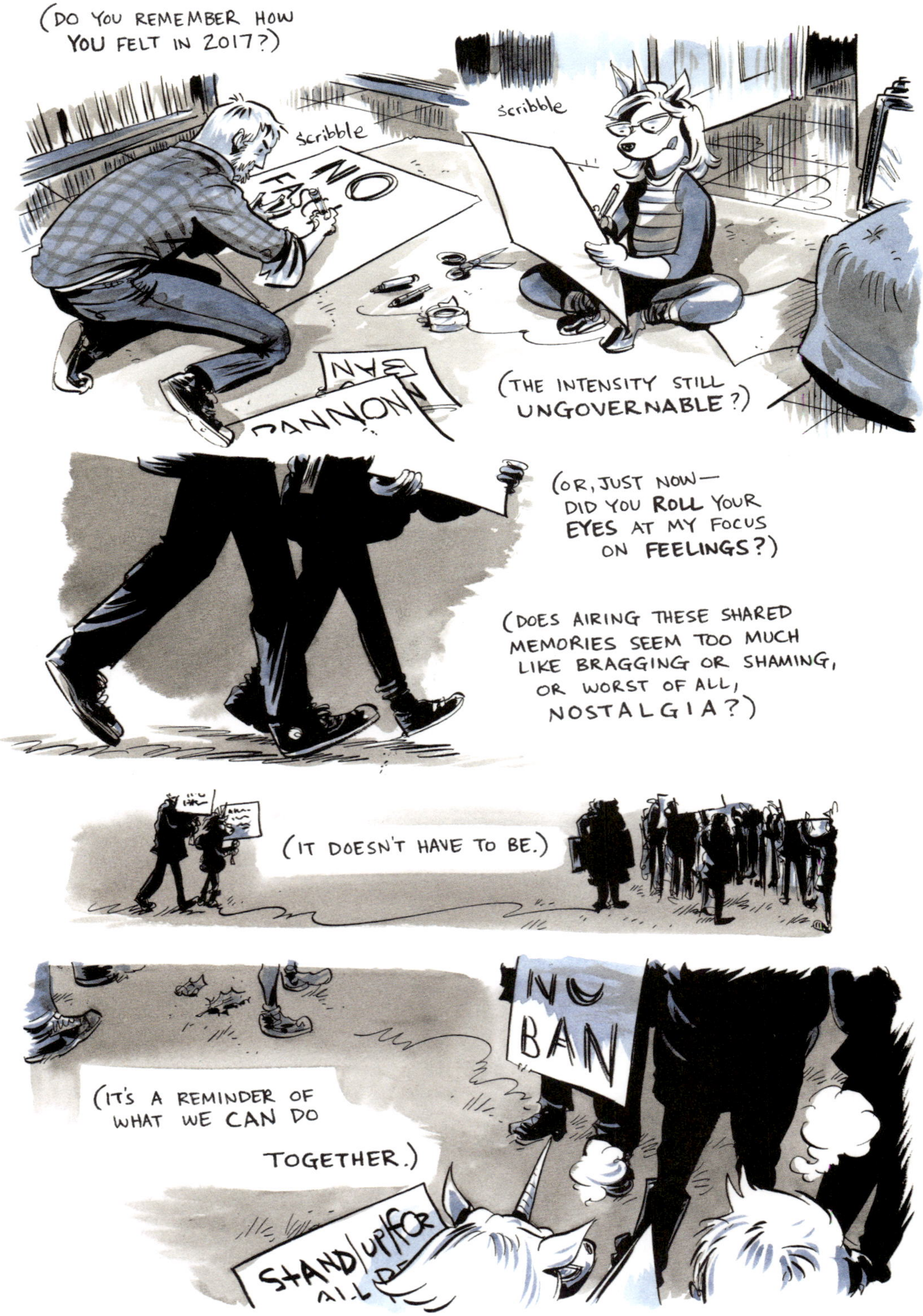
(DO YOU REMEMBER HOW YOU FELT IN 2017?)
scribble
scribble
NO FAS
BAN
NO BANNON
(THE INTENSITY STILL UNGOVERNABLE?)
(OR, JUST NOW— DID YOU ROLL YOUR EYES AT MY FOCUS ON FEELINGS?)
(DOES AIRING THESE SHARED MEMORIES SEEM TOO MUCH LIKE BRAGGING OR SHAMING, OR WORST OF ALL, NOSTALGIA?)
(IT DOESN'T HAVE TO BE.)
NO BAN
(IT'S A REMINDER OF WHAT WE CAN DO
TOGETHER.)
STAND UP FOR

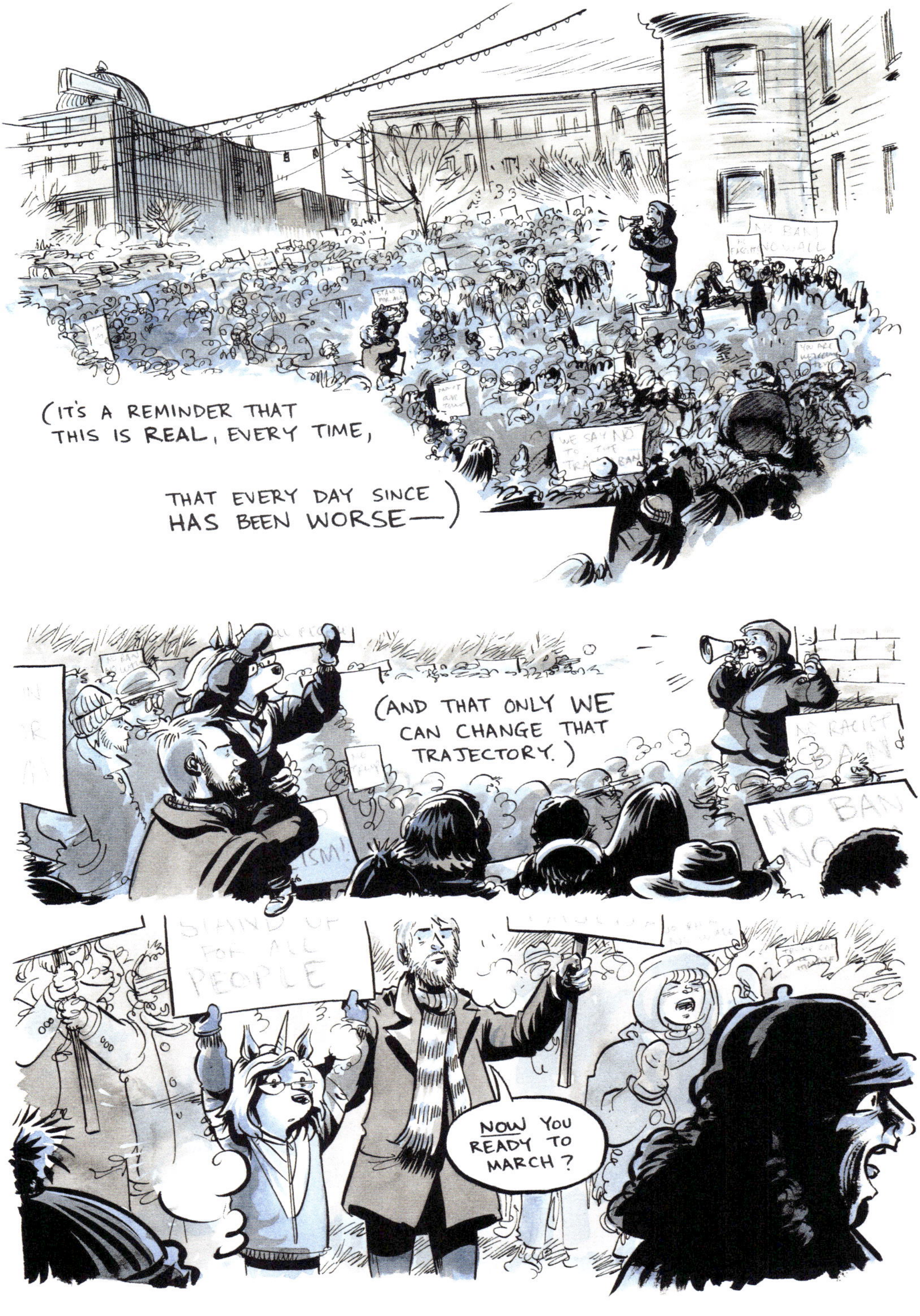
(IT'S A REMINDER THAT THIS IS REAL, EVERY TIME,
THAT EVERY DAY SINCE HAS BEEN WORSE—)
(AND THAT ONLY WE CAN CHANGE THAT TRAJECTORY.)
NO RACIST BAN
STAND UP FOR ALL PEOPLE
NOW YOU READY TO MARCH?

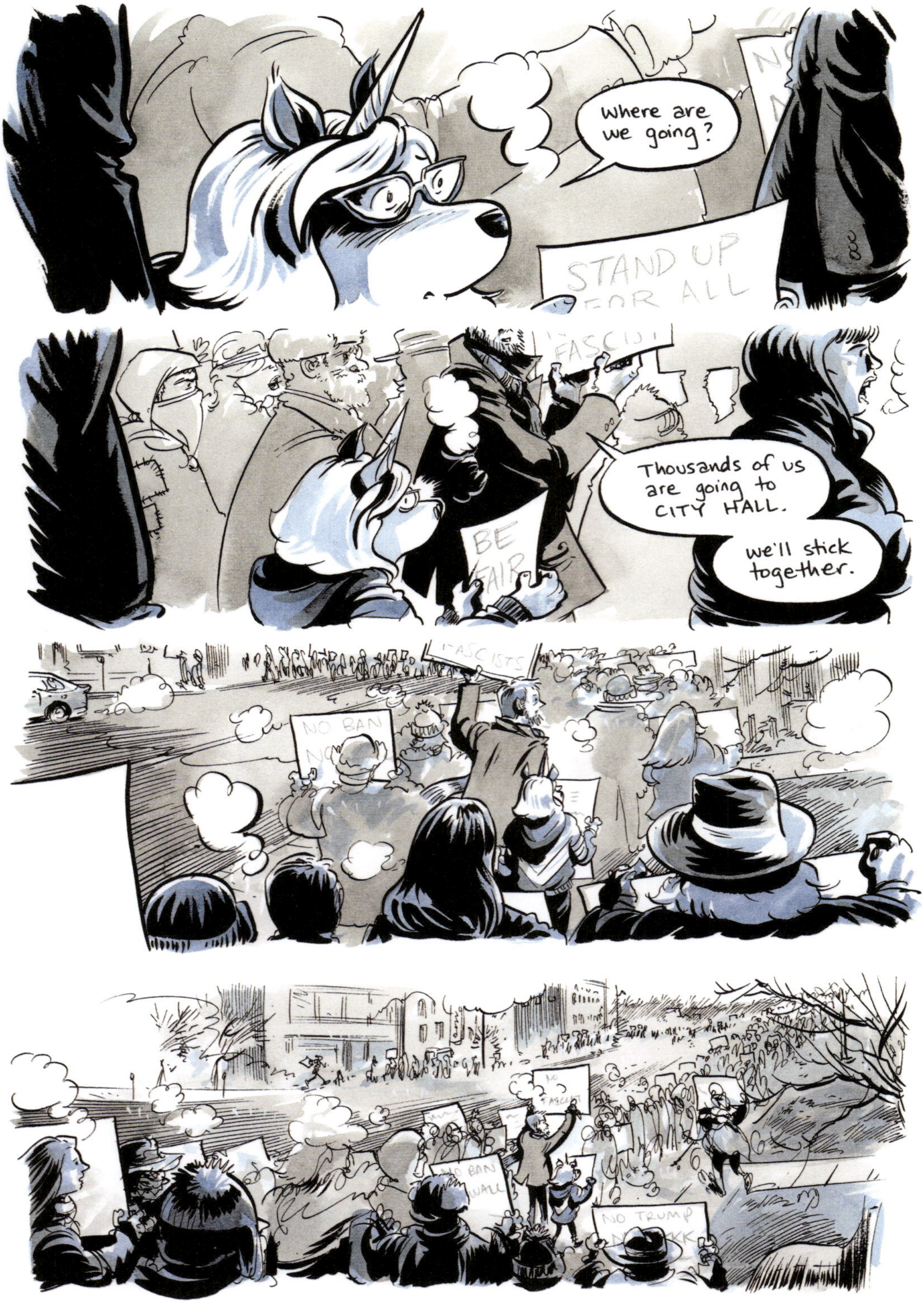
Where are we going?
STAND UP
Thousands of us are going to CITY HALL.
We'll stick together.
BE FAIR
FASCISTS
NO BAN
NO TRUMP

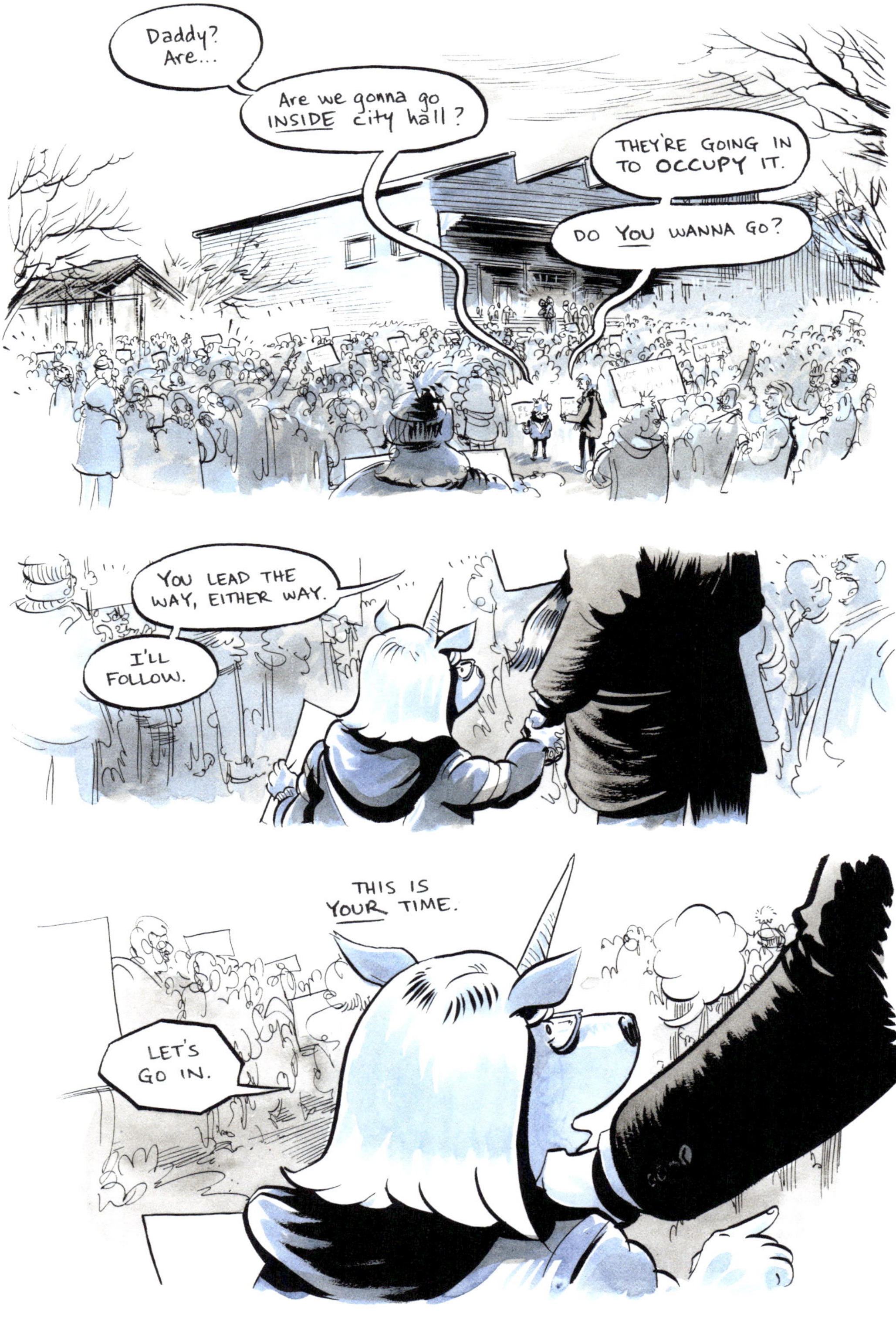

Daddy? Are...
Are we gonna go INSIDE city hall?
THEY'RE GOING IN TO OCCUPY IT.
DO YOU WANNA GO?
YOU LEAD THE WAY, EITHER WAY.
I'LL FOLLOW.
THIS IS YOUR TIME.
LET'S GO IN.

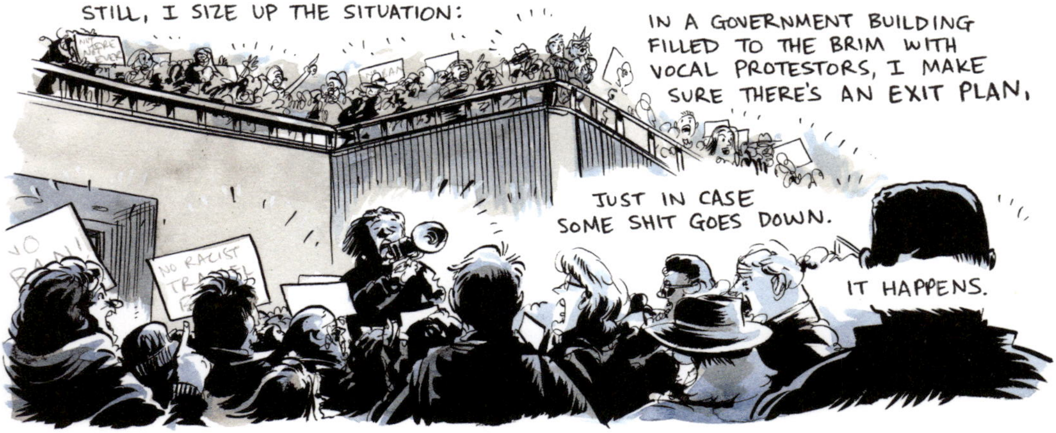
STILL, I SIZE UP THE SITUATION:
IN A GOVERNMENT BUILDING FILLED TO THE BRIM WITH VOCAL PROTESTORS, I MAKE SURE THERE'S AN EXIT PLAN,
JUST IN CASE SOME SHIT GOES DOWN.
IT HAPPENS.

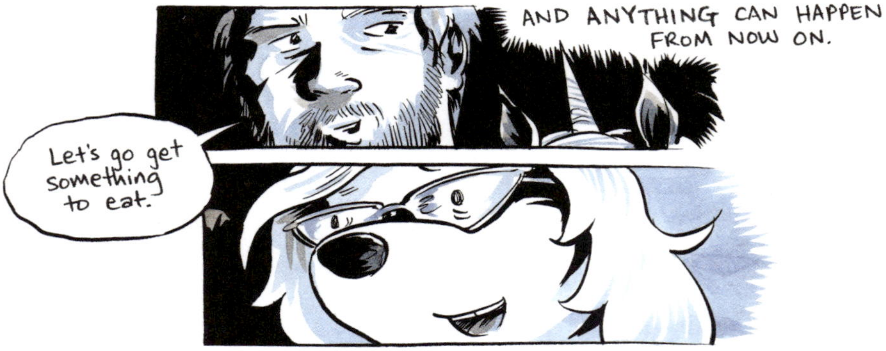
AND ANYTHING CAN HAPPEN FROM NOW ON.
Let's go get something to eat.

THE FOLLOWING YEAR, THE REGIME DID SUCCEED IN UPHOLDING THEIR TRAVEL BAN BY ATTRITION WARFARE, AND NOBODY IN TOWN, TO MY KNOWLEDGE, ORGANIZED AGAINST IT.

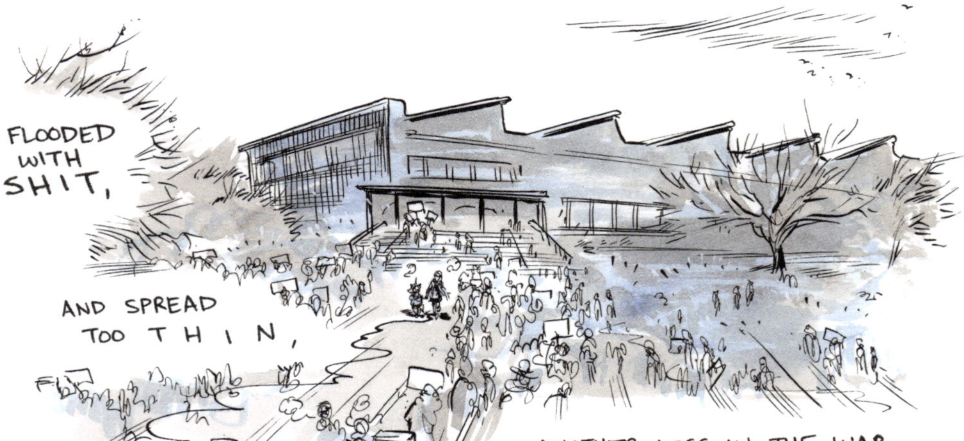
FLOODED WITH SHIT,
AND SPREAD TOO T H I N,
ANOTHER LOSS IN THE WAR AGAINST NORMALIZED AUTOCRACY.

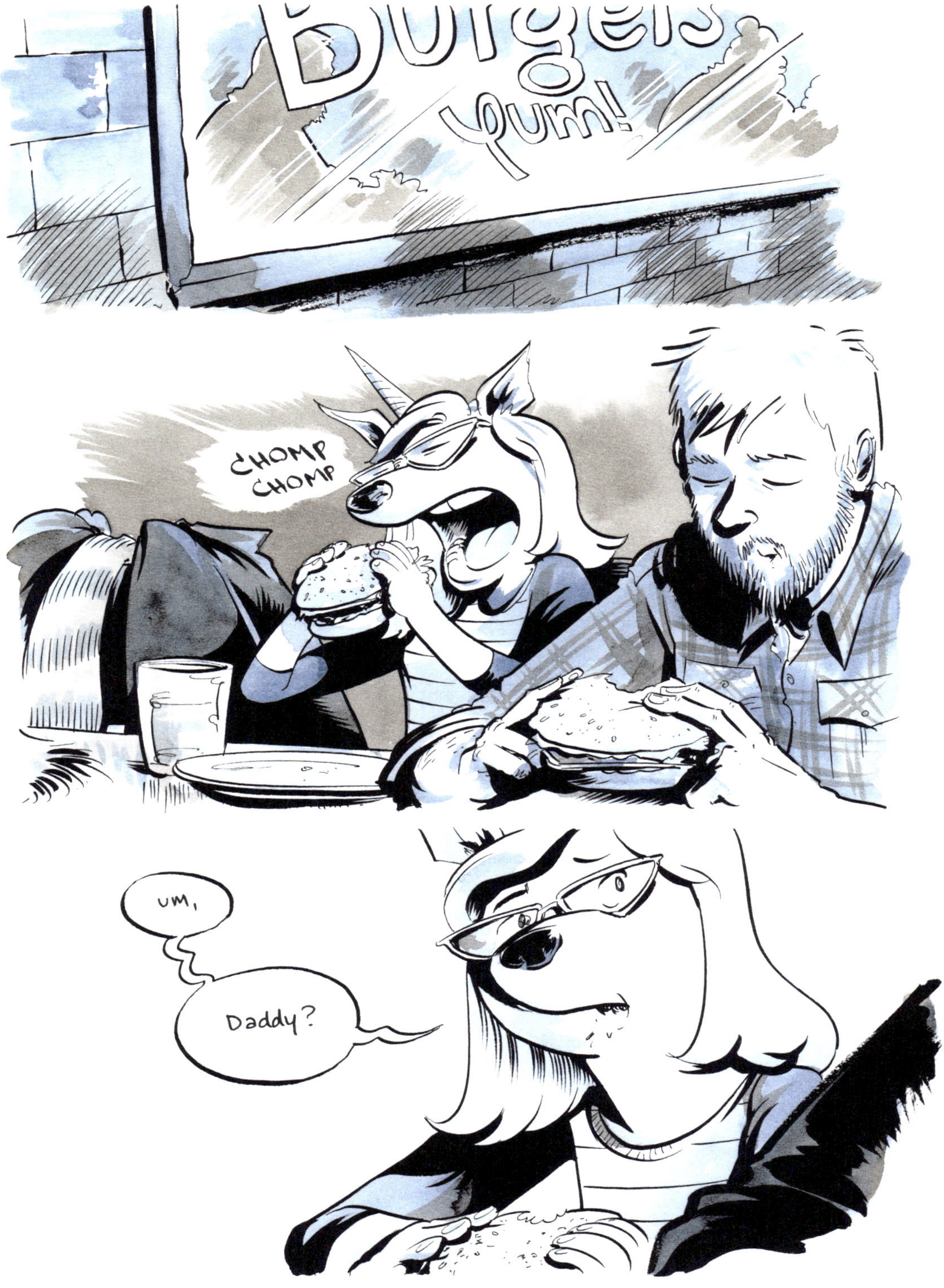
Burgers
yum!
CHOMP CHOMP
um,
Daddy?

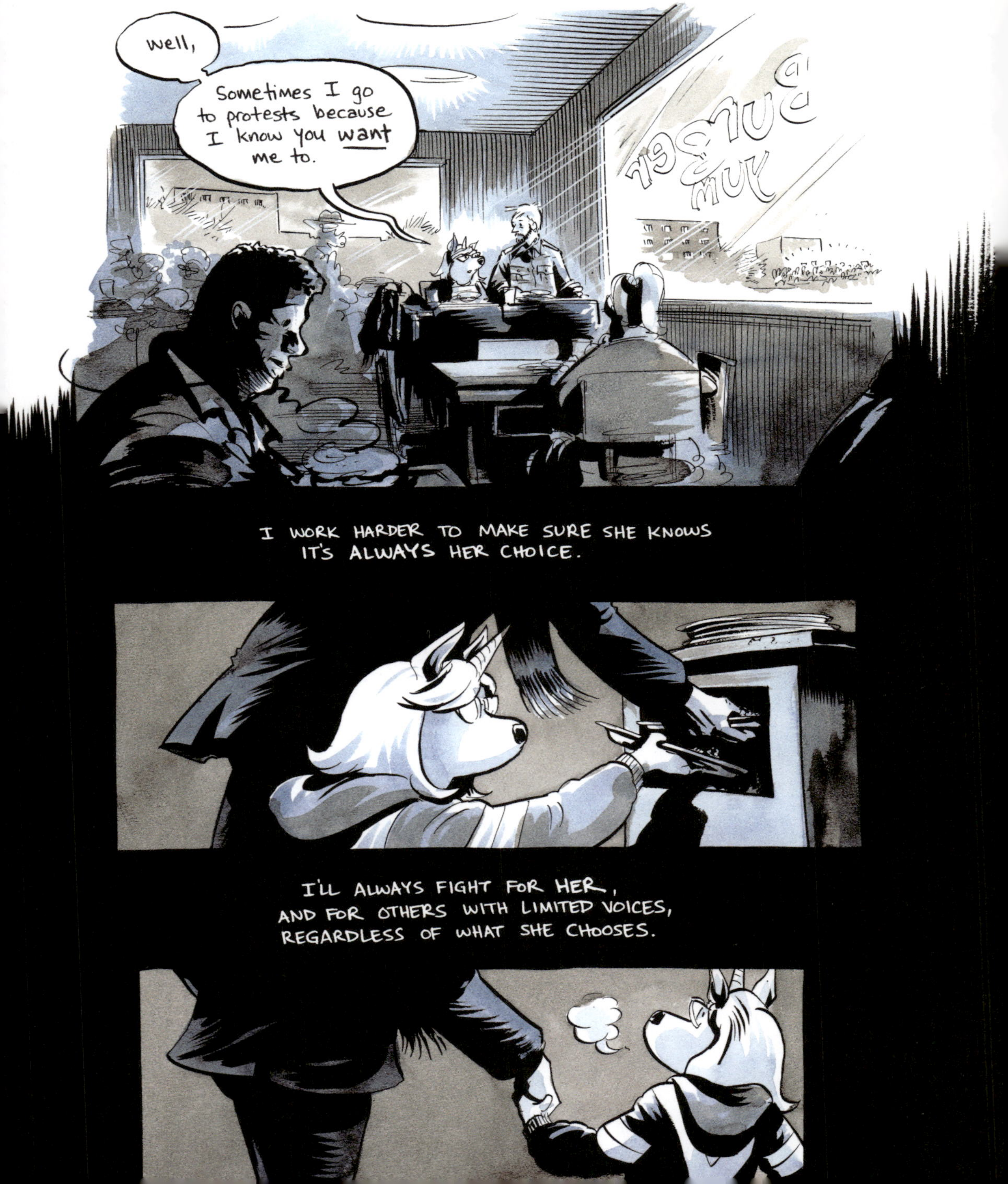

Well,
Sometimes I go to protests because I know you want me to.
I WORK HARDER TO MAKE SURE SHE KNOWS IT'S ALWAYS HER CHOICE.
I'LL ALWAYS FIGHT FOR HER, AND FOR OTHERS WITH LIMITED VOICES, REGARDLESS OF WHAT SHE CHOOSES.

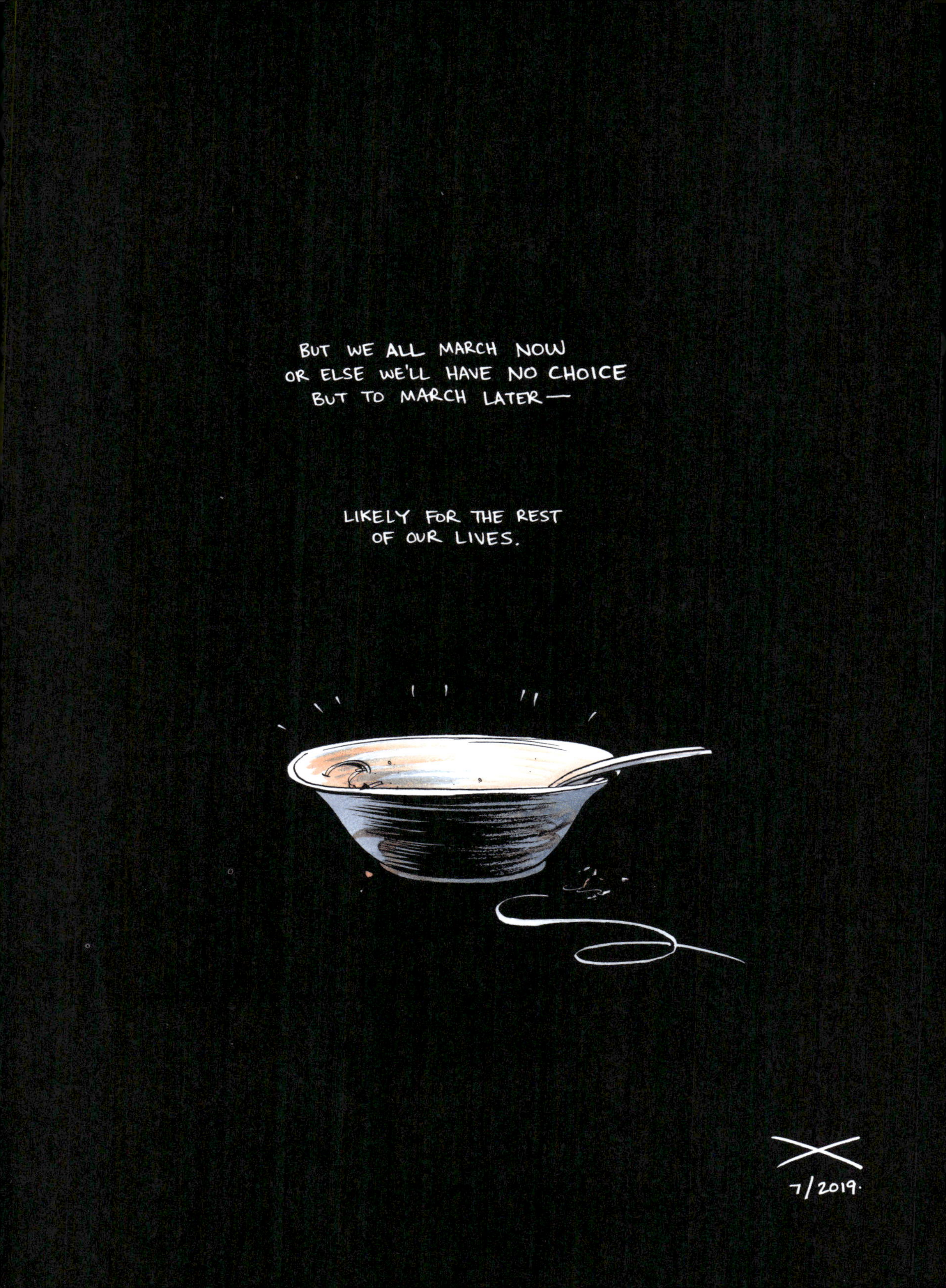
BUT WE ALL MARCH NOW
OR ELSE WE'LL HAVE NO CHOICE
BUT TO MARCH LATER—
LIKELY FOR THE REST
OF OUR LIVES.
7/2019.

2
PROMISES

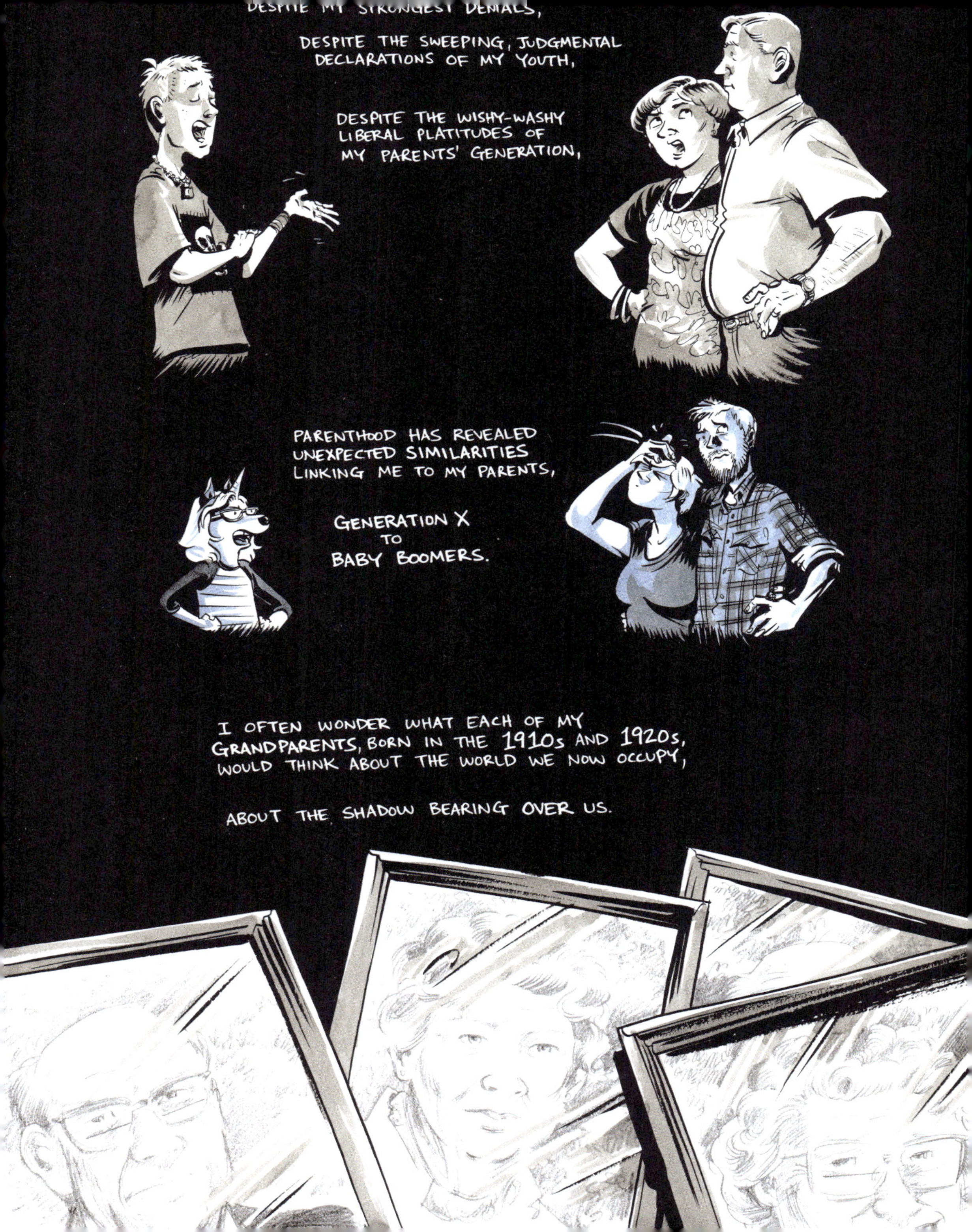
DESPITE MY STRONGEST DENIALS,
DESPITE THE SWEEPING, JUDGMENTAL DECLARATIONS OF MY YOUTH,
DESPITE THE WISHY-WASHY LIBERAL PLATITUDES OF MY PARENTS' GENERATION,
PARENTHOOD HAS REVEALED UNEXPECTED SIMILARITIES LINKING ME TO MY PARENTS,
GENERATION X TO BABY BOOMERS.
I OFTEN WONDER WHAT EACH OF MY GRANDPARENTS, BORN IN THE 1910s AND 1920s, WOULD THINK ABOUT THE WORLD WE NOW OCCUPY,
ABOUT THE SHADOW BEARING OVER US.

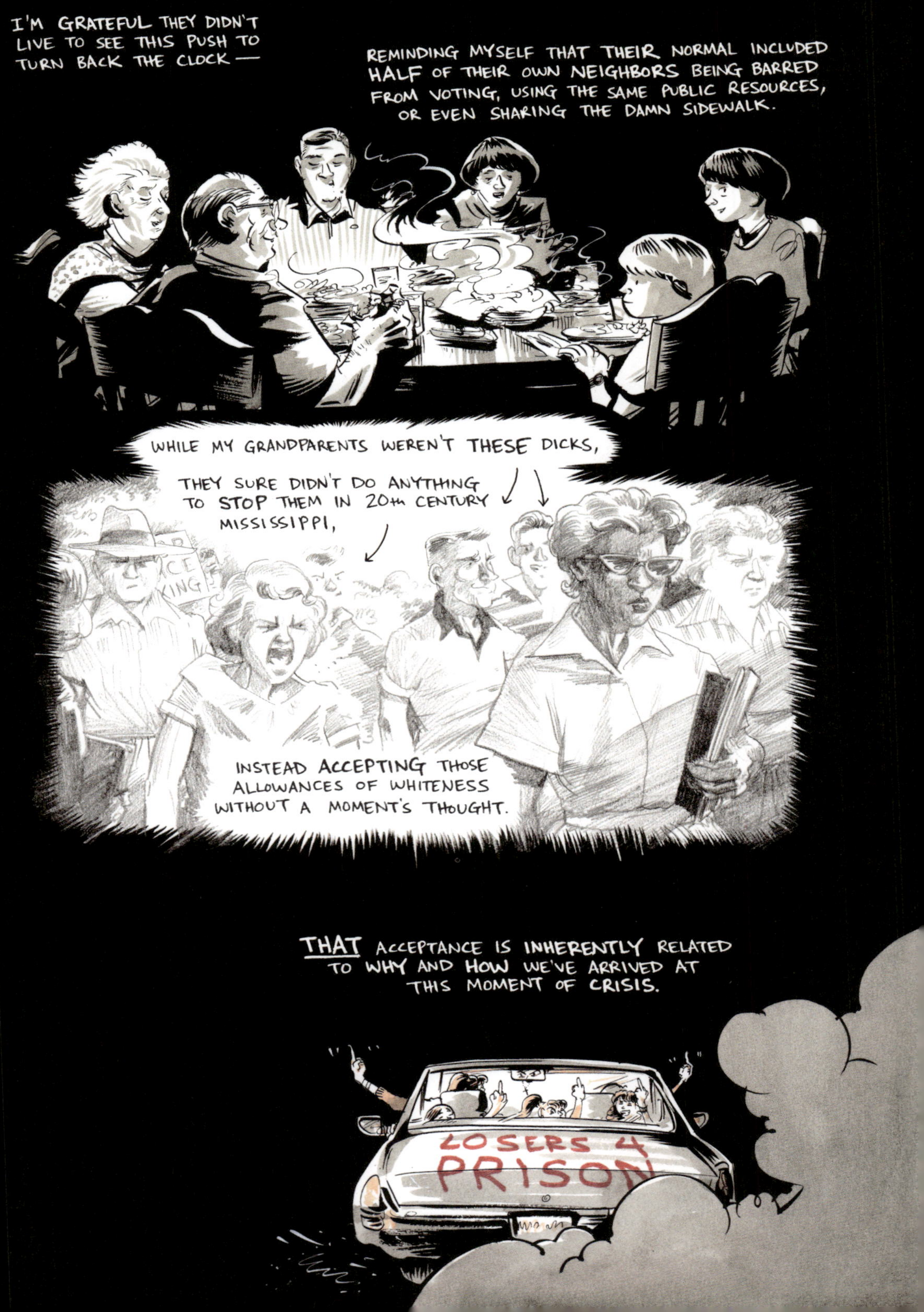
I'M GRATEFUL THEY DIDN'T LIVE TO SEE THIS PUSH TO TURN BACK THE CLOCK —
REMINDING MYSELF THAT THEIR NORMAL INCLUDED HALF OF THEIR OWN NEIGHBORS BEING BARRED FROM VOTING, USING THE SAME PUBLIC RESOURCES, OR EVEN SHARING THE DAMN SIDEWALK.
WHILE MY GRANDPARENTS WEREN'T THESE DICKS,
THEY SURE DIDN'T DO ANYTHING TO STOP THEM IN 20th CENTURY MISSISSIPPI,
INSTEAD ACCEPTING THOSE ALLOWANCES OF WHITENESS WITHOUT A MOMENT'S THOUGHT.
THAT ACCEPTANCE IS INHERENTLY RELATED TO WHY AND HOW WE'VE ARRIVED AT THIS MOMENT OF CRISIS.
LOSERS 4 PRISON

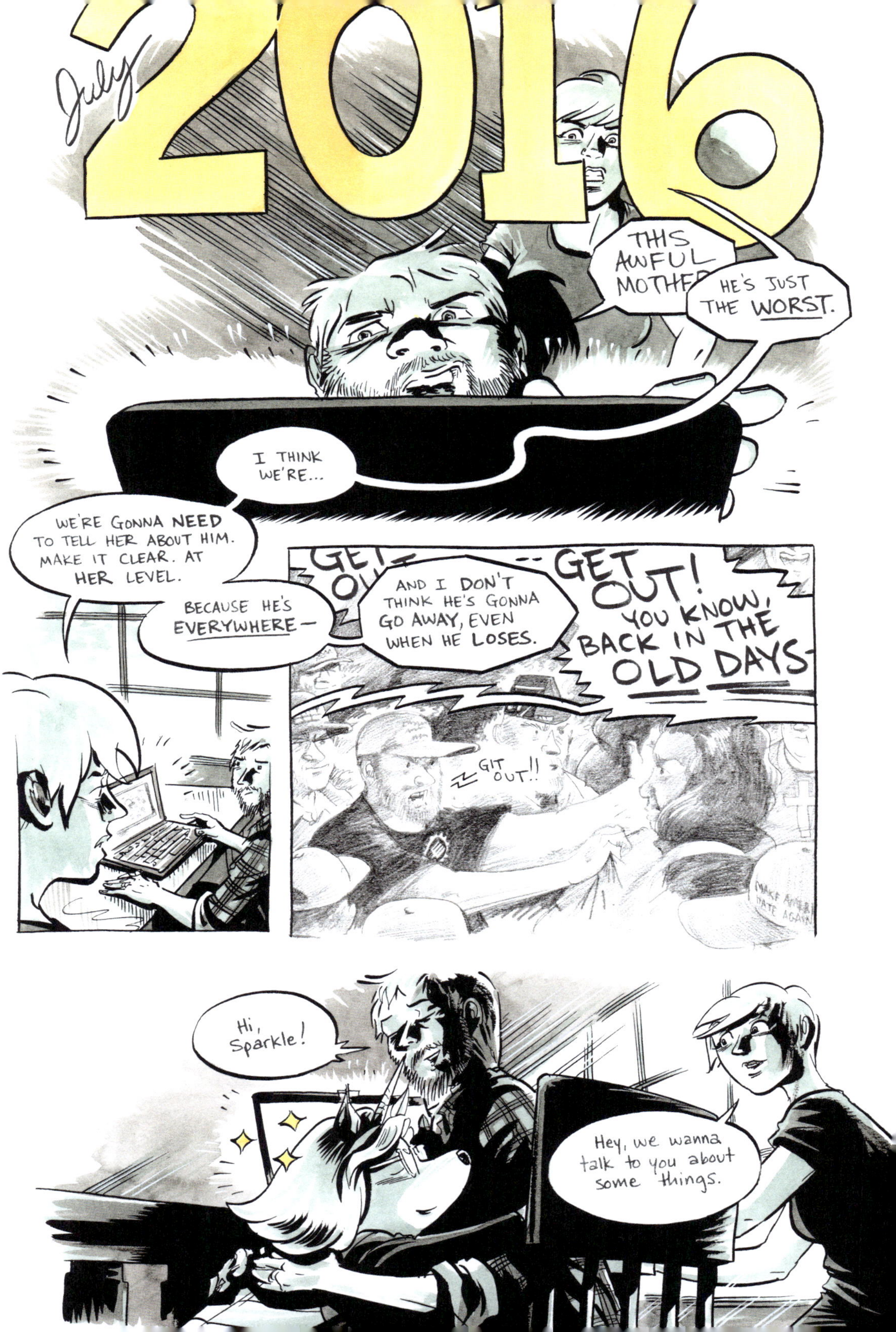
July
2016
THIS AWFUL MOTHER
HE'S JUST THE WORST.
I THINK WE'RE...
WE'RE GONNA NEED TO TELL HER ABOUT HIM. MAKE IT CLEAR. AT HER LEVEL.
BECAUSE HE'S EVERYWHERE—
AND I DON'T THINK HE'S GONNA GO AWAY, EVEN WHEN HE LOSES.
GET OUT! YOU KNOW, BACK IN THE OLD DAYS—
GIT OUT!!
Hi, Sparkle!
Hey, we wanna talk to you about some things.

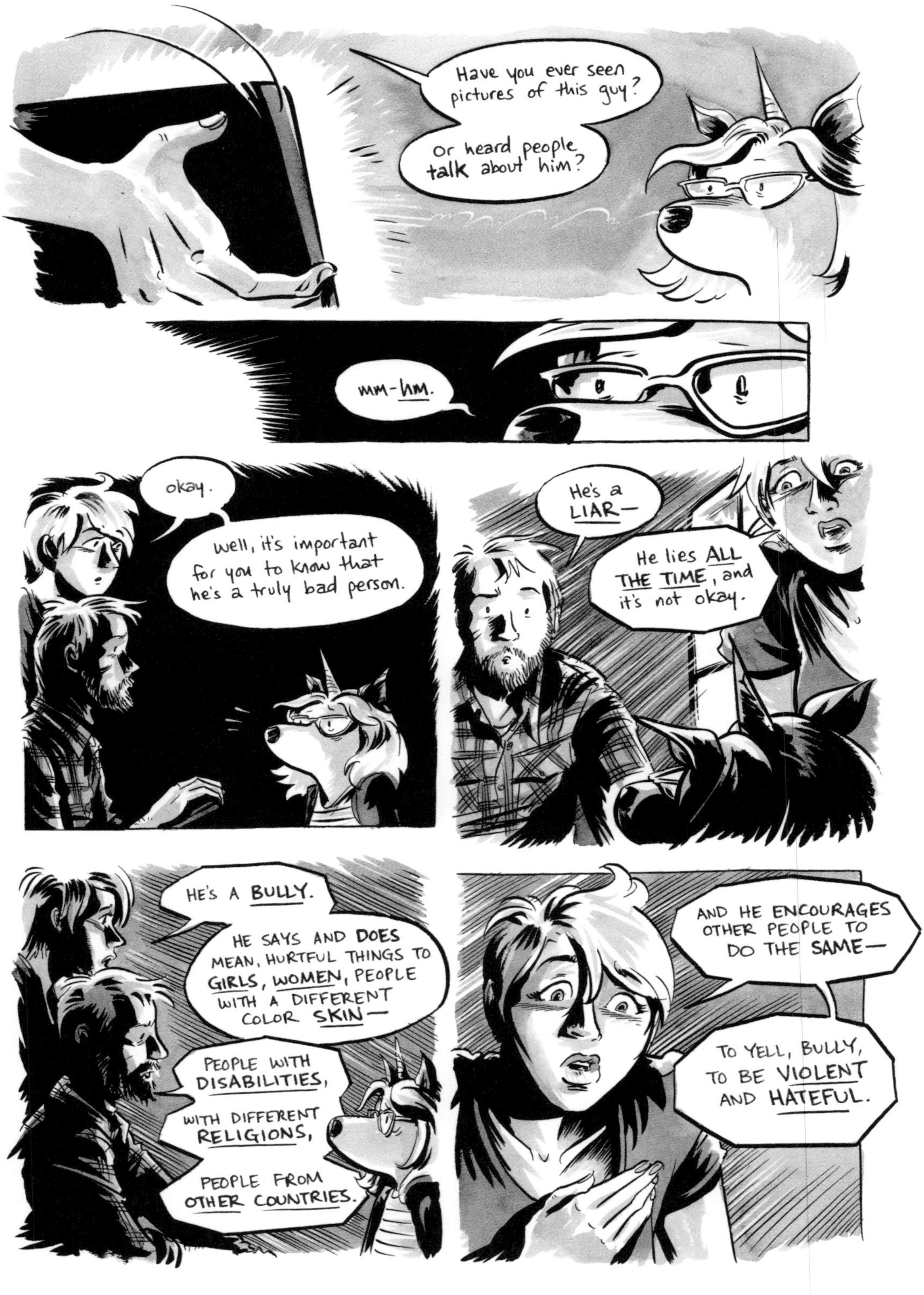

Have you ever seen pictures of this guy?
Or heard people talk about him?
mm-hm.
okay.
Well, it's important for you to know that he's a truly bad person.
He's a LIAR—
He lies ALL THE TIME, and it's not okay.
HE'S A BULLY.
HE SAYS AND DOES MEAN, HURTFUL THINGS TO GIRLS, WOMEN, PEOPLE WITH A DIFFERENT COLOR SKIN—
PEOPLE WITH DISABILITIES,
WITH DIFFERENT RELIGIONS,
PEOPLE FROM OTHER COUNTRIES.
AND HE ENCOURAGES OTHER PEOPLE TO DO THE SAME—
TO YELL, BULLY, TO BE VIOLENT AND HATEFUL.

"YOU'RE GOING TO BE SEEING AND HEARING ABOUT HIM A LOT, AND PEOPLE MIGHT ACT LIKE THIS IS ALL NORMAL—

BUT IT'S NOT.

THERE ARE ALWAYS PEOPLE WE DISAGREE WITH, AND THEY MIGHT ALSO HAVE BAD IDEAS OR BE BULLIES—

BUT THIS IS DIFFERENT.

THIS IS WRONG.

(THERE, I SAID IT.)

"Uhh, I dunno what I said, I don't rememberrr..."

Is... he mean to his friends?

HE PROBABLY DOESN'T HAVE ANY.

He may have NEVER had a real friend in his whole LIFE.

gasp!

Something is BROKEN in his mind.

He doesn't THINK or FEEL the way that people usually do.

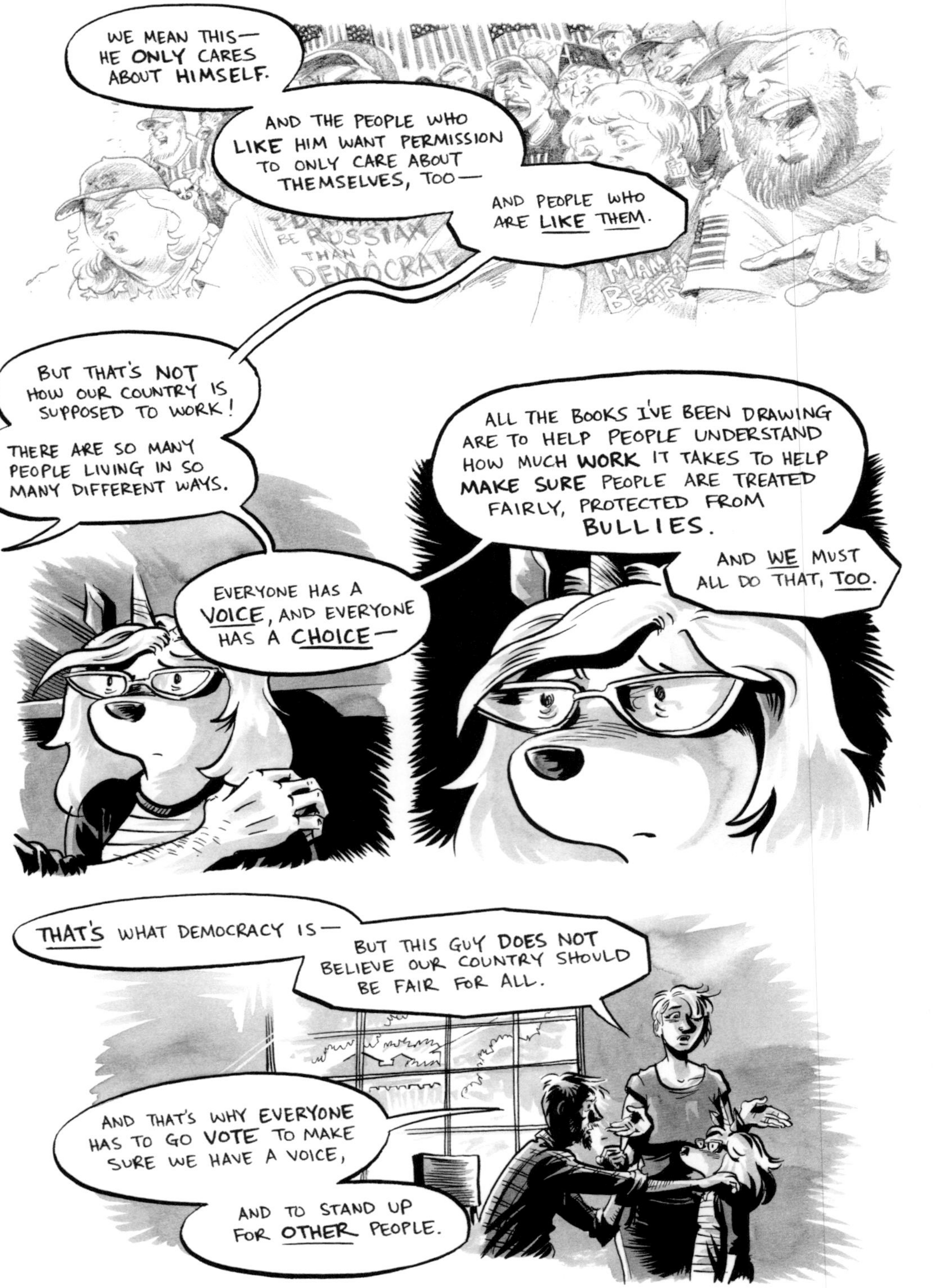
WE MEAN THIS— HE ONLY CARES ABOUT HIMSELF.
AND THE PEOPLE WHO LIKE HIM WANT PERMISSION TO ONLY CARE ABOUT THEMSELVES, TOO—
AND PEOPLE WHO ARE LIKE THEM.
BE RUSSIAN THAN A DEMOCRAT
MAMA BEAR
BUT THAT'S NOT HOW OUR COUNTRY IS SUPPOSED TO WORK!
THERE ARE SO MANY PEOPLE LIVING IN SO MANY DIFFERENT WAYS.
EVERYONE HAS A VOICE, AND EVERYONE HAS A CHOICE—
ALL THE BOOKS I'VE BEEN DRAWING ARE TO HELP PEOPLE UNDERSTAND HOW MUCH WORK IT TAKES TO HELP MAKE SURE PEOPLE ARE TREATED FAIRLY, PROTECTED FROM BULLIES.
AND WE MUST ALL DO THAT, TOO.
THAT'S WHAT DEMOCRACY IS—
BUT THIS GUY DOES NOT BELIEVE OUR COUNTRY SHOULD BE FAIR FOR ALL.
AND THAT'S WHY EVERYONE HAS TO GO VOTE TO MAKE SURE WE HAVE A VOICE,
AND TO STAND UP FOR OTHER PEOPLE.

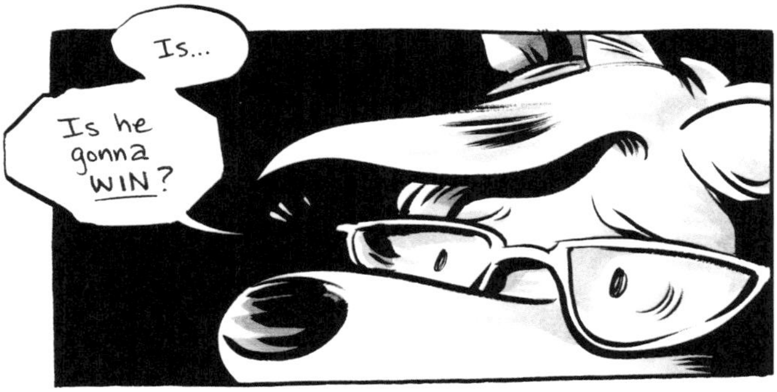
Is...
Is he gonna WIN?

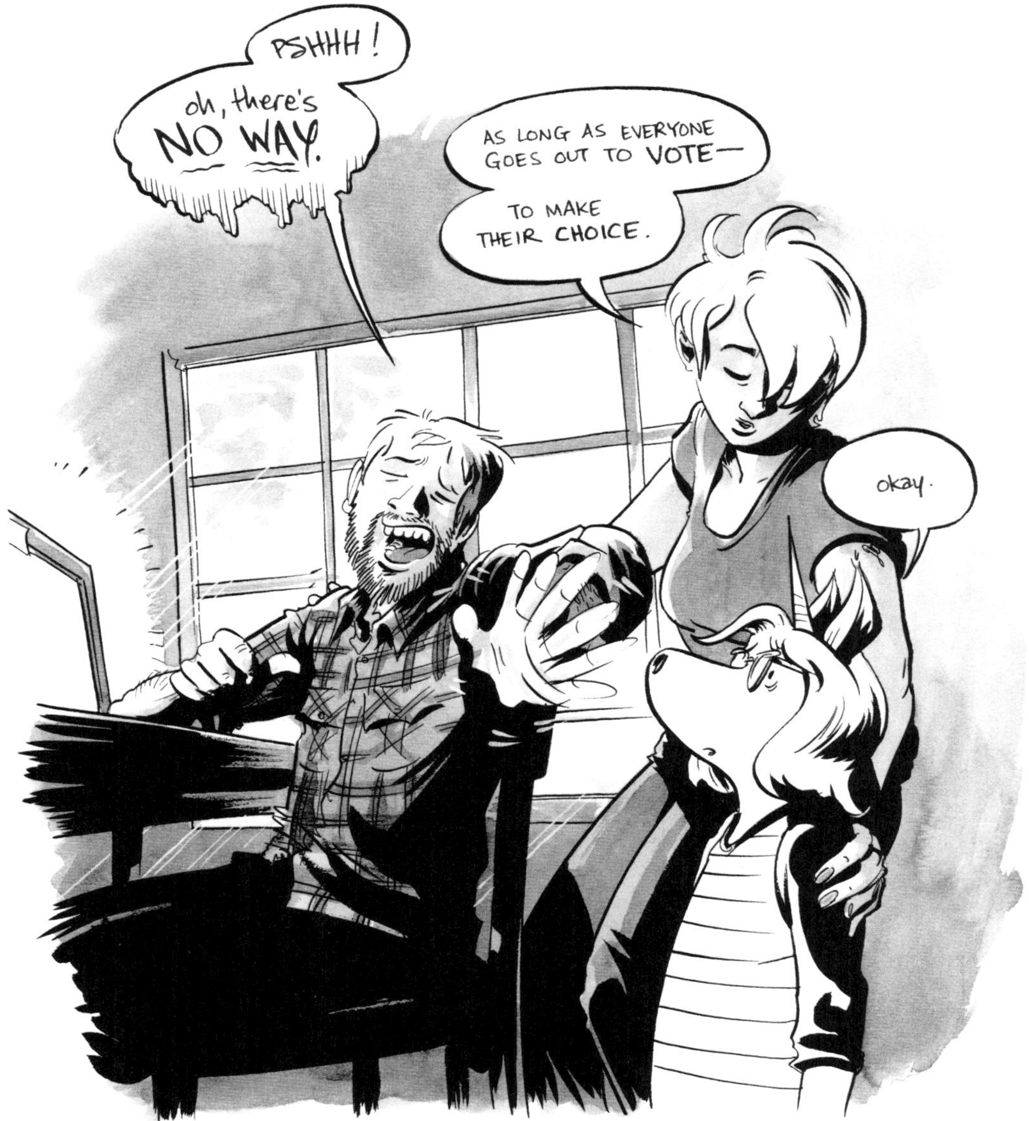
PSHHH!
oh, there's NO WAY.
AS LONG AS EVERYONE GOES OUT TO VOTE—
TO MAKE THEIR CHOICE.
okay.

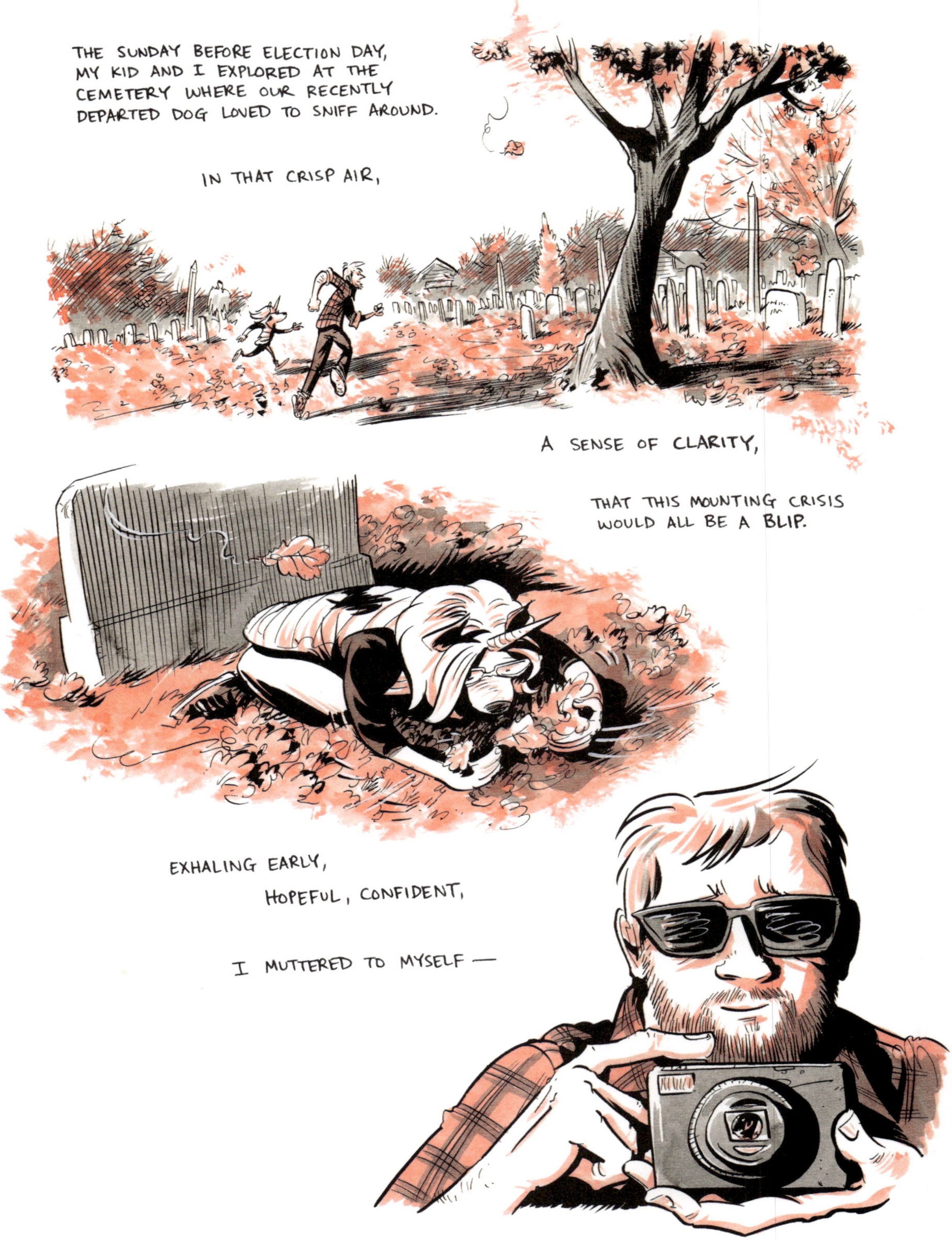
THE SUNDAY BEFORE ELECTION DAY, MY KID AND I EXPLORED AT THE CEMETERY WHERE OUR RECENTLY DEPARTED DOG LOVED TO SNIFF AROUND.
IN THAT CRISP AIR,
A SENSE OF CLARITY,
THAT THIS MOUNTING CRISIS WOULD ALL BE A BLIP.
EXHALING EARLY,
HOPEFUL, CONFIDENT,
I MUTTERED TO MYSELF —

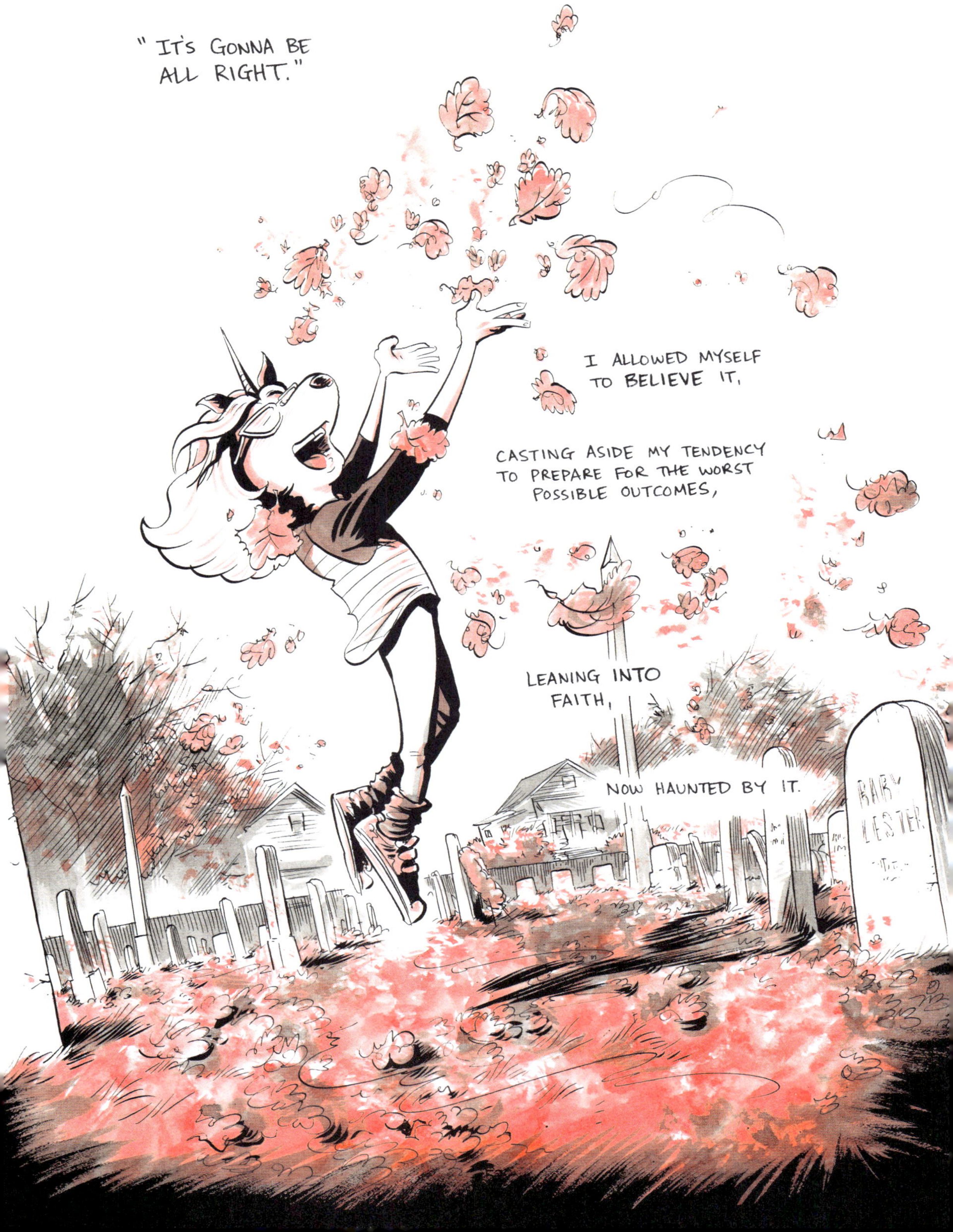
"IT'S GONNA BE ALL RIGHT."
I ALLOWED MYSELF TO BELIEVE IT,
CASTING ASIDE MY TENDENCY TO PREPARE FOR THE WORST POSSIBLE OUTCOMES,
LEANING INTO FAITH,
NOW HAUNTED BY IT.
BABY LESTER

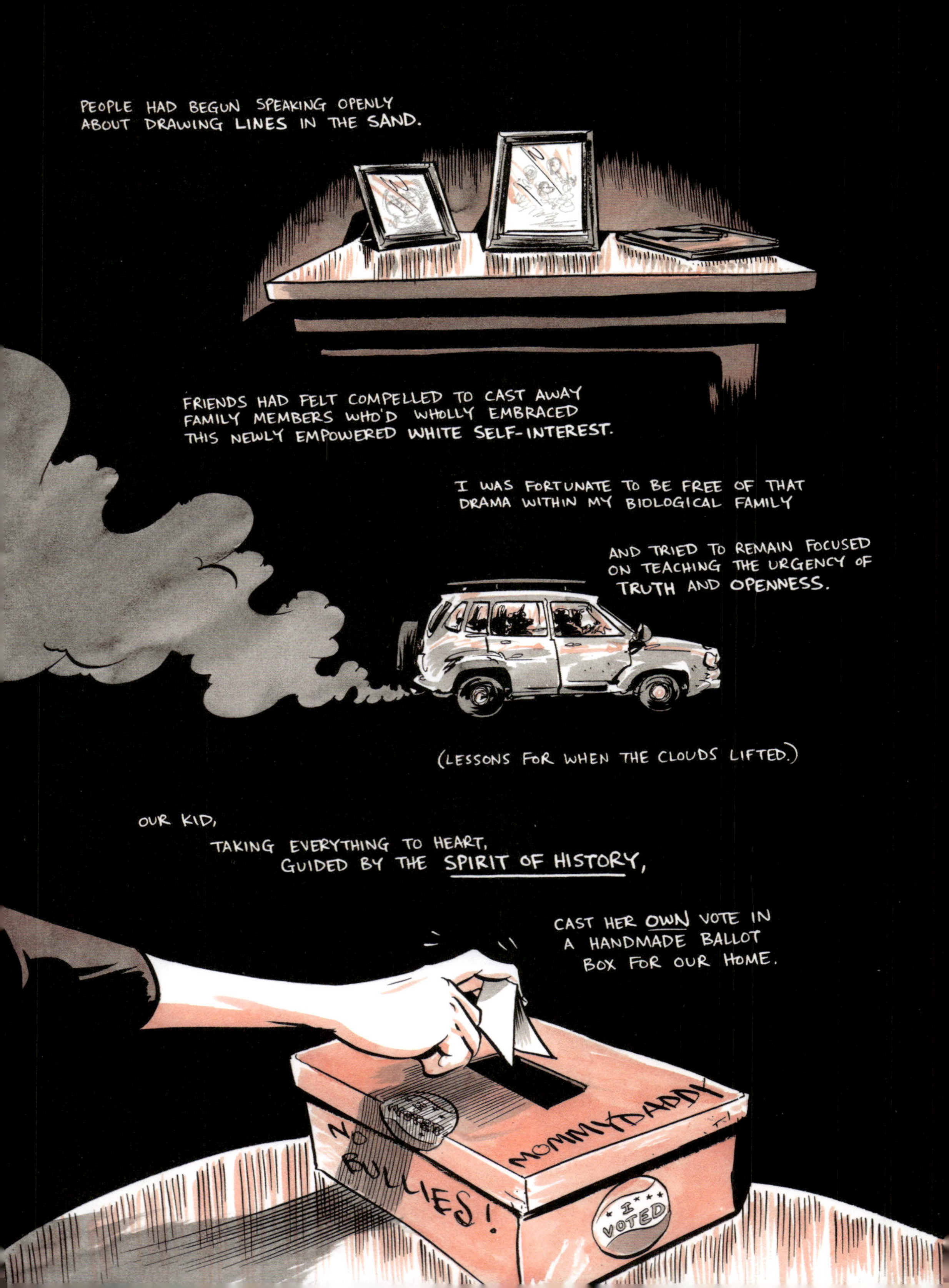
PEOPLE HAD BEGUN SPEAKING OPENLY ABOUT DRAWING LINES IN THE SAND.
FRIENDS HAD FELT COMPELLED TO CAST AWAY FAMILY MEMBERS WHO'D WHOLLY EMBRACED THIS NEWLY EMPOWERED WHITE SELF-INTEREST.
I WAS FORTUNATE TO BE FREE OF THAT DRAMA WITHIN MY BIOLOGICAL FAMILY
AND TRIED TO REMAIN FOCUSED ON TEACHING THE URGENCY OF TRUTH AND OPENNESS.
(LESSONS FOR WHEN THE CLOUDS LIFTED.)
OUR KID,
TAKING EVERYTHING TO HEART,
GUIDED BY THE SPIRIT OF HISTORY,
CAST HER OWN VOTE IN A HANDMADE BALLOT BOX FOR OUR HOME.
MOMMY DADDY
NO BULLIES!
I VOTED

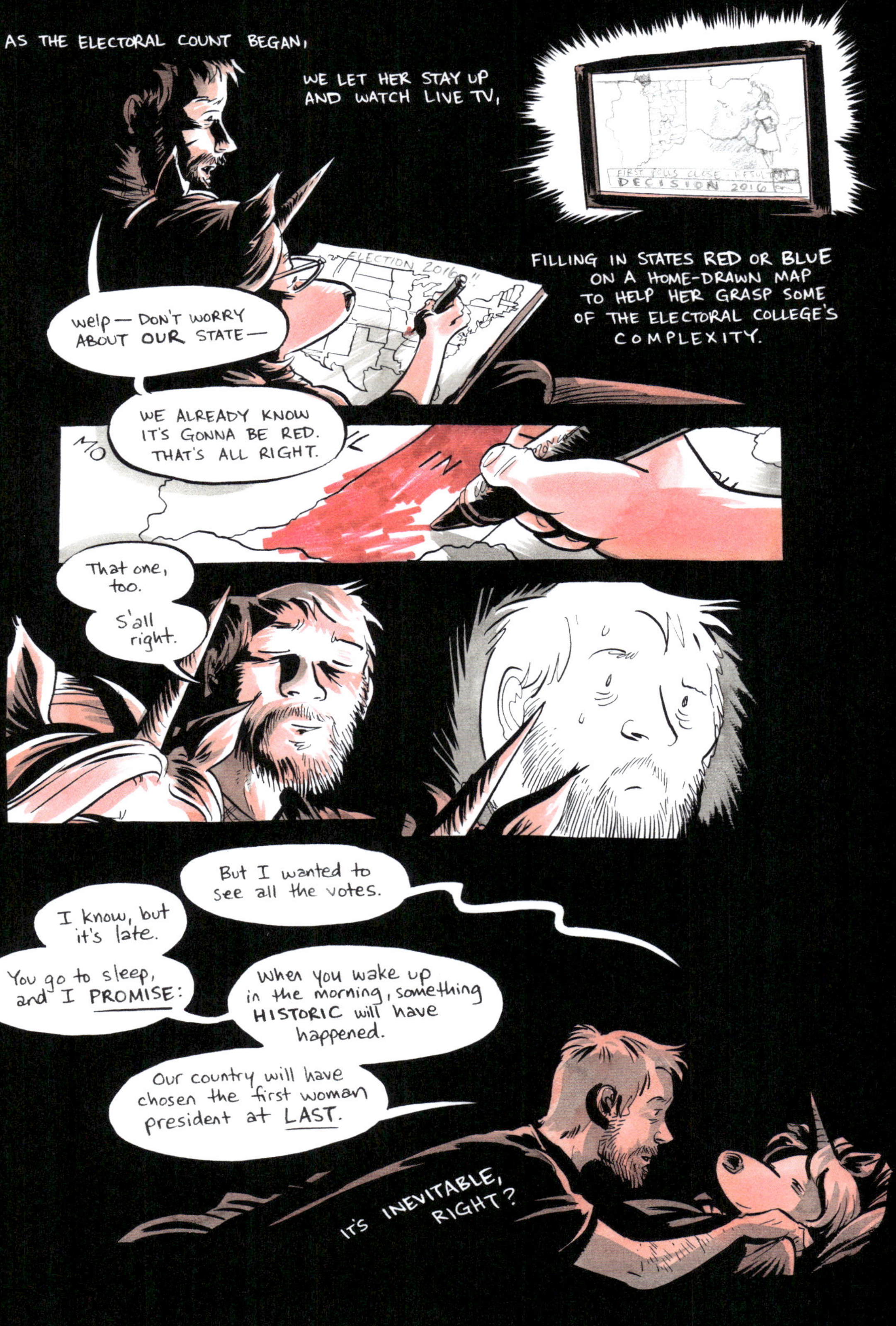
AS THE ELECTORAL COUNT BEGAN,
WE LET HER STAY UP AND WATCH LIVE TV,
DECISION 2016
FILLING IN STATES RED OR BLUE ON A HOME-DRAWN MAP TO HELP HER GRASP SOME OF THE ELECTORAL COLLEGE'S COMPLEXITY.
ELECTION 2016!!
welp— DON'T WORRY ABOUT OUR STATE—
WE ALREADY KNOW IT'S GONNA BE RED. THAT'S ALL RIGHT.
MO
That one, too.
S'all right.
But I wanted to see all the votes.
I know, but it's late.
You go to sleep, and I PROMISE:
When you wake up in the morning, something HISTORIC will have happened.
Our country will have chosen the first woman president at LAST.
IT'S INEVITABLE, RIGHT?

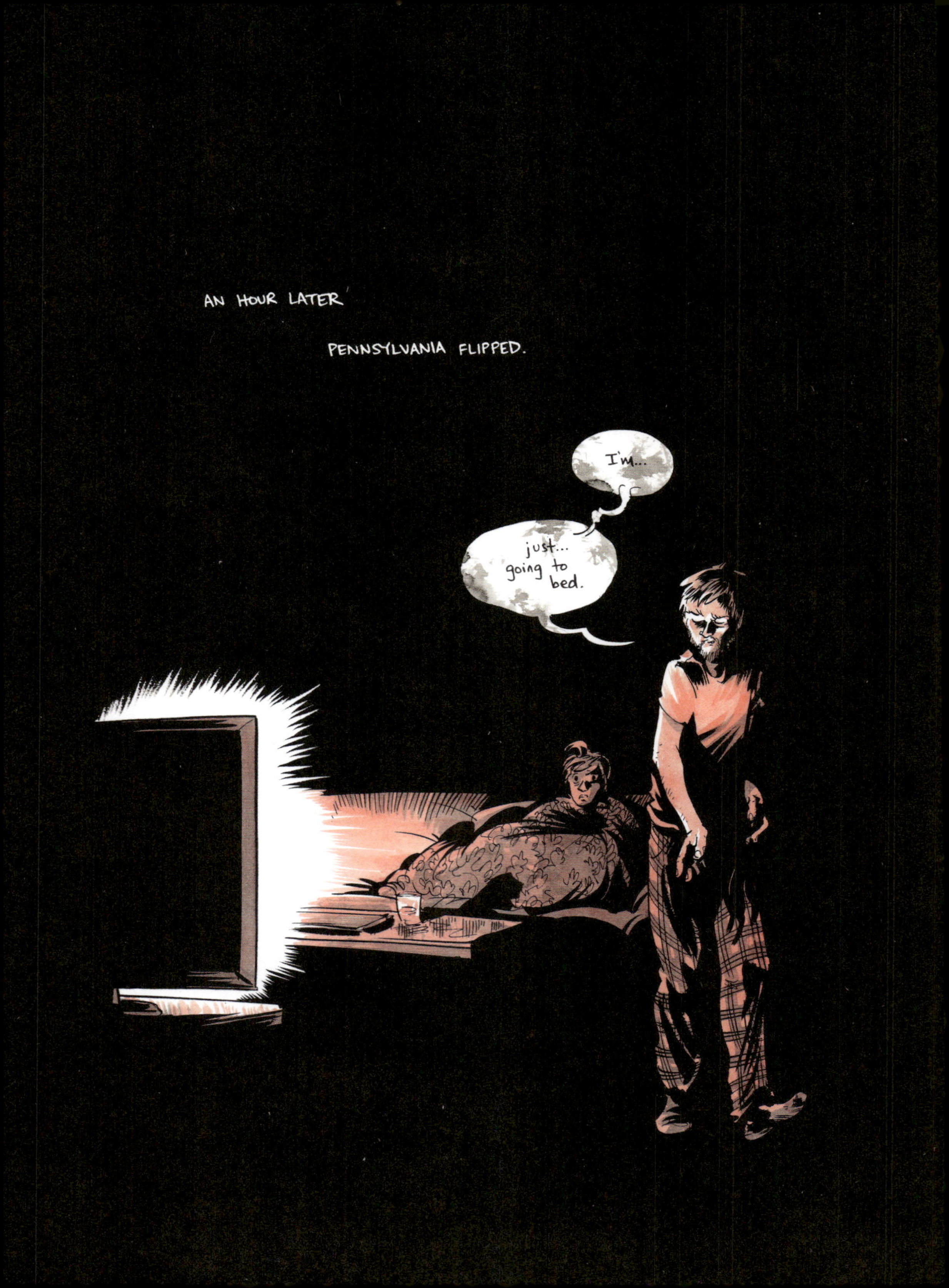
AN HOUR LATER
PENNSYLVANIA FLIPPED.
I'm...
just... going to bed.

FAITH IN INEVITABILITY—

A FATAL ERROR OF BOTH GENERATION X AND THE BOOMERS BEFORE US,

OUR WHITE, MIDDLE-CLASS OUTLOOKS SHAPED THROUGH A FAIRLY STABLE SOCIAL AND POLITICAL REALITY.

OUR FAITH IN MECHANISMS SLOWLY PUSHING SOCIETY FORWARD,

CLEARLY AN ERROR OF FAITH IN A SELF-PROPELLED MORAL ARC OF THE UNIVERSE.

YES, THE PENDULUM SWINGS,

BUT THIS IS SOMETHING ELSE.

Daddy?

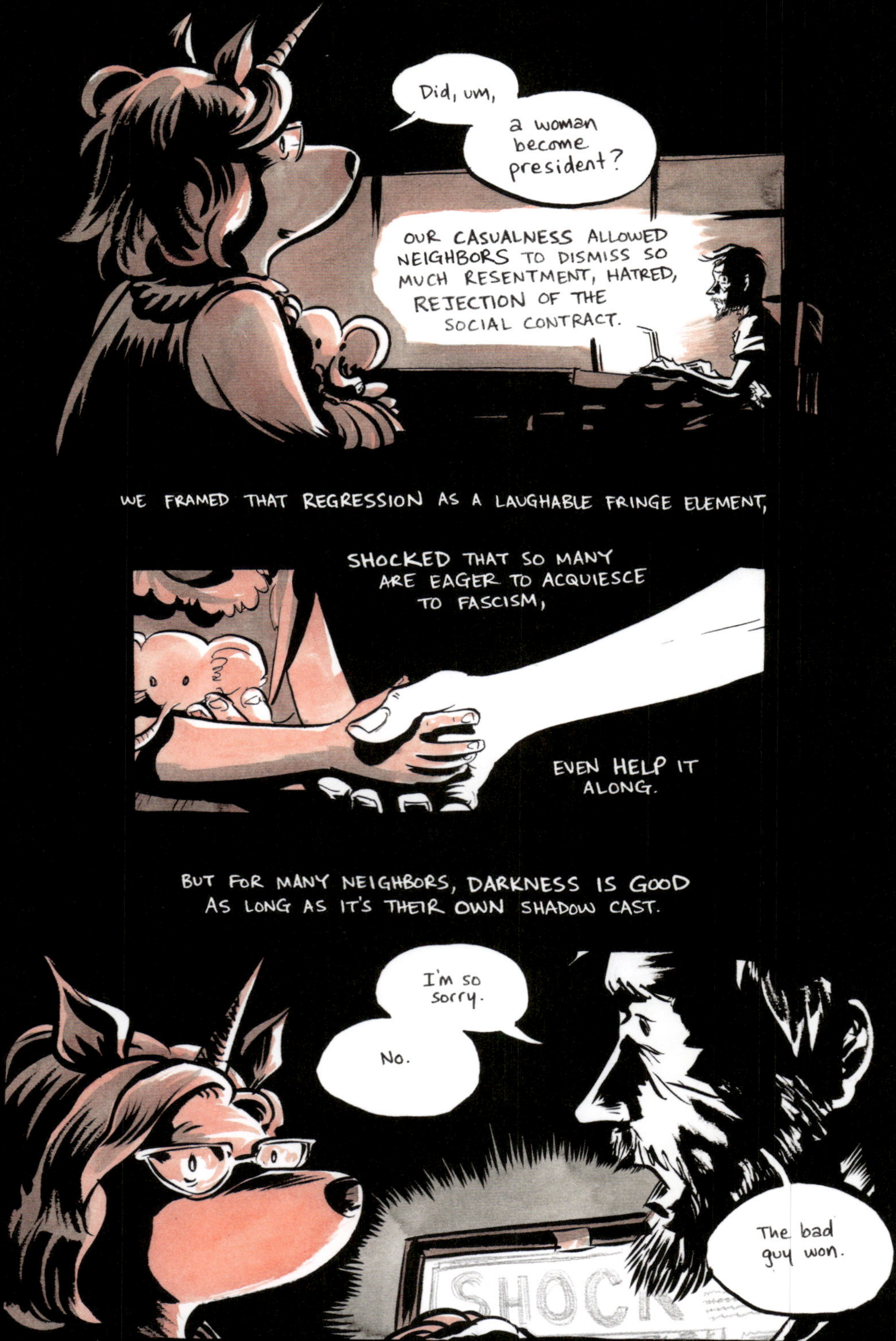
Did, um,
a woman become president?
OUR CASUALNESS ALLOWED NEIGHBORS TO DISMISS SO MUCH RESENTMENT, HATRED, REJECTION OF THE SOCIAL CONTRACT.
WE FRAMED THAT REGRESSION AS A LAUGHABLE FRINGE ELEMENT,
SHOCKED THAT SO MANY ARE EAGER TO ACQUIESCE TO FASCISM,
EVEN HELP IT ALONG.
BUT FOR MANY NEIGHBORS, DARKNESS IS GOOD AS LONG AS IT'S THEIR OWN SHADOW CAST.
I'm so sorry.
No.
The bad guy won.
SHOCK

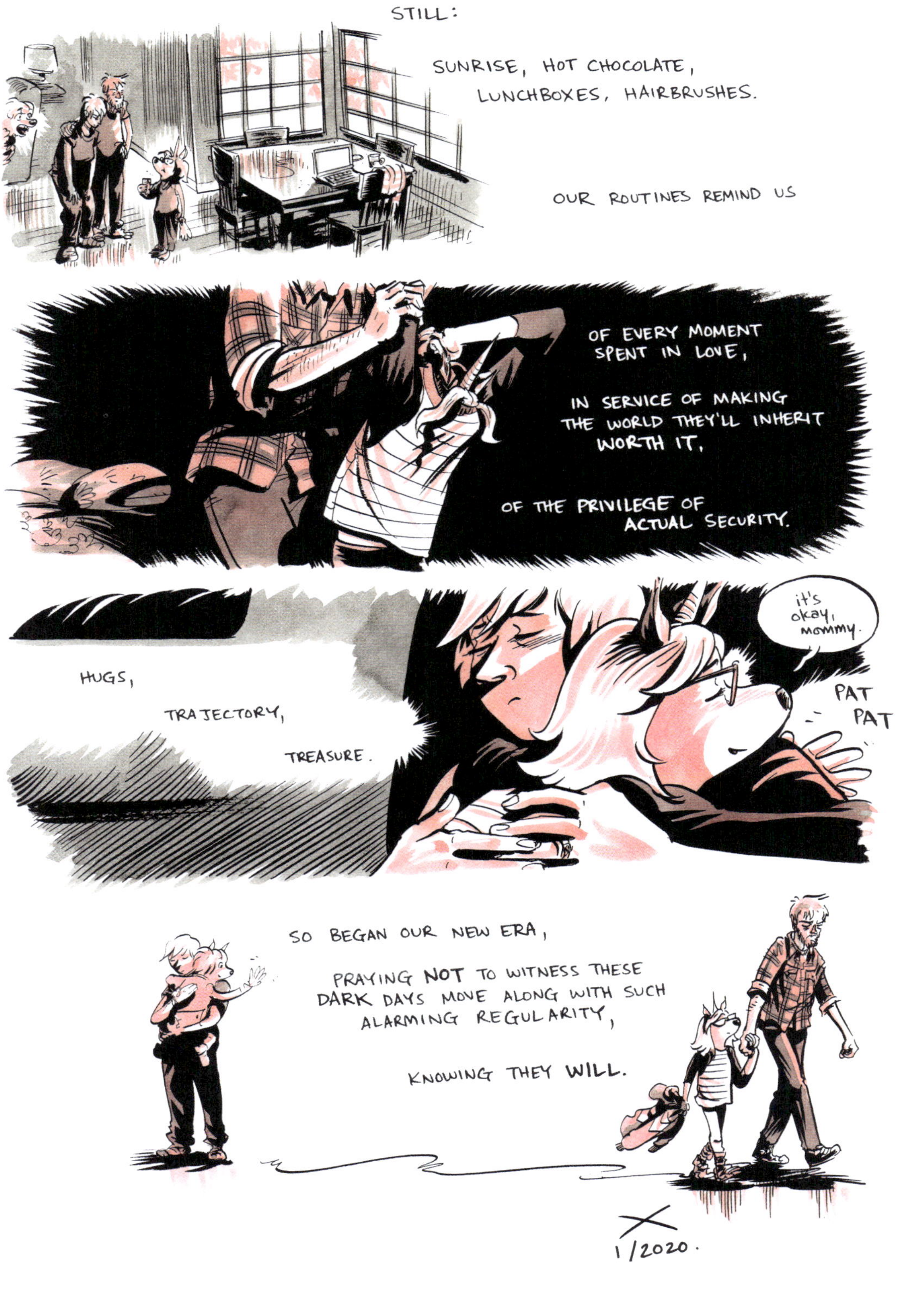
STILL:
SUNRISE, HOT CHOCOLATE, LUNCHBOXES, HAIRBRUSHES.
OUR ROUTINES REMIND US
OF EVERY MOMENT SPENT IN LOVE,
IN SERVICE OF MAKING THE WORLD THEY'LL INHERIT WORTH IT,
OF THE PRIVILEGE OF ACTUAL SECURITY.
HUGS,
TRAJECTORY,
TREASURE.
it's okay, mommy.
PAT PAT
SO BEGAN OUR NEW ERA,
PRAYING NOT TO WITNESS THESE DARK DAYS MOVE ALONG WITH SUCH ALARMING REGULARITY,
KNOWING THEY WILL.
1/2020.

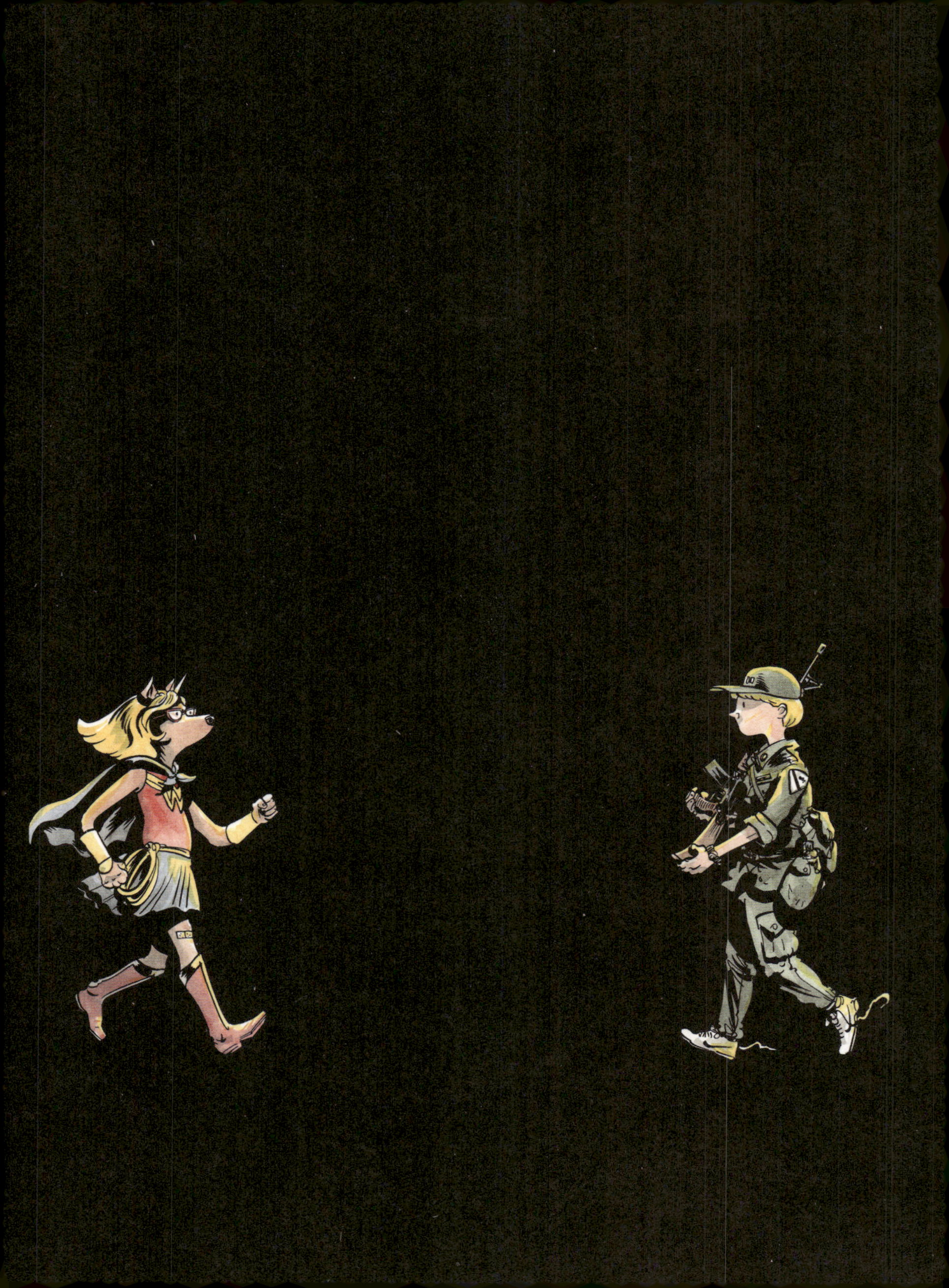

3

GOOD TROUBLE, BAD FLAGS

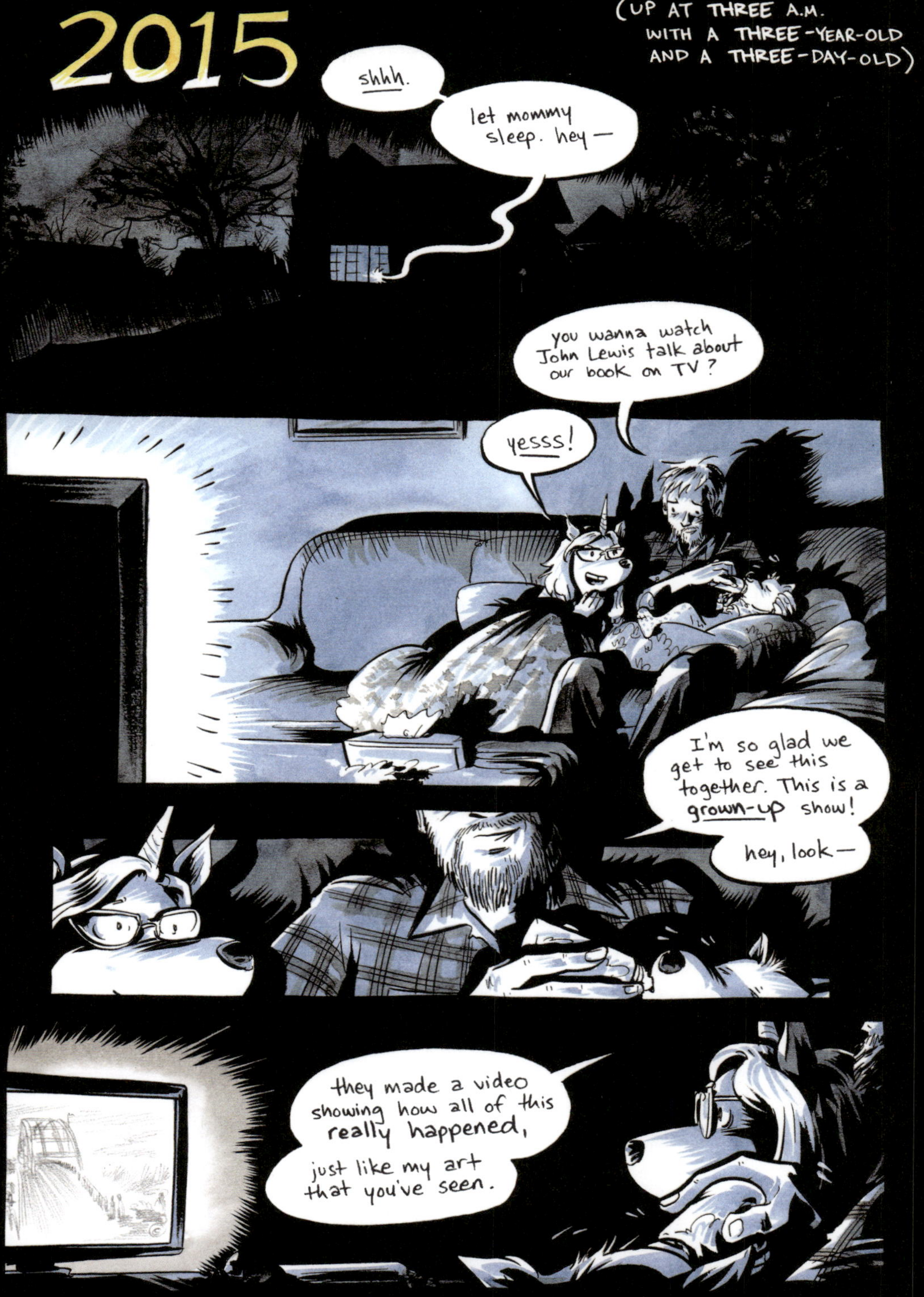
2015
(UP AT THREE A.M. WITH A THREE-YEAR-OLD AND A THREE-DAY-OLD)
shhh.
let mommy sleep. hey—
you wanna watch John Lewis talk about our book on TV?
yesss!
I'm so glad we get to see this together. This is a grown-up show!
hey, look—
they made a video showing how all of this really happened,
just like my art that you've seen.

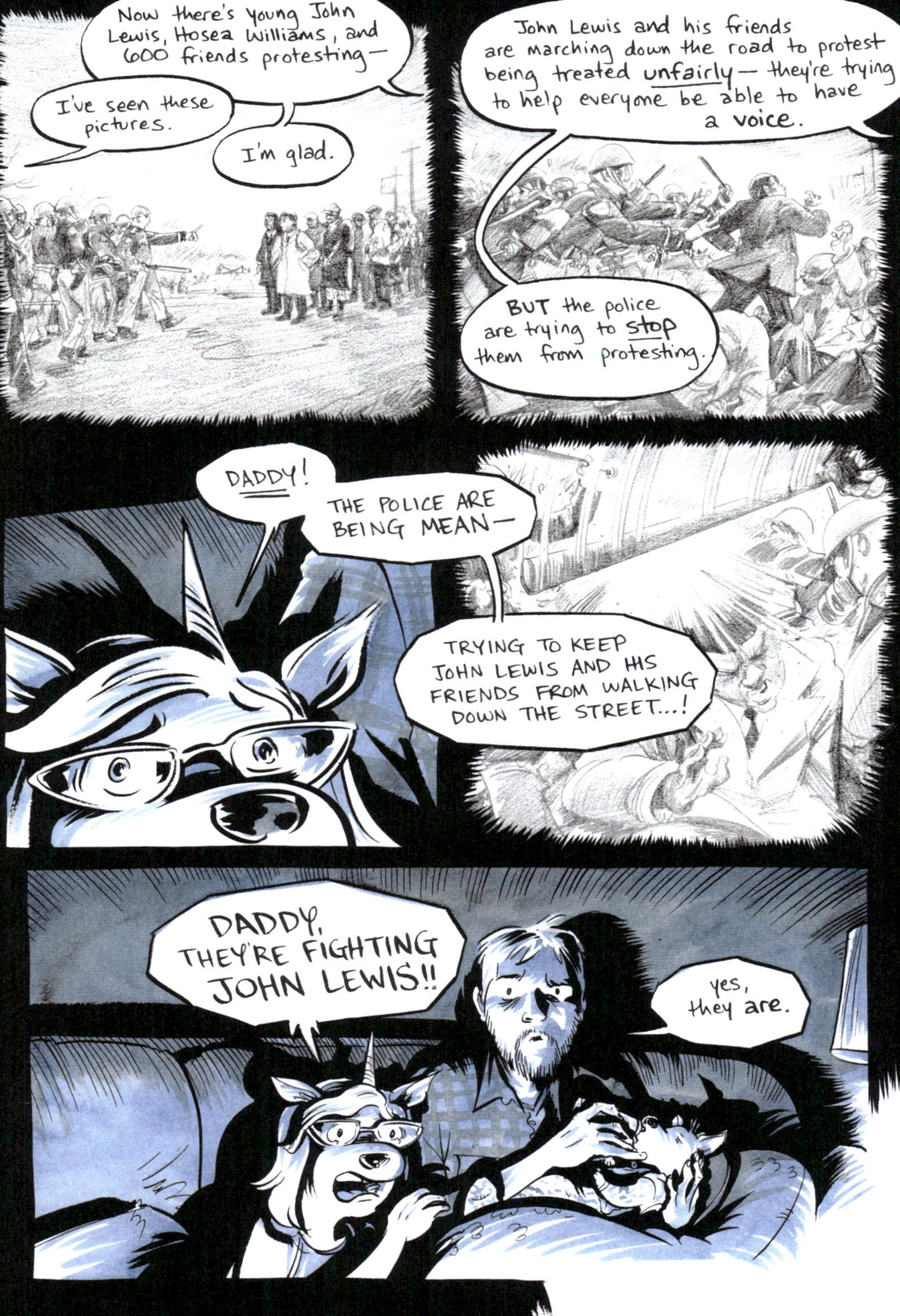
Now there's young John Lewis, Hosea Williams, and 600 friends protesting—
I've seen these pictures.
I'm glad.
John Lewis and his friends are marching down the road to protest being treated unfairly— they're trying to help everyone be able to have a voice.
BUT the police are trying to stop them from protesting.
DADDY!
THE POLICE ARE BEING MEAN—
TRYING TO KEEP JOHN LEWIS AND HIS FRIENDS FROM WALKING DOWN THE STREET...!
DADDY, THEY'RE FIGHTING JOHN LEWIS!!
yes, they are.

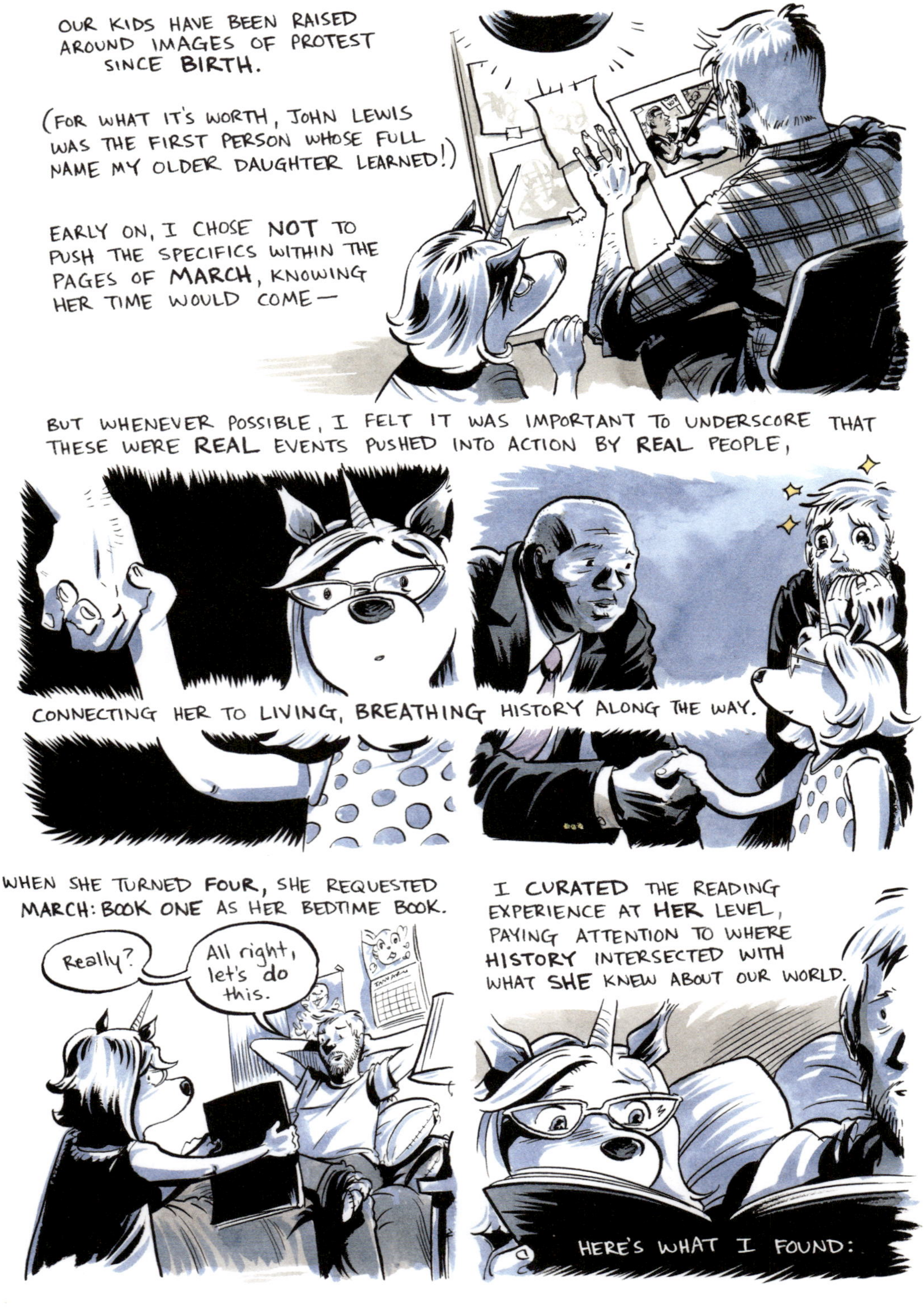
OUR KIDS HAVE BEEN RAISED AROUND IMAGES OF PROTEST SINCE BIRTH.
(FOR WHAT IT'S WORTH, JOHN LEWIS WAS THE FIRST PERSON WHOSE FULL NAME MY OLDER DAUGHTER LEARNED!)
EARLY ON, I CHOSE NOT TO PUSH THE SPECIFICS WITHIN THE PAGES OF MARCH, KNOWING HER TIME WOULD COME—
BUT WHENEVER POSSIBLE, I FELT IT WAS IMPORTANT TO UNDERSCORE THAT THESE WERE REAL EVENTS PUSHED INTO ACTION BY REAL PEOPLE,
CONNECTING HER TO LIVING, BREATHING HISTORY ALONG THE WAY.
WHEN SHE TURNED FOUR, SHE REQUESTED MARCH: BOOK ONE AS HER BEDTIME BOOK.
Really?
All right, let's do this.
I CURATED THE READING EXPERIENCE AT HER LEVEL, PAYING ATTENTION TO WHERE HISTORY INTERSECTED WITH WHAT SHE KNEW ABOUT OUR WORLD.
HERE'S WHAT I FOUND:

EVERY FOUR-YEAR-OLD HAS A PRETTY CLEAR RADAR FOR FAIRNESS AND INJUSTICE, AS SMALL AS THAT SCALE MAY OFTEN BE—

AND EVERY FOUR-YEAR OLD HAS ALREADY EXPERIENCED A BULLY.

OUR FIRST TIME THROUGH, IT WAS MOST IMPORTANT TO HIGHLIGHT THE POSITIVE **WORK** BY THESE YOUNG PEOPLE WHO HELPED MAKE OUR COUNTRY **FAIRER** BY SPEAKING OUT, PROTESTING AGAINST **INJUSTICE**.

(that's it.)

THE NEXT TIME, THE ACTIONS OF BULLIES WERE WOVEN INTO THAT INJUSTICE— AND HOW BULLIES WITH **POWER** WORK TO **KEEP** THINGS UNFAIR.

THE **THIRD** TIME WE READ IT, MY KID WAS FOCUSED ON UNFAIR TREATMENT DUE TO **DIFFERENCE**,

JUST DIFFERENCE **ITSELF**.

WHITE

COLORED

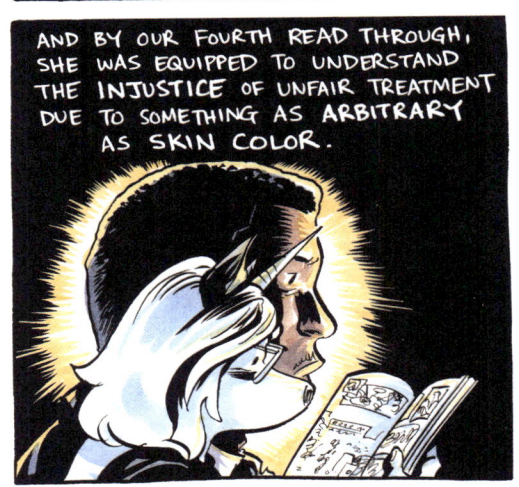

AND BY OUR FOURTH READ THROUGH, SHE WAS EQUIPPED TO UNDERSTAND THE **INJUSTICE** OF UNFAIR TREATMENT DUE TO SOMETHING AS **ARBITRARY** AS SKIN COLOR.

KIDS GET IT IMMEDIATELY— AND A HELL OF A LOT BETTER THAN ADULTS DO—

STILL ALLOWING THEMSELVES TO BE **MOVED** WITHOUT RESERVATION.

AS SHE SAW MORE IMAGES OF ACTIVIST ARRESTS, IT BECAME **NECESSARY** TO POINT OUT THAT THESE ACTIVISTS WERE OFTEN, IN FACT, **BREAKING THE LAW**—

BUT THAT LAWS CAN BE WRONG, HAVE **OFTEN** BEEN,

"you wanna VOTE?!"

"then how many JELLY BEANS in this hea'h JAR?"

AND SPACE FOR **FAIRER** LAWS IS ONLY CARVED OUT BY CHALLENGING THE **UNJUST** ONES.

IN BEING **ARRESTED** AND EVEN **BEATEN** BY POLICE EMPLOYED TO UPHOLD THOSE UNJUST LAWS, YOUNG PEOPLE FOUND **A WAY** TO MAKE MORE PEOPLE **PAY ATTENTION** TO INJUSTICES AFFECTING **MILLIONS** OF NEIGHBORS,

AND EVENTUALLY MADE OTHERWISE COMFORTABLE WHITE PEOPLE **JOIN** THE EFFORT TO **FIX** THAT INJUSTICE.

GIVE US

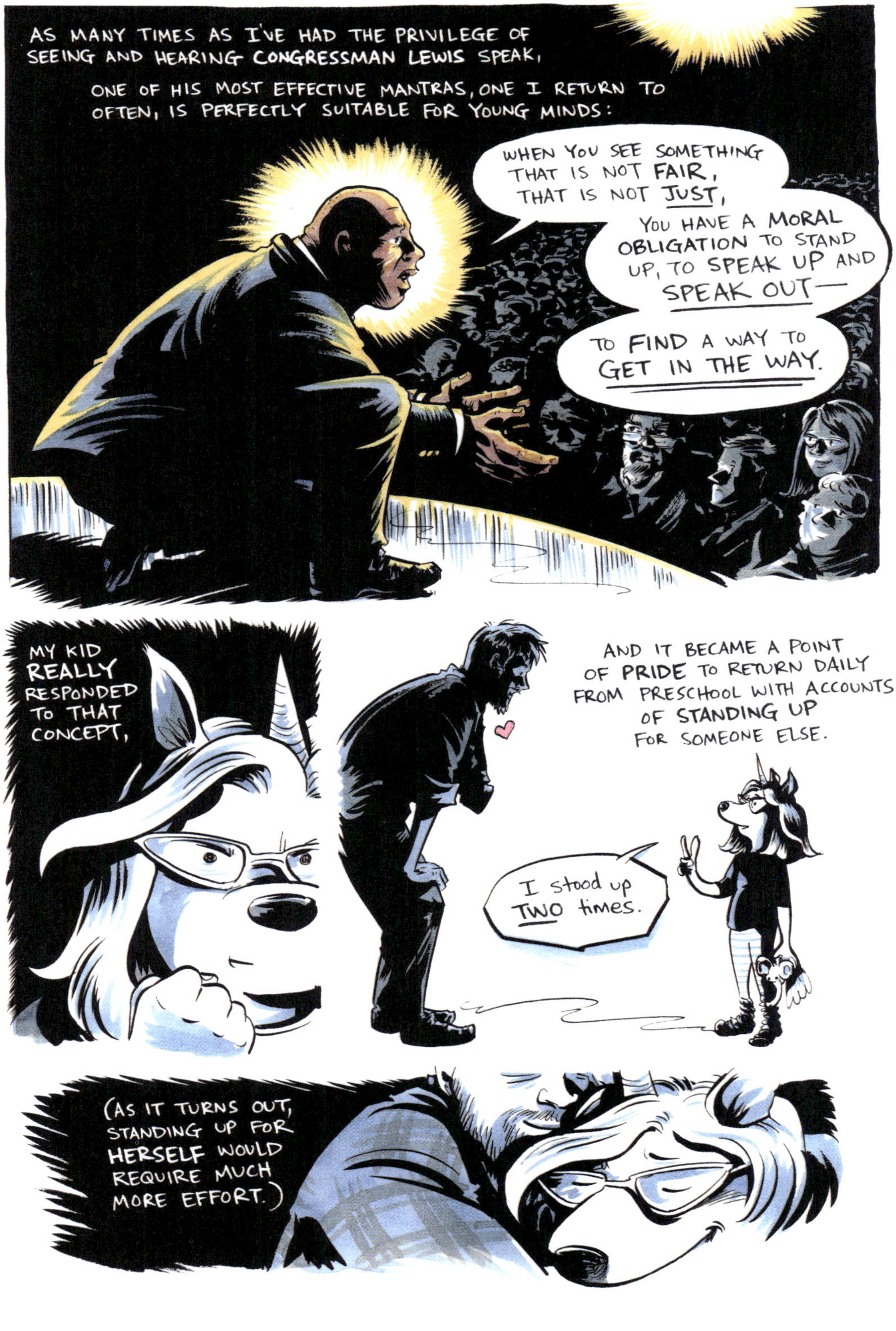
AS MANY TIMES AS I'VE HAD THE PRIVILEGE OF SEEING AND HEARING CONGRESSMAN LEWIS SPEAK,
ONE OF HIS MOST EFFECTIVE MANTRAS, ONE I RETURN TO OFTEN, IS PERFECTLY SUITABLE FOR YOUNG MINDS:
WHEN YOU SEE SOMETHING THAT IS NOT FAIR, THAT IS NOT JUST,
YOU HAVE A MORAL OBLIGATION TO STAND UP, TO SPEAK UP AND SPEAK OUT—
TO FIND A WAY TO GET IN THE WAY.
MY KID REALLY RESPONDED TO THAT CONCEPT,
AND IT BECAME A POINT OF PRIDE TO RETURN DAILY FROM PRESCHOOL WITH ACCOUNTS OF STANDING UP FOR SOMEONE ELSE.
I stood up TWO times.
(AS IT TURNS OUT, STANDING UP FOR HERSELF WOULD REQUIRE MUCH MORE EFFORT.)

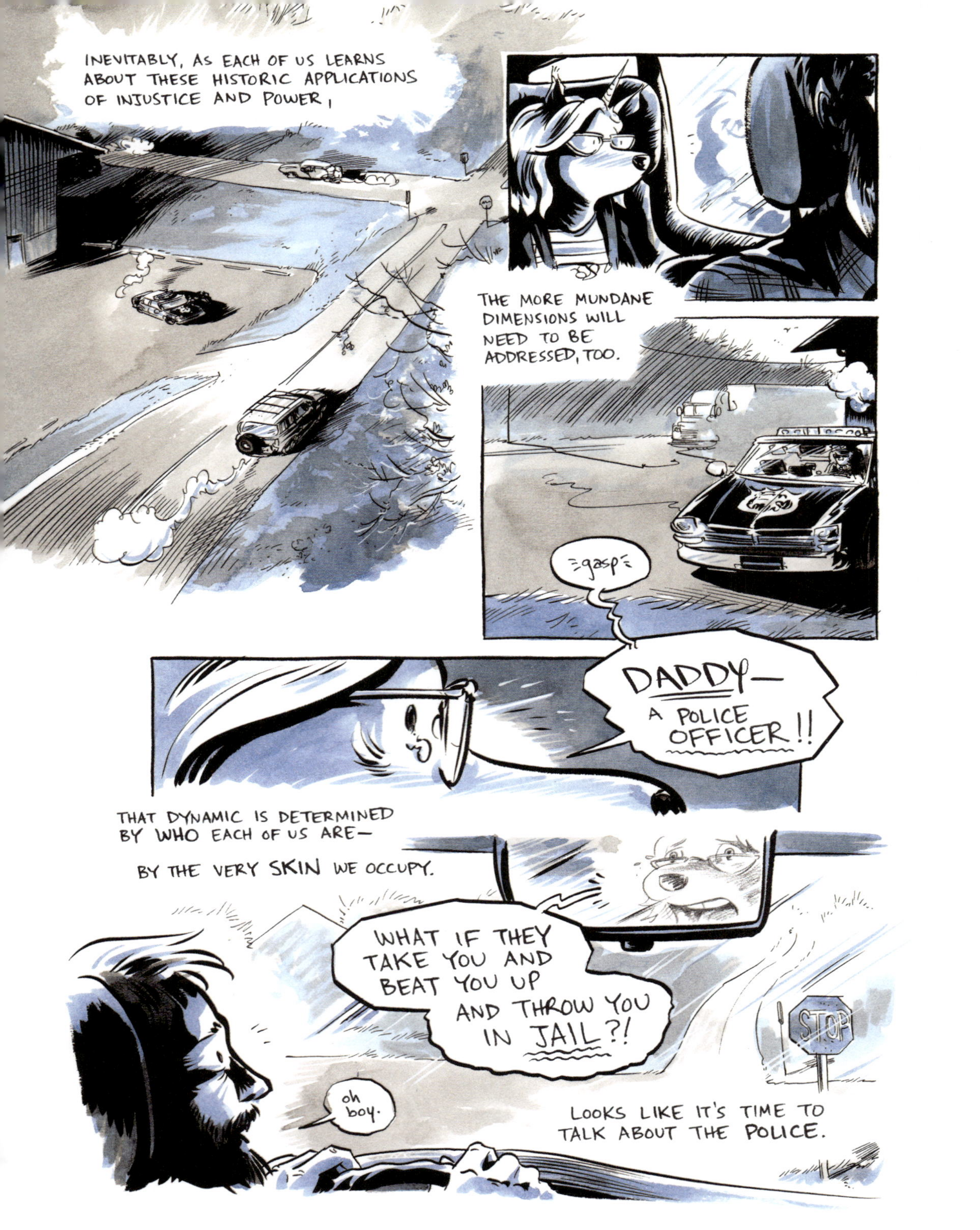
INEVITABLY, AS EACH OF US LEARNS ABOUT THESE HISTORIC APPLICATIONS OF INJUSTICE AND POWER,
THE MORE MUNDANE DIMENSIONS WILL NEED TO BE ADDRESSED, TOO.
gasp
DADDY— A POLICE OFFICER!!
THAT DYNAMIC IS DETERMINED BY WHO EACH OF US ARE—
BY THE VERY SKIN WE OCCUPY.
WHAT IF THEY TAKE YOU AND BEAT YOU UP AND THROW YOU IN JAIL?!
oh boy.
STOP
LOOKS LIKE IT'S TIME TO TALK ABOUT THE POLICE.

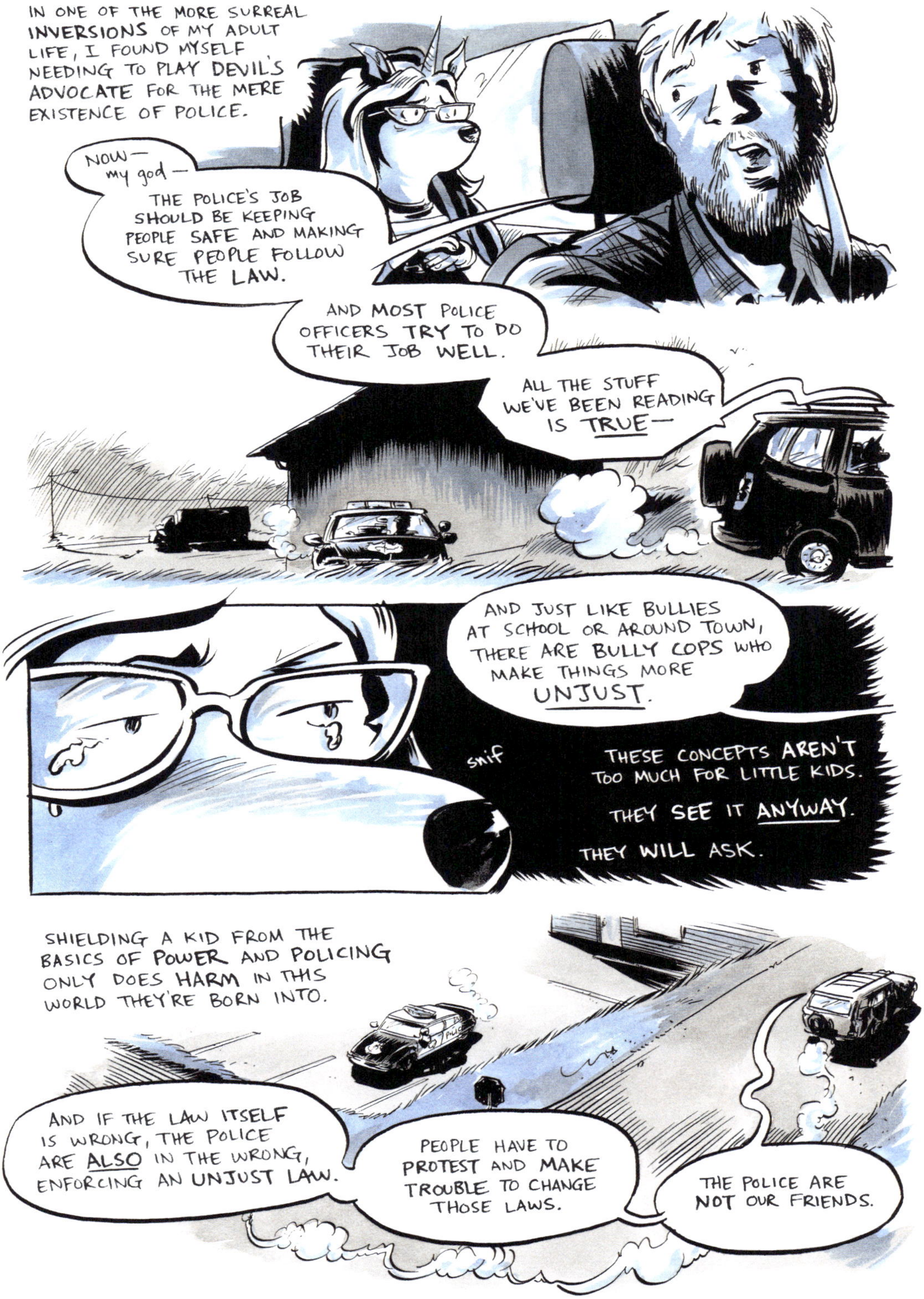
IN ONE OF THE MORE SURREAL INVERSIONS OF MY ADULT LIFE, I FOUND MYSELF NEEDING TO PLAY DEVIL'S ADVOCATE FOR THE MERE EXISTENCE OF POLICE.
NOW— my god— THE POLICE'S JOB SHOULD BE KEEPING PEOPLE SAFE AND MAKING SURE PEOPLE FOLLOW THE LAW.
AND MOST POLICE OFFICERS TRY TO DO THEIR JOB WELL.
ALL THE STUFF WE'VE BEEN READING IS TRUE—
AND JUST LIKE BULLIES AT SCHOOL OR AROUND TOWN, THERE ARE BULLY COPS WHO MAKE THINGS MORE UNJUST.
snif
THESE CONCEPTS AREN'T TOO MUCH FOR LITTLE KIDS.
THEY SEE IT ANYWAY.
THEY WILL ASK.
SHIELDING A KID FROM THE BASICS OF POWER AND POLICING ONLY DOES HARM IN THIS WORLD THEY'RE BORN INTO.
AND IF THE LAW ITSELF IS WRONG, THE POLICE ARE ALSO IN THE WRONG, ENFORCING AN UNJUST LAW.
PEOPLE HAVE TO PROTEST AND MAKE TROUBLE TO CHANGE THOSE LAWS.
THE POLICE ARE NOT OUR FRIENDS.

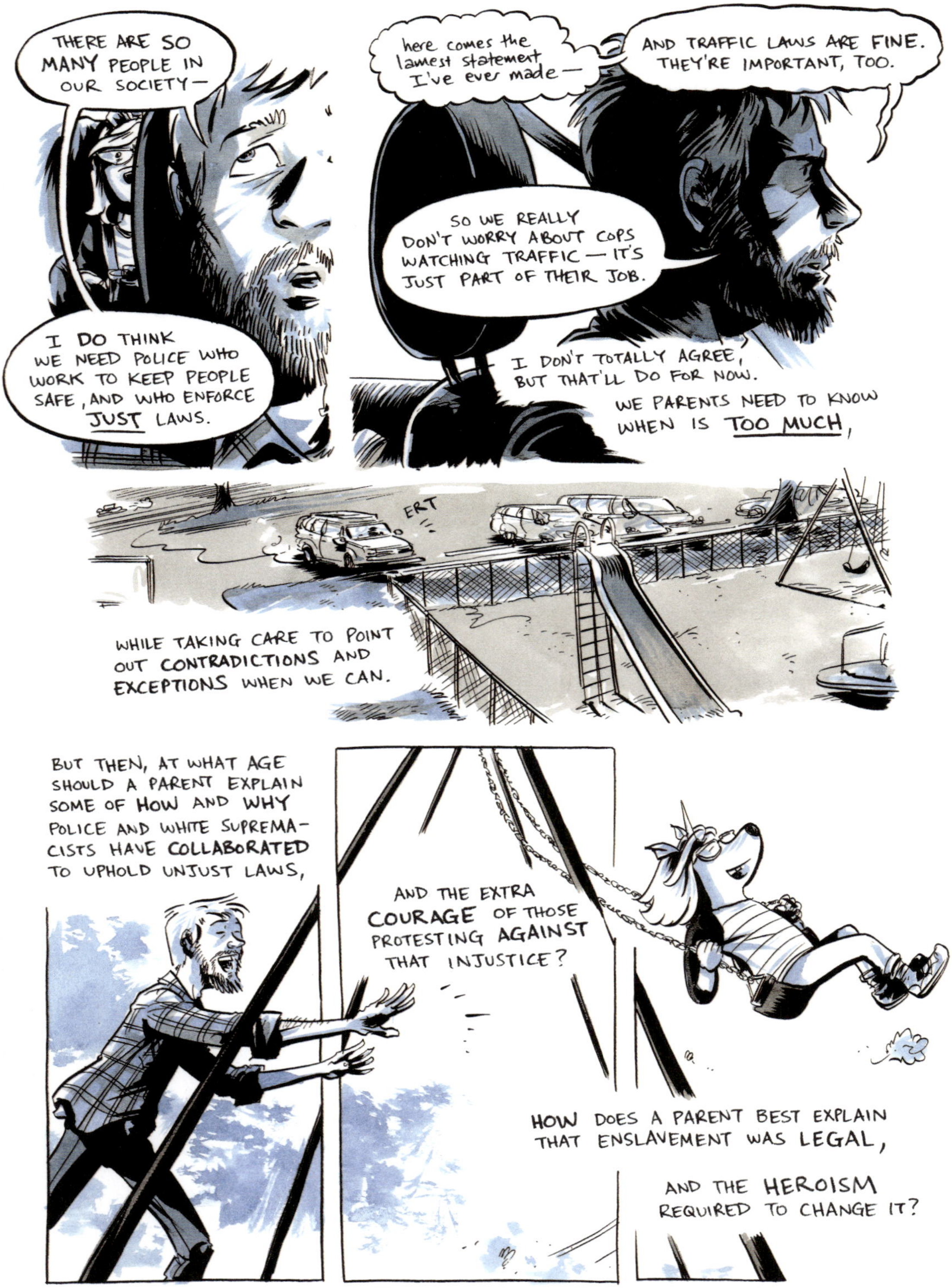
THERE ARE SO MANY PEOPLE IN OUR SOCIETY—
I DO THINK WE NEED POLICE WHO WORK TO KEEP PEOPLE SAFE, AND WHO ENFORCE JUST LAWS.
here comes the lamest statement I've ever made—
AND TRAFFIC LAWS ARE FINE. THEY'RE IMPORTANT, TOO.
SO WE REALLY DON'T WORRY ABOUT COPS WATCHING TRAFFIC— IT'S JUST PART OF THEIR JOB.
I DON'T TOTALLY AGREE, BUT THAT'LL DO FOR NOW.
WE PARENTS NEED TO KNOW WHEN IS TOO MUCH,
ERT
WHILE TAKING CARE TO POINT OUT CONTRADICTIONS AND EXCEPTIONS WHEN WE CAN.
BUT THEN, AT WHAT AGE SHOULD A PARENT EXPLAIN SOME OF HOW AND WHY POLICE AND WHITE SUPREMACISTS HAVE COLLABORATED TO UPHOLD UNJUST LAWS,
AND THE EXTRA COURAGE OF THOSE PROTESTING AGAINST THAT INJUSTICE?
HOW DOES A PARENT BEST EXPLAIN THAT ENSLAVEMENT WAS LEGAL,
AND THE HEROISM REQUIRED TO CHANGE IT?

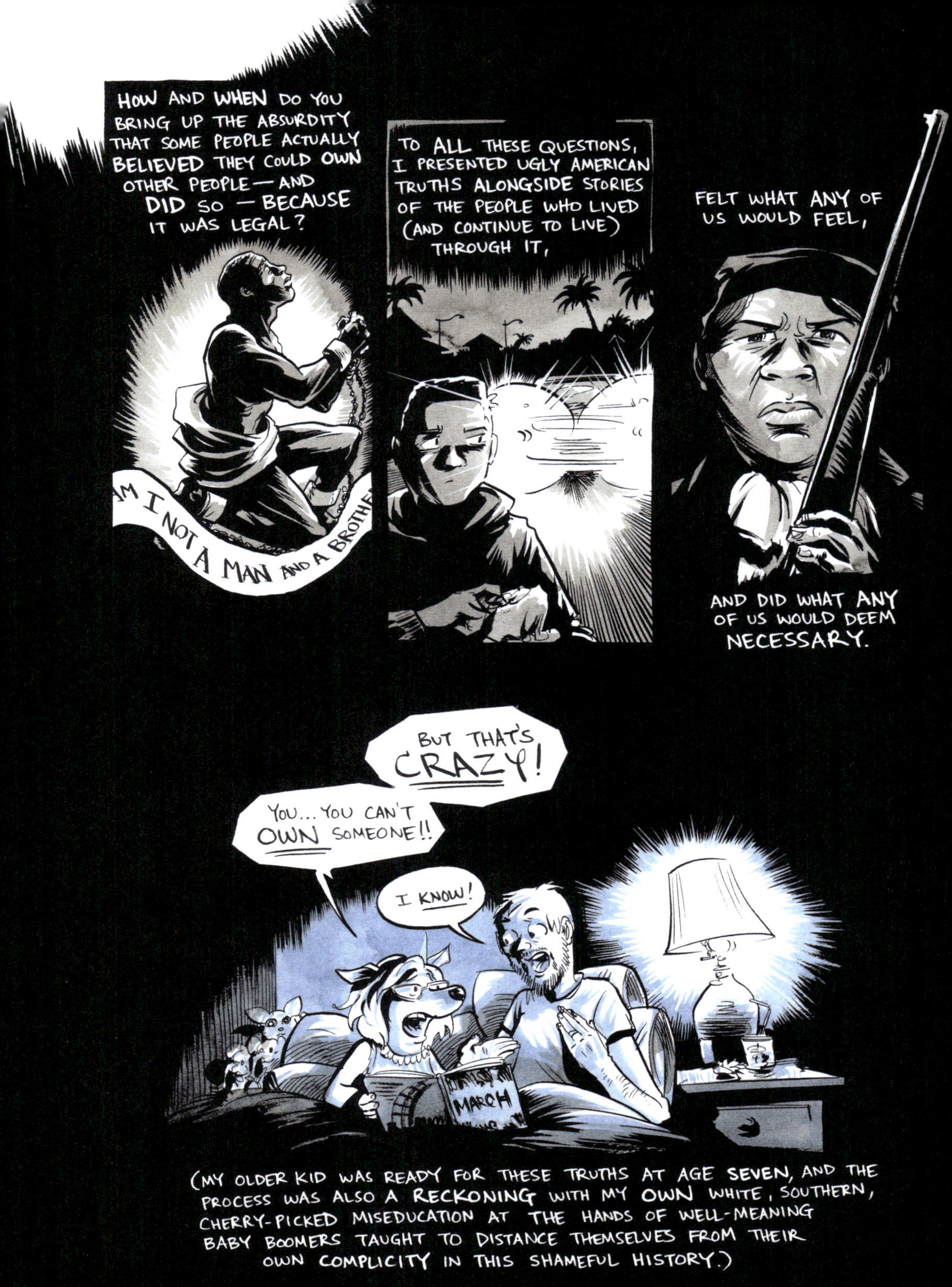
HOW AND WHEN DO YOU BRING UP THE ABSURDITY THAT SOME PEOPLE ACTUALLY BELIEVED THEY COULD OWN OTHER PEOPLE—AND DID SO—BECAUSE IT WAS LEGAL?
AM I NOT A MAN AND A BROTHER
TO ALL THESE QUESTIONS, I PRESENTED UGLY AMERICAN TRUTHS ALONGSIDE STORIES OF THE PEOPLE WHO LIVED (AND CONTINUE TO LIVE) THROUGH IT,
FELT WHAT ANY OF US WOULD FEEL,
AND DID WHAT ANY OF US WOULD DEEM NECESSARY.
BUT THAT'S CRAZY!
YOU... YOU CAN'T OWN SOMEONE!!
I KNOW!
MARCH
(MY OLDER KID WAS READY FOR THESE TRUTHS AT AGE SEVEN, AND THE PROCESS WAS ALSO A RECKONING WITH MY OWN WHITE, SOUTHERN, CHERRY-PICKED MISEDUCATION AT THE HANDS OF WELL-MEANING BABY BOOMERS TAUGHT TO DISTANCE THEMSELVES FROM THEIR OWN COMPLICITY IN THIS SHAMEFUL HISTORY.)

HEROISM IS MORAL AND PHYSICAL COURAGE IN THE FACE OF DANGER, OFTEN IN THE SERVICE OF **STRANGERS**.

IT'S WHAT KIDS HER AGE ABSORB EVERY DAY IN POP-CULTURE ENTERTAINMENT,

(A BIT DEFANGED, BUT STILL.)

AND KIDS ARE HUNGRY TO SEE EXAMPLES OF REAL HEROES USING EVERYDAY STRENGTHS — THEIR OWN STRENGTHS — TO RIGHT A WRONG.

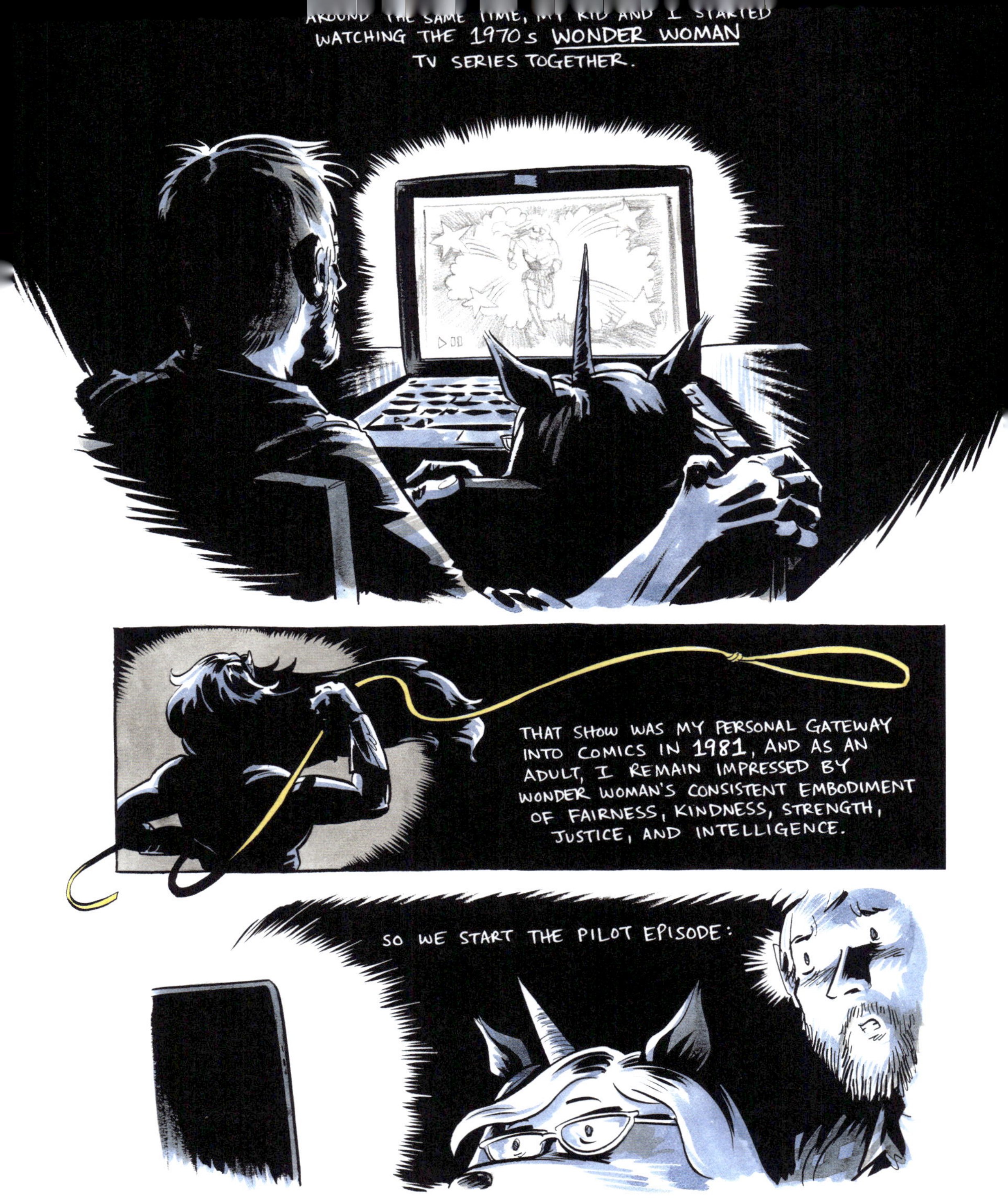
AROUND THE SAME TIME, MY KID AND I STARTED WATCHING THE 1970s WONDER WOMAN TV SERIES TOGETHER.
THAT SHOW WAS MY PERSONAL GATEWAY INTO COMICS IN 1981, AND AS AN ADULT, I REMAIN IMPRESSED BY WONDER WOMAN'S CONSISTENT EMBODIMENT OF FAIRNESS, KINDNESS, STRENGTH, JUSTICE, AND INTELLIGENCE.
SO WE START THE PILOT EPISODE:

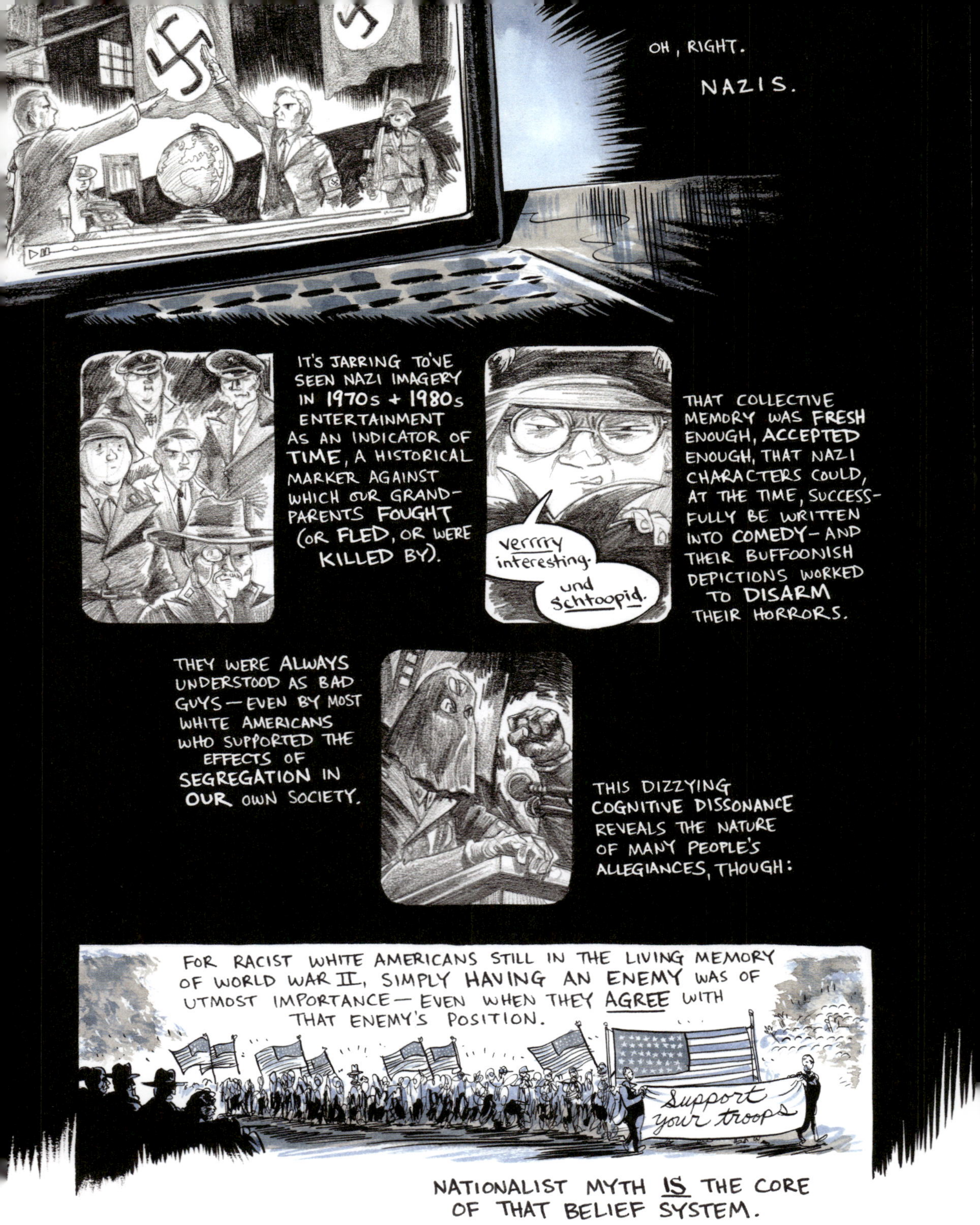
OH, RIGHT.
NAZIS.
IT'S JARRING TO'VE SEEN NAZI IMAGERY IN 1970s + 1980s ENTERTAINMENT AS AN INDICATOR OF TIME, A HISTORICAL MARKER AGAINST WHICH OUR GRANDPARENTS FOUGHT (OR FLED, OR WERE KILLED BY).
verrrry interesting.
und schtoopid.
THAT COLLECTIVE MEMORY WAS FRESH ENOUGH, ACCEPTED ENOUGH, THAT NAZI CHARACTERS COULD, AT THE TIME, SUCCESSFULLY BE WRITTEN INTO COMEDY– AND THEIR BUFFOONISH DEPICTIONS WORKED TO DISARM THEIR HORRORS.
THEY WERE ALWAYS UNDERSTOOD AS BAD GUYS– EVEN BY MOST WHITE AMERICANS WHO SUPPORTED THE EFFECTS OF SEGREGATION IN OUR OWN SOCIETY.
THIS DIZZYING COGNITIVE DISSONANCE REVEALS THE NATURE OF MANY PEOPLE'S ALLEGIANCES, THOUGH:
FOR RACIST WHITE AMERICANS STILL IN THE LIVING MEMORY OF WORLD WAR II, SIMPLY HAVING AN ENEMY WAS OF UTMOST IMPORTANCE– EVEN WHEN THEY AGREE WITH THAT ENEMY'S POSITION.
Support your troops
NATIONALIST MYTH IS THE CORE OF THAT BELIEF SYSTEM.

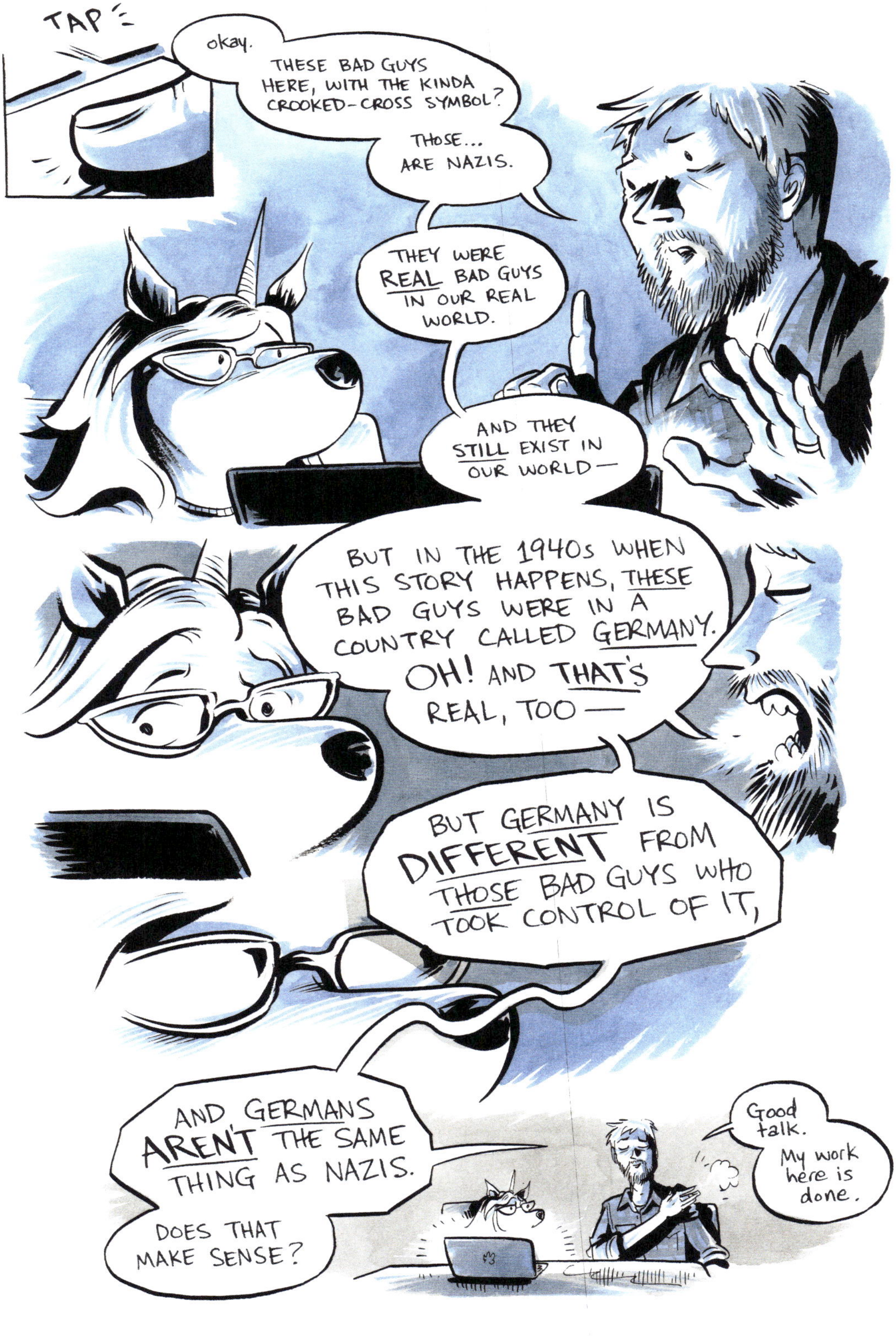
TAP
okay. THESE BAD GUYS HERE, WITH THE KINDA CROOKED-CROSS SYMBOL?
THOSE... ARE NAZIS.
THEY WERE REAL BAD GUYS IN OUR REAL WORLD.
AND THEY STILL EXIST IN OUR WORLD—
BUT IN THE 1940s WHEN THIS STORY HAPPENS, THESE BAD GUYS WERE IN A COUNTRY CALLED GERMANY. OH! AND THAT'S REAL, TOO—
BUT GERMANY IS DIFFERENT FROM THOSE BAD GUYS WHO TOOK CONTROL OF IT,
AND GERMANS AREN'T THE SAME THING AS NAZIS.
DOES THAT MAKE SENSE?
Good talk.
My work here is done.

WHEN YOUNG PEOPLE PRETEND, VILLAINY HAS AN IRRESISTIBLE ALLURE—

BUT SOMETHING TELLS ME MY GENERATION FAILED TO ASK WHY.

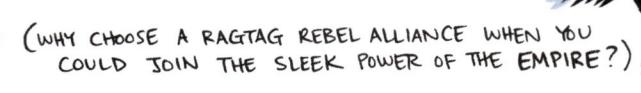

(WHY CHOOSE A RAGTAG REBEL ALLIANCE WHEN YOU COULD JOIN THE SLEEK POWER OF THE EMPIRE?)

"HEY THERE—"

"WHAT'S THIS ON YOUR ARM?"

"What were you drawing there?"

76

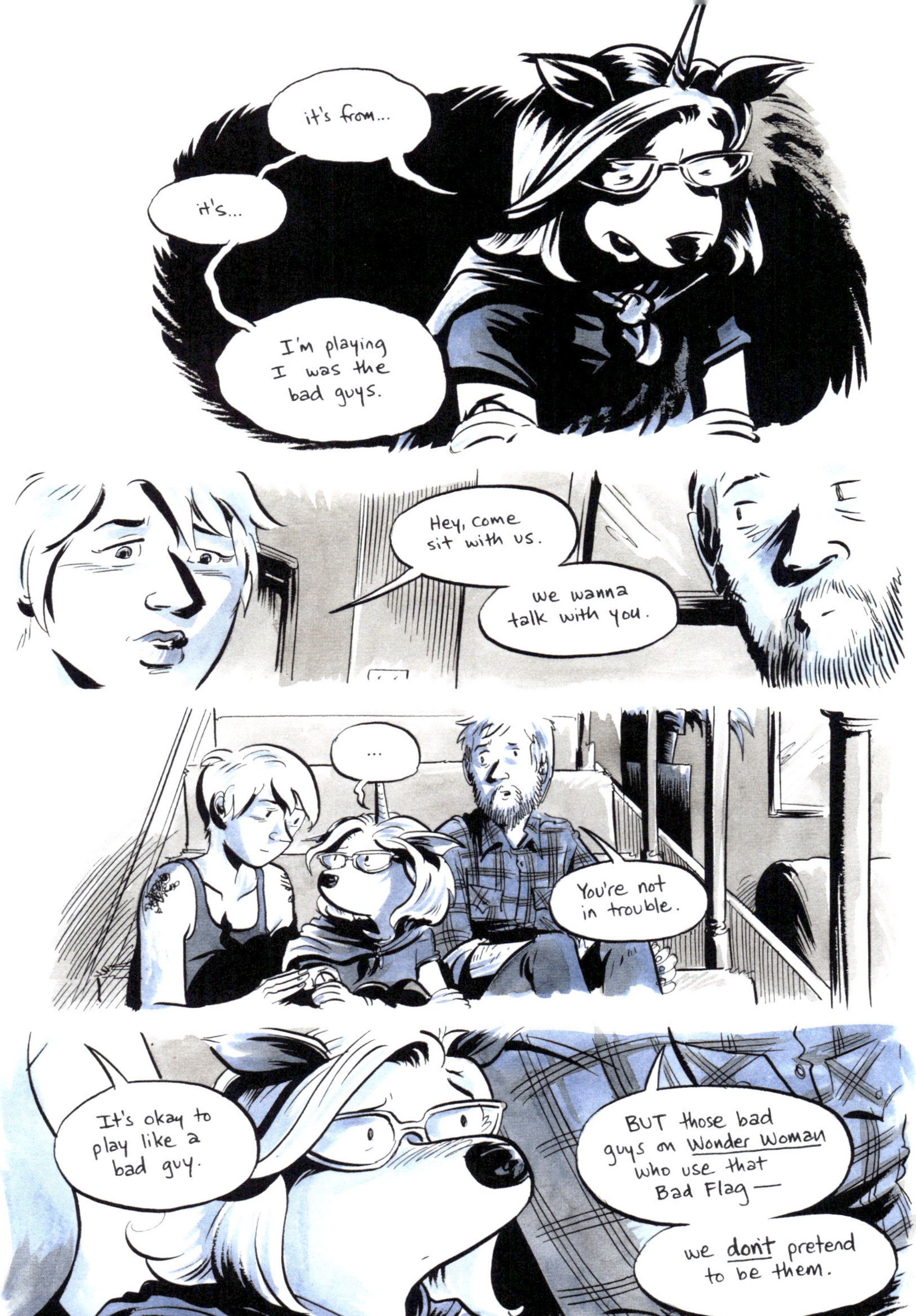
it's...
it's from...
I'm playing I was the bad guys.
Hey, come sit with us.
we wanna talk with you.
...
You're not in trouble.
It's okay to play like a bad guy.
BUT those bad guys on Wonder Woman who use that Bad Flag—
we don't pretend to be them.

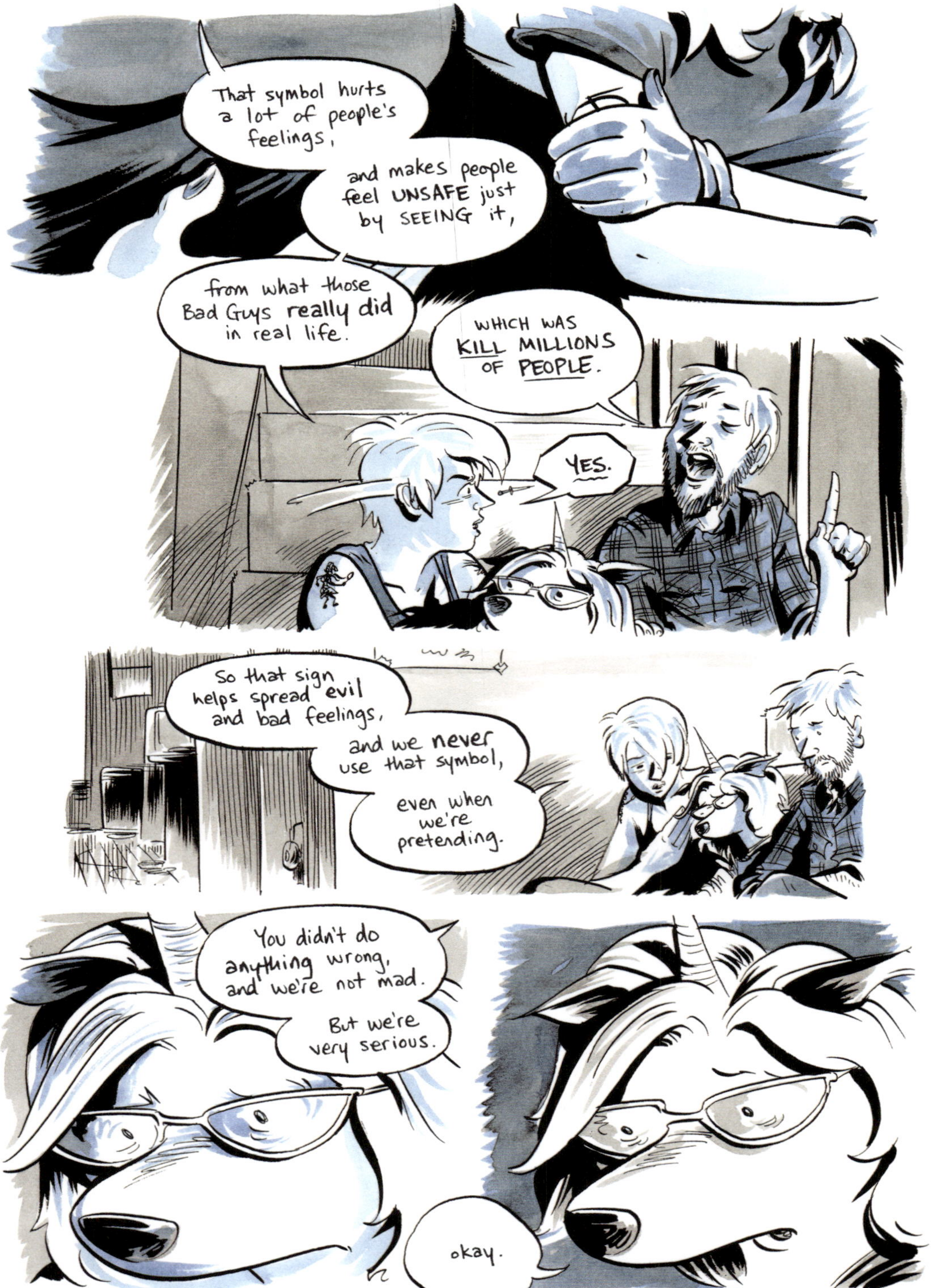
That symbol hurts a lot of people's feelings,
and makes people feel UNSAFE just by SEEING it,
from what those Bad Guys really did in real life.
WHICH WAS KILL MILLIONS OF PEOPLE.
YES.
So that sign helps spread evil and bad feelings,
and we never use that symbol,
even when we're pretending.
You didn't do anything wrong, and we're not mad.
But we're very serious.
okay.

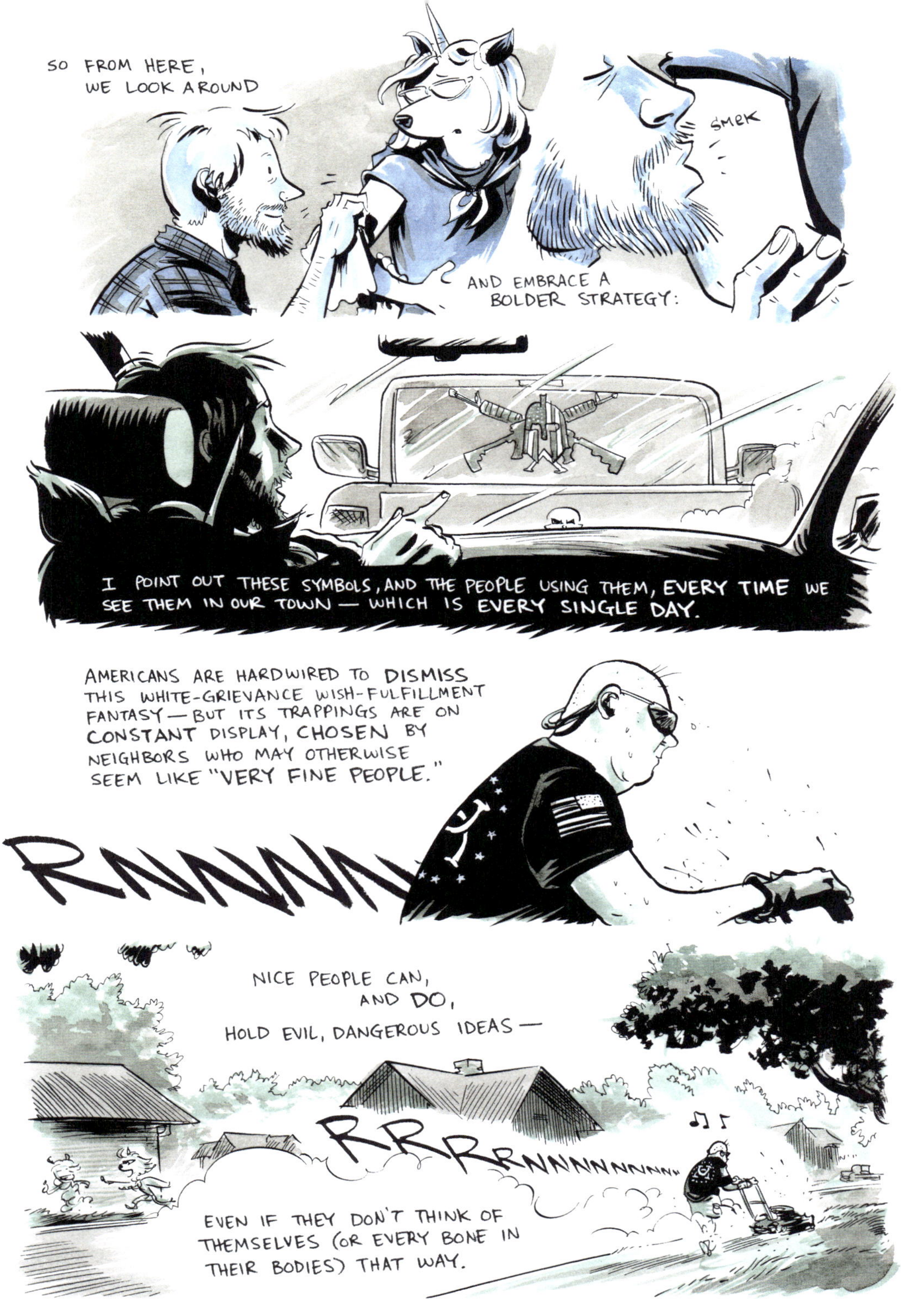
SO FROM HERE, WE LOOK AROUND
SMEK
AND EMBRACE A BOLDER STRATEGY:
I POINT OUT THESE SYMBOLS, AND THE PEOPLE USING THEM, EVERY TIME WE SEE THEM IN OUR TOWN — WHICH IS EVERY SINGLE DAY.
AMERICANS ARE HARDWIRED TO DISMISS THIS WHITE-GRIEVANCE WISH-FULFILLMENT FANTASY — BUT ITS TRAPPINGS ARE ON CONSTANT DISPLAY, CHOSEN BY NEIGHBORS WHO MAY OTHERWISE SEEM LIKE "VERY FINE PEOPLE."
RNNNNN
NICE PEOPLE CAN, AND DO, HOLD EVIL, DANGEROUS IDEAS —
RRRRNNNNNNNNN
EVEN IF THEY DON'T THINK OF THEMSELVES (OR EVERY BONE IN THEIR BODIES) THAT WAY.

EVEN TEACHING ABOUT THE **SOCIAL CONTRACT** BY WHICH CHILDREN **SHOULD** BE ABLE TO ASK AN ADULT FOR HELP, I'VE CHOSEN TO MAKE AN EXCEPTION:

IF YOU SEE SOMEONE WITH ONE OF THE TWO MAIN **BAD FLAGS**, YOU NEED TO **GET AWAY** FROM THEM, EVEN IF YOU NEED HELP.

(I'll wait for the White Tears.)

TO ALL THE WHITE BABY BOOMERS IN THE BACK:

LET ME SPEAK TO THE **MANAGER**.

ONLY THE **SKIN** INTO WHICH MY KID WAS **BORN** AFFORDS HER THE ASSUMPTION OF SAFETY IN THE PRESENCE OF SOMEONE BEARING THOSE SYMBOLS.

WHAT MESSAGE WOULD IT SEND TO EMPHASIZE THAT **HER** SAFETY ALONE IS WORTHY OF CONCERN IN DISREGARD OF HER NEIGHBORS AND CLASSMATES?

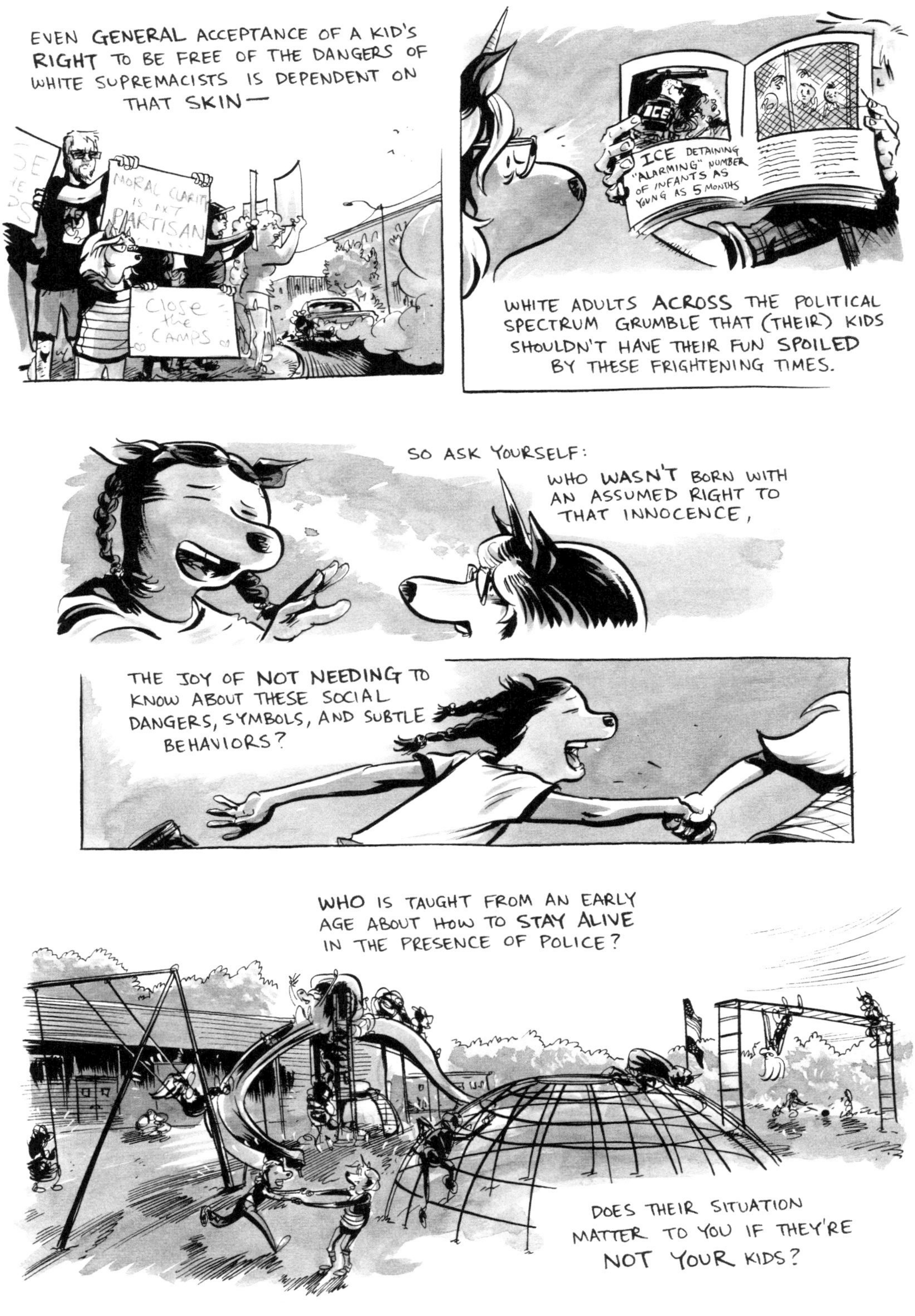
EVEN GENERAL ACCEPTANCE OF A KID'S RIGHT TO BE FREE OF THE DANGERS OF WHITE SUPREMACISTS IS DEPENDENT ON THAT SKIN—
PARTISAN
Close the CAMPS
ICE
ICE DETAINING "ALARMING" NUMBER OF INFANTS AS YOUNG AS 5 MONTHS
WHITE ADULTS ACROSS THE POLITICAL SPECTRUM GRUMBLE THAT (THEIR) KIDS SHOULDN'T HAVE THEIR FUN SPOILED BY THESE FRIGHTENING TIMES.
SO ASK YOURSELF:
WHO WASN'T BORN WITH AN ASSUMED RIGHT TO THAT INNOCENCE,
THE JOY OF NOT NEEDING TO KNOW ABOUT THESE SOCIAL DANGERS, SYMBOLS, AND SUBTLE BEHAVIORS?
WHO IS TAUGHT FROM AN EARLY AGE ABOUT HOW TO STAY ALIVE IN THE PRESENCE OF POLICE?
DOES THEIR SITUATION MATTER TO YOU IF THEY'RE NOT YOUR KIDS?

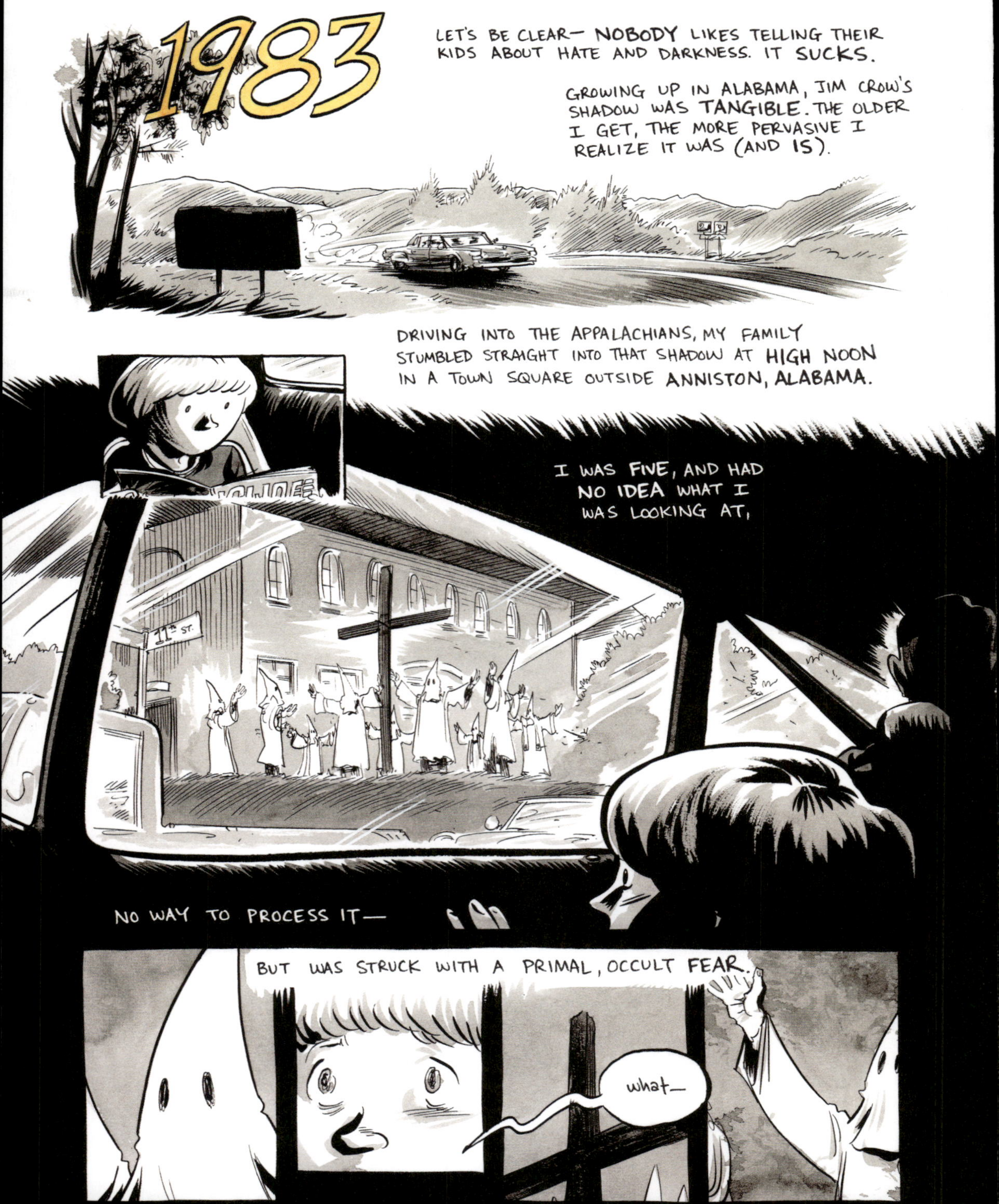
1983
LET'S BE CLEAR— NOBODY LIKES TELLING THEIR KIDS ABOUT HATE AND DARKNESS. IT SUCKS.
GROWING UP IN ALABAMA, JIM CROW'S SHADOW WAS TANGIBLE. THE OLDER I GET, THE MORE PERVASIVE I REALIZE IT WAS (AND IS).
DRIVING INTO THE APPALACHIANS, MY FAMILY STUMBLED STRAIGHT INTO THAT SHADOW AT HIGH NOON IN A TOWN SQUARE OUTSIDE ANNISTON, ALABAMA.
I WAS FIVE, AND HAD NO IDEA WHAT I WAS LOOKING AT,
11TH ST.
NO WAY TO PROCESS IT—
BUT WAS STRUCK WITH A PRIMAL, OCCULT FEAR.
what_

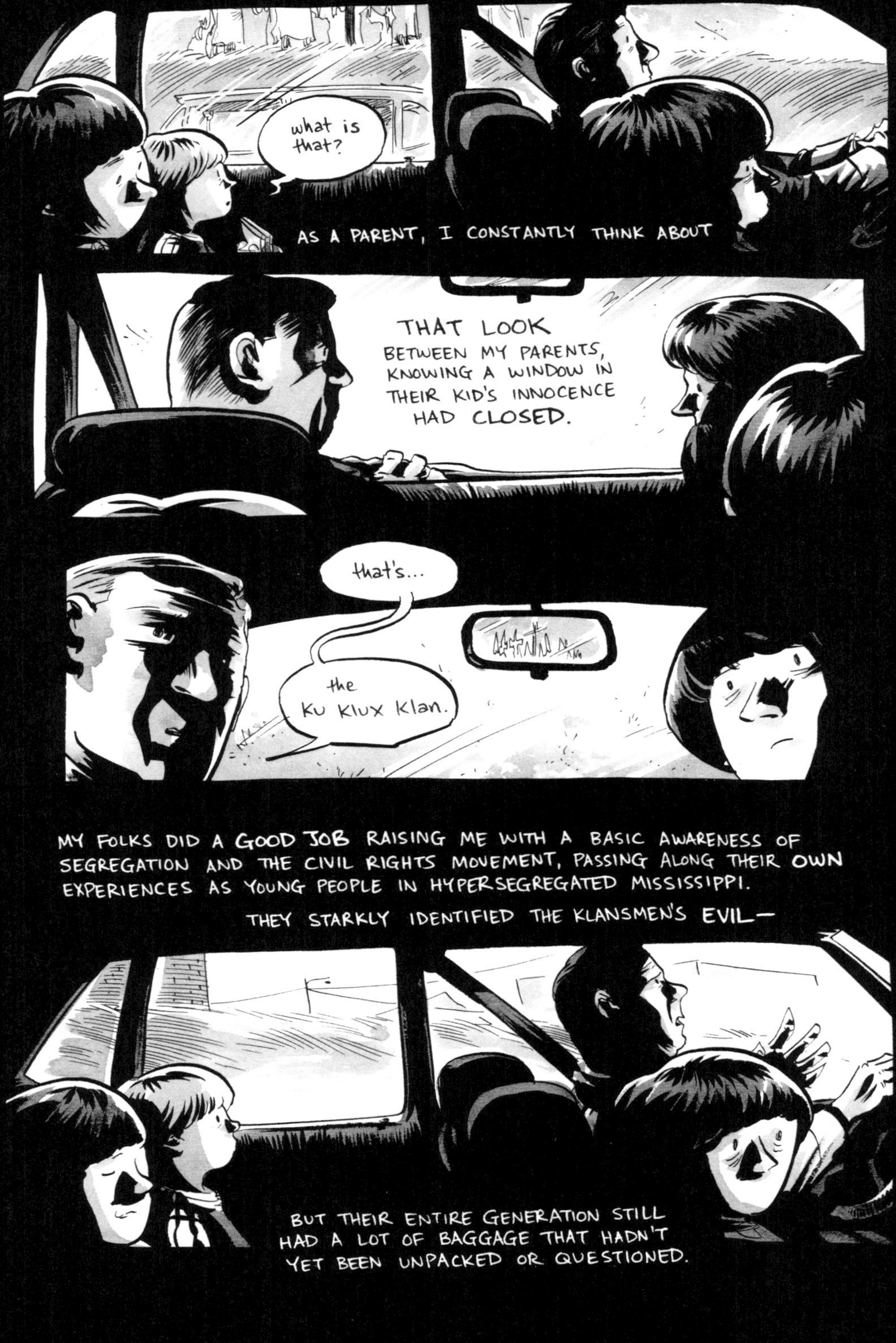
what is that?
AS A PARENT, I CONSTANTLY THINK ABOUT
THAT LOOK BETWEEN MY PARENTS, KNOWING A WINDOW IN THEIR KID'S INNOCENCE HAD CLOSED.
that's...
the Ku Klux Klan.
MY FOLKS DID A GOOD JOB RAISING ME WITH A BASIC AWARENESS OF SEGREGATION AND THE CIVIL RIGHTS MOVEMENT, PASSING ALONG THEIR OWN EXPERIENCES AS YOUNG PEOPLE IN HYPERSEGREGATED MISSISSIPPI.
THEY STARKLY IDENTIFIED THE KLANSMEN'S EVIL—
BUT THEIR ENTIRE GENERATION STILL HAD A LOT OF BAGGAGE THAT HADN'T YET BEEN UNPACKED OR QUESTIONED.

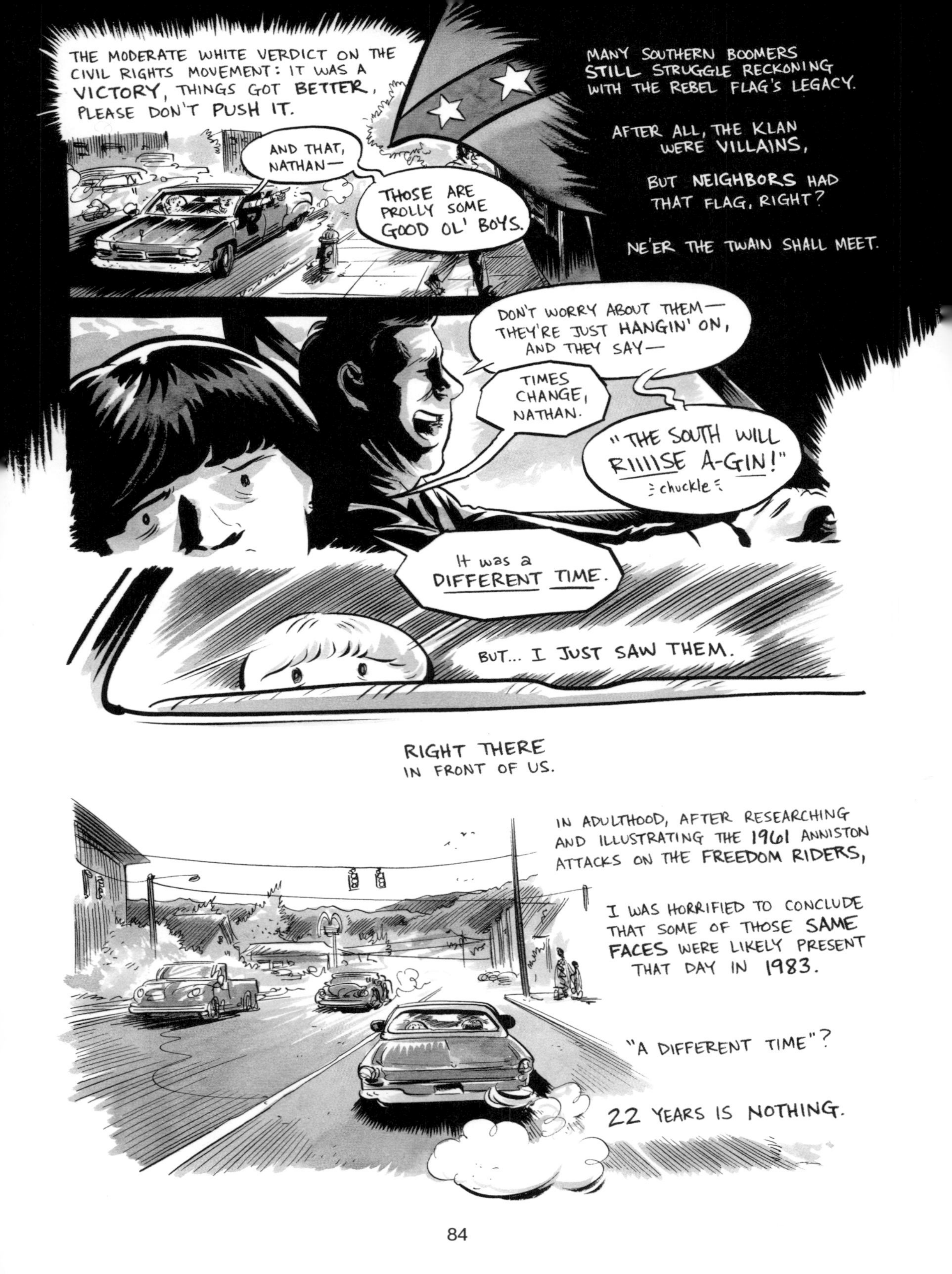
THE MODERATE WHITE VERDICT ON THE CIVIL RIGHTS MOVEMENT: IT WAS A VICTORY, THINGS GOT BETTER, PLEASE DON'T PUSH IT.
AND THAT, NATHAN—
THOSE ARE PROLLY SOME GOOD OL' BOYS.
MANY SOUTHERN BOOMERS STILL STRUGGLE RECKONING WITH THE REBEL FLAG'S LEGACY.
AFTER ALL, THE KLAN WERE VILLAINS,
BUT NEIGHBORS HAD THAT FLAG, RIGHT?
NE'ER THE TWAIN SHALL MEET.
DON'T WORRY ABOUT THEM— THEY'RE JUST HANGIN' ON, AND THEY SAY—
"THE SOUTH WILL RIIIISE A-GIN!"
chuckle
TIMES CHANGE, NATHAN.
It was a DIFFERENT TIME.
BUT... I JUST SAW THEM.
RIGHT THERE IN FRONT OF US.
IN ADULTHOOD, AFTER RESEARCHING AND ILLUSTRATING THE 1961 ANNISTON ATTACKS ON THE FREEDOM RIDERS,
I WAS HORRIFIED TO CONCLUDE THAT SOME OF THOSE SAME FACES WERE LIKELY PRESENT THAT DAY IN 1983.
"A DIFFERENT TIME"?
22 YEARS IS NOTHING.

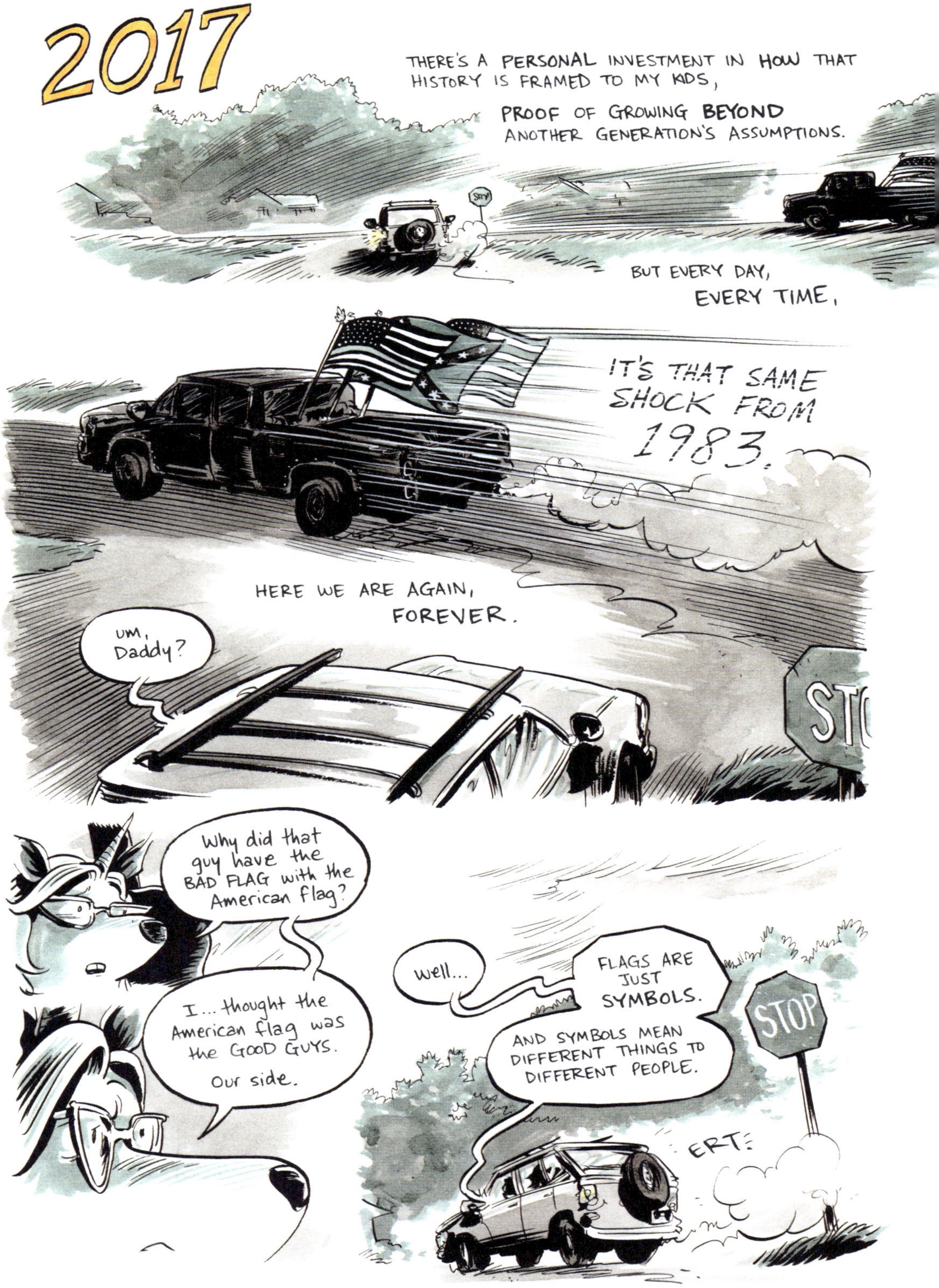

2017
THERE'S A PERSONAL INVESTMENT IN HOW THAT HISTORY IS FRAMED TO MY KIDS,
PROOF OF GROWING BEYOND ANOTHER GENERATION'S ASSUMPTIONS.
STOP
BUT EVERY DAY, EVERY TIME,
IT'S THAT SAME SHOCK FROM 1983.
HERE WE ARE AGAIN, FOREVER.
um, Daddy?
STO
Why did that guy have the BAD FLAG with the American flag?
I... thought the American flag was the GOOD GUYS.
Our side.
well...
FLAGS ARE JUST SYMBOLS.
AND SYMBOLS MEAN DIFFERENT THINGS TO DIFFERENT PEOPLE.
STOP
ERT

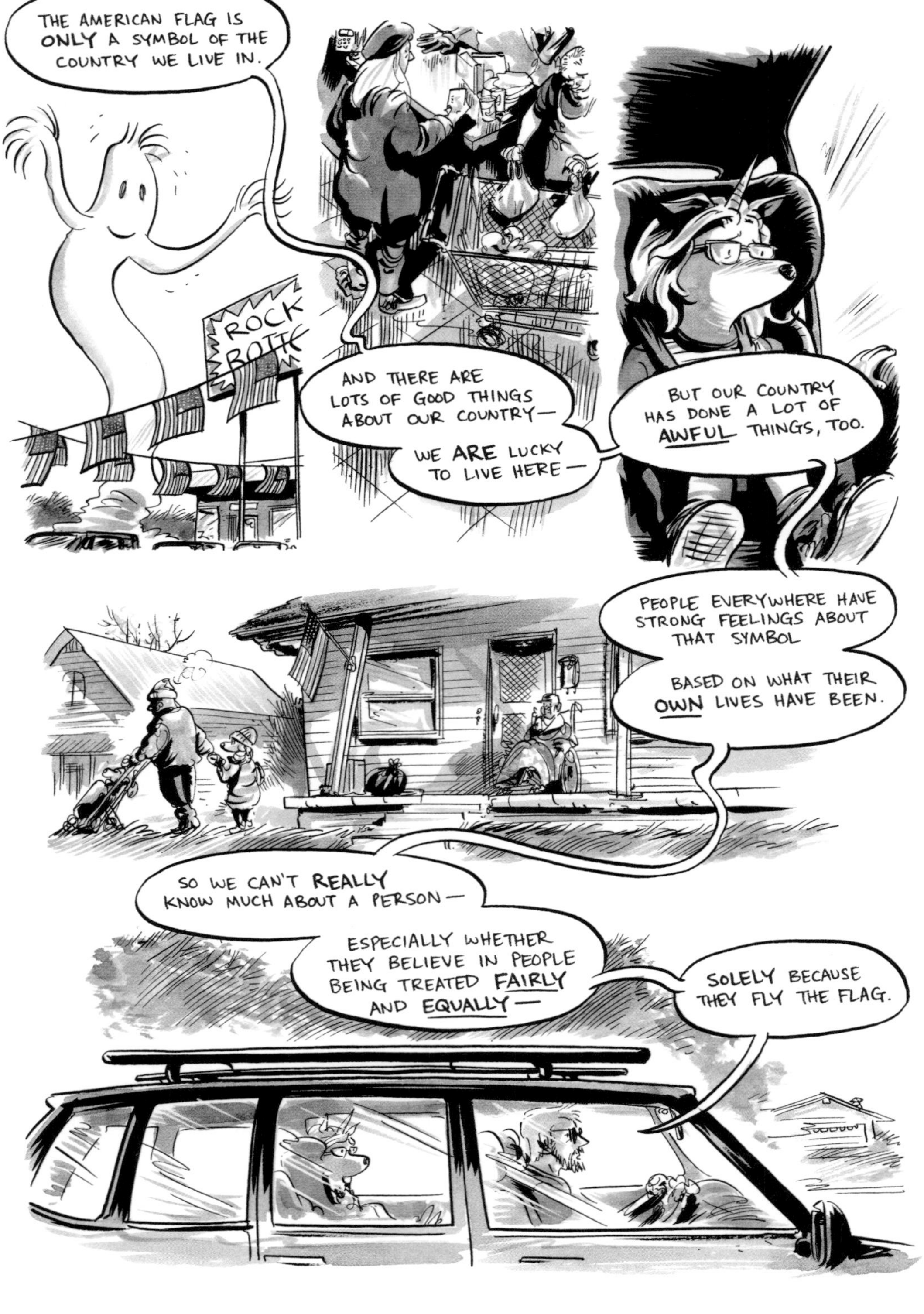
THE AMERICAN FLAG IS ONLY A SYMBOL OF THE COUNTRY WE LIVE IN.
ROCK BOTT
AND THERE ARE LOTS OF GOOD THINGS ABOUT OUR COUNTRY—
WE ARE LUCKY TO LIVE HERE—
BUT OUR COUNTRY HAS DONE A LOT OF AWFUL THINGS, TOO.
PEOPLE EVERYWHERE HAVE STRONG FEELINGS ABOUT THAT SYMBOL
BASED ON WHAT THEIR OWN LIVES HAVE BEEN.
SO WE CAN'T REALLY KNOW MUCH ABOUT A PERSON—
ESPECIALLY WHETHER THEY BELIEVE IN PEOPLE BEING TREATED FAIRLY AND EQUALLY—
SOLELY BECAUSE THEY FLY THE FLAG.

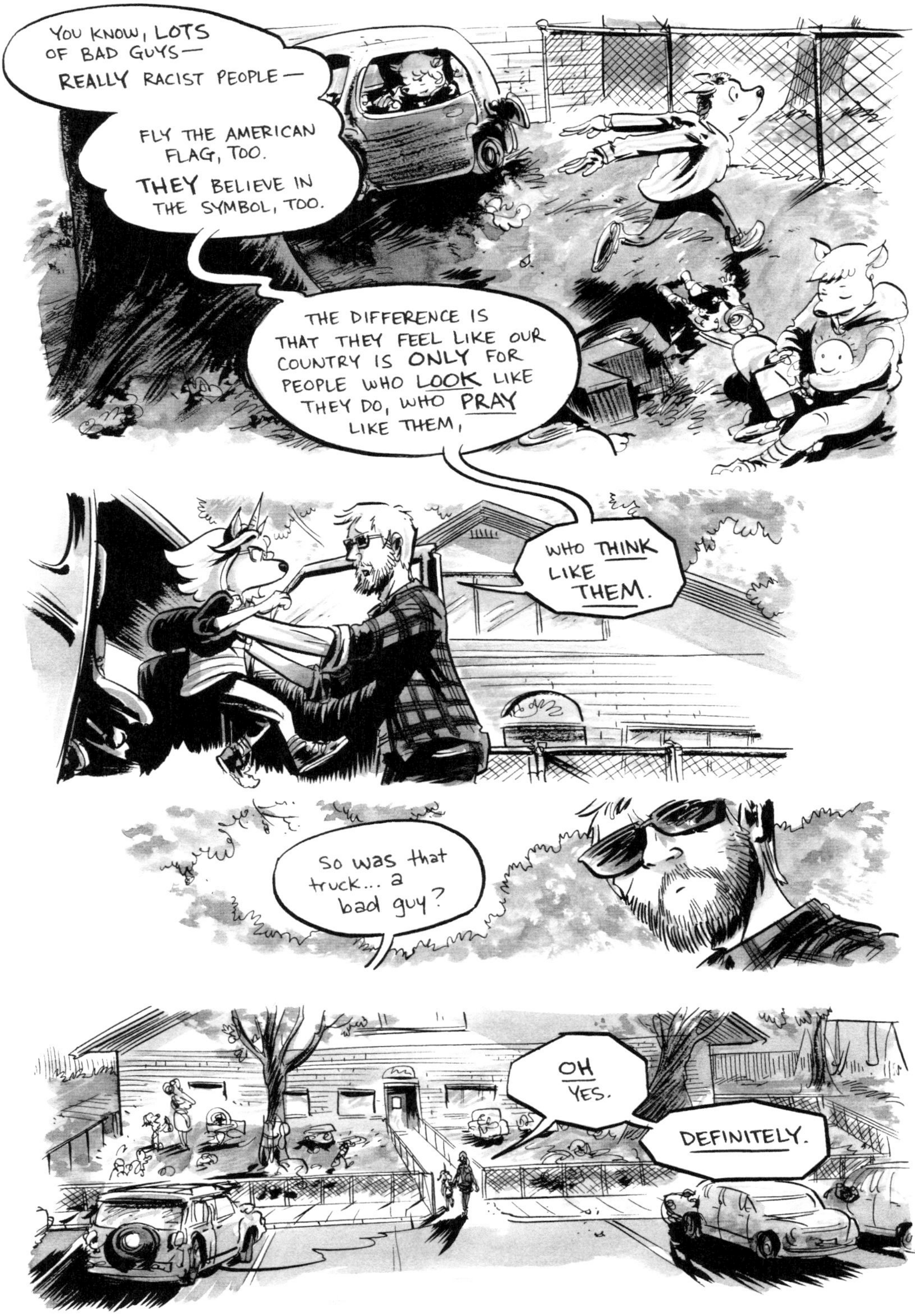

YOU KNOW, LOTS OF BAD GUYS— REALLY RACIST PEOPLE—
FLY THE AMERICAN FLAG, TOO.
THEY BELIEVE IN THE SYMBOL, TOO.
THE DIFFERENCE IS THAT THEY FEEL LIKE OUR COUNTRY IS ONLY FOR PEOPLE WHO LOOK LIKE THEY DO, WHO PRAY LIKE THEM,
WHO THINK LIKE THEM.
So was that truck... a bad guy?
OH YES.
DEFINITELY.

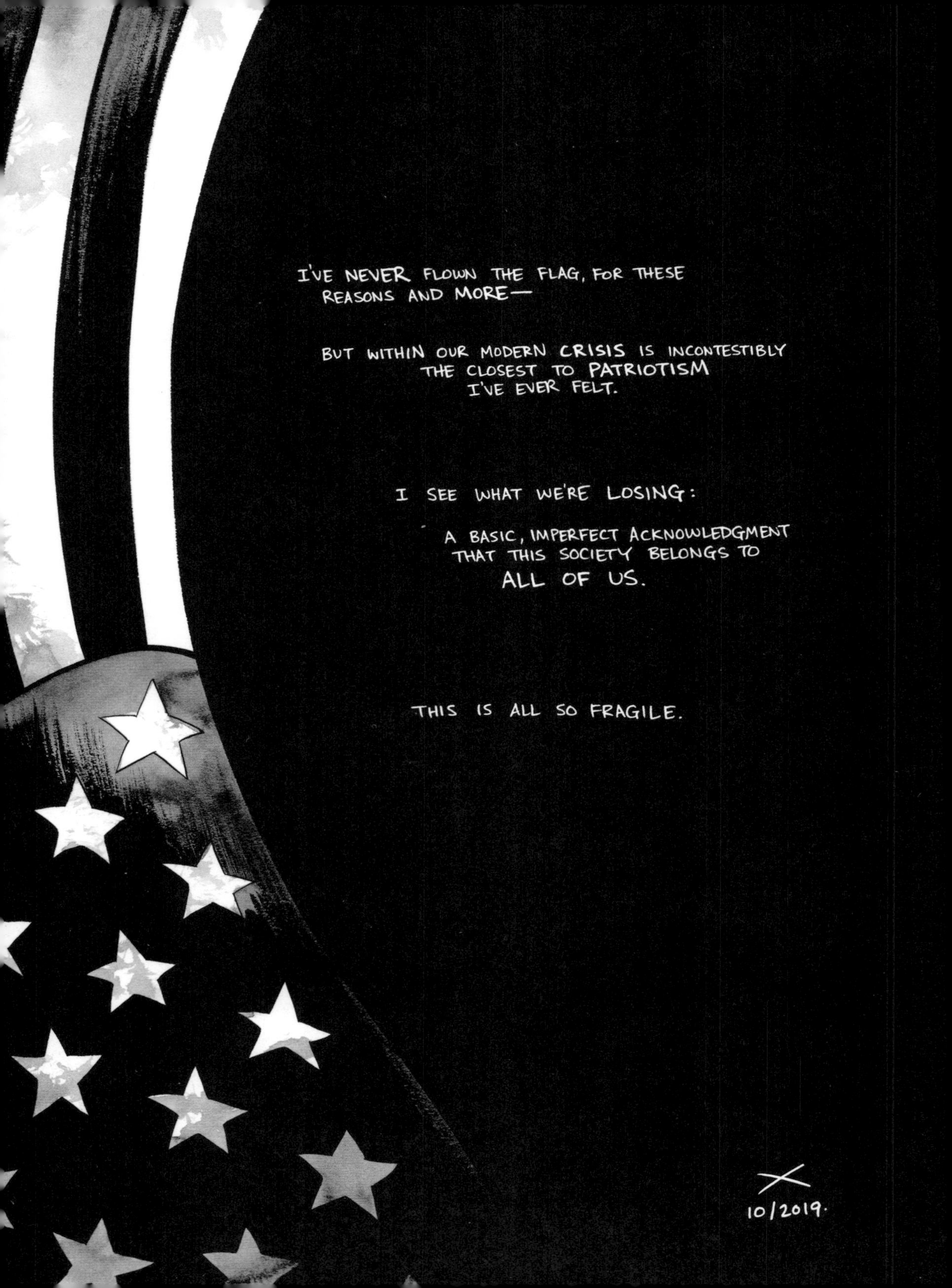
I'VE NEVER FLOWN THE FLAG, FOR THESE REASONS AND MORE—
BUT WITHIN OUR MODERN CRISIS IS INCONTESTIBLY THE CLOSEST TO PATRIOTISM I'VE EVER FELT.
I SEE WHAT WE'RE LOSING:
A BASIC, IMPERFECT ACKNOWLEDGMENT THAT THIS SOCIETY BELONGS TO ALL OF US.
THIS IS ALL SO FRAGILE.
X
10/2019.

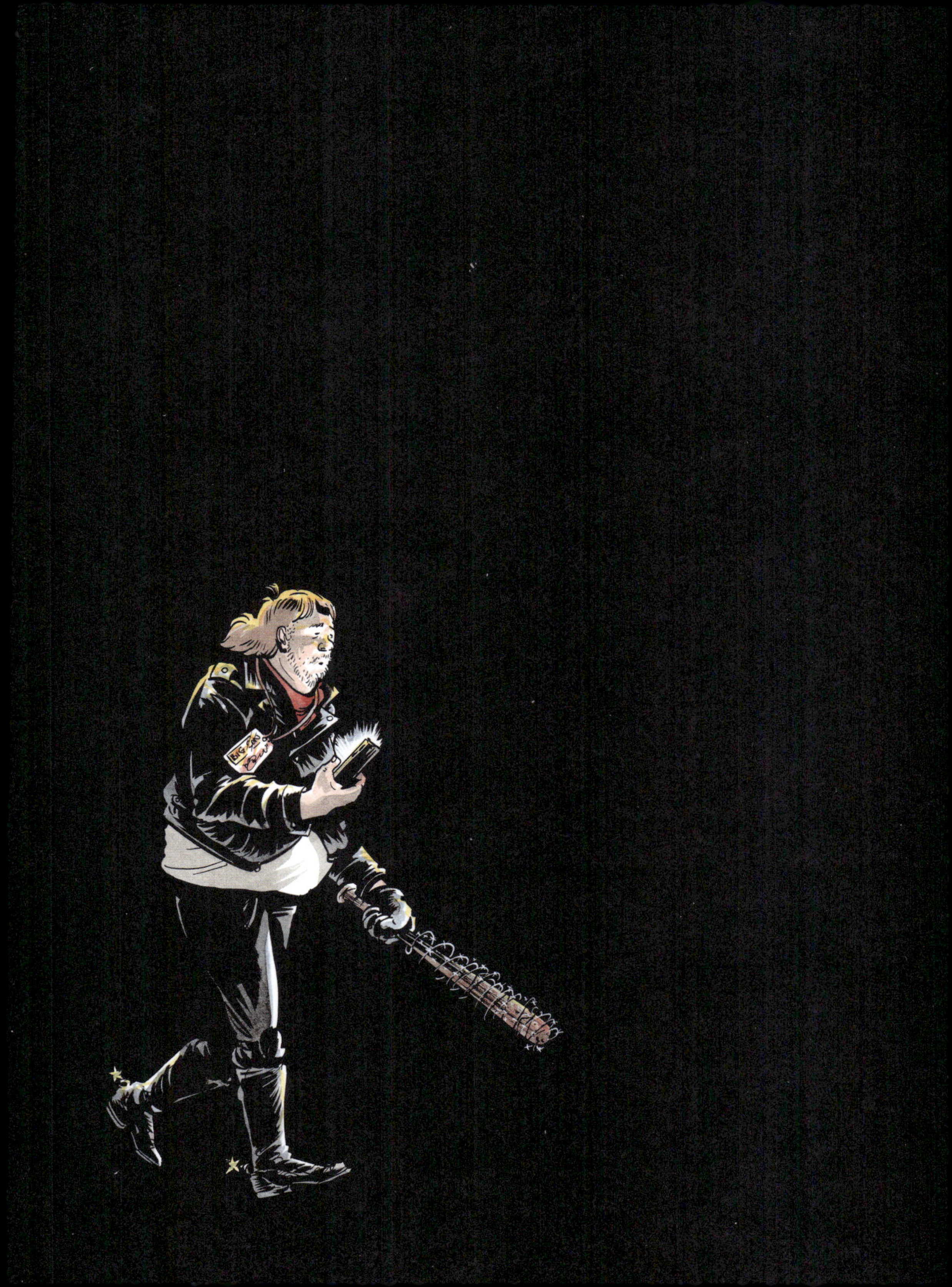

4

PECKING ORDER

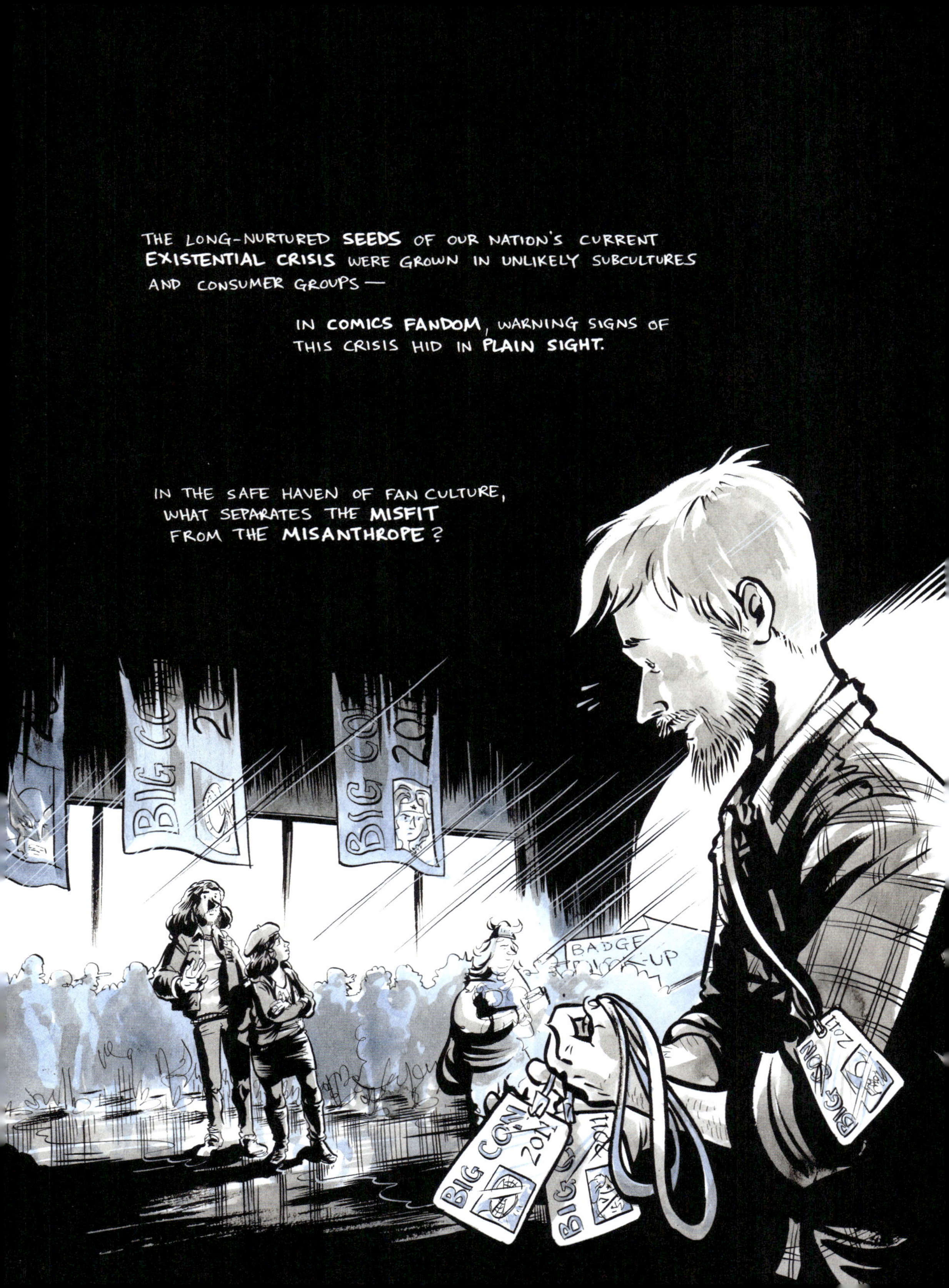
THE LONG-NURTURED SEEDS OF OUR NATION'S CURRENT EXISTENTIAL CRISIS WERE GROWN IN UNLIKELY SUBCULTURES AND CONSUMER GROUPS—
IN COMICS FANDOM, WARNING SIGNS OF THIS CRISIS HID IN PLAIN SIGHT.
IN THE SAFE HAVEN OF FAN CULTURE, WHAT SEPARATES THE MISFIT FROM THE MISANTHROPE?
BADGE
BIG CON 2011

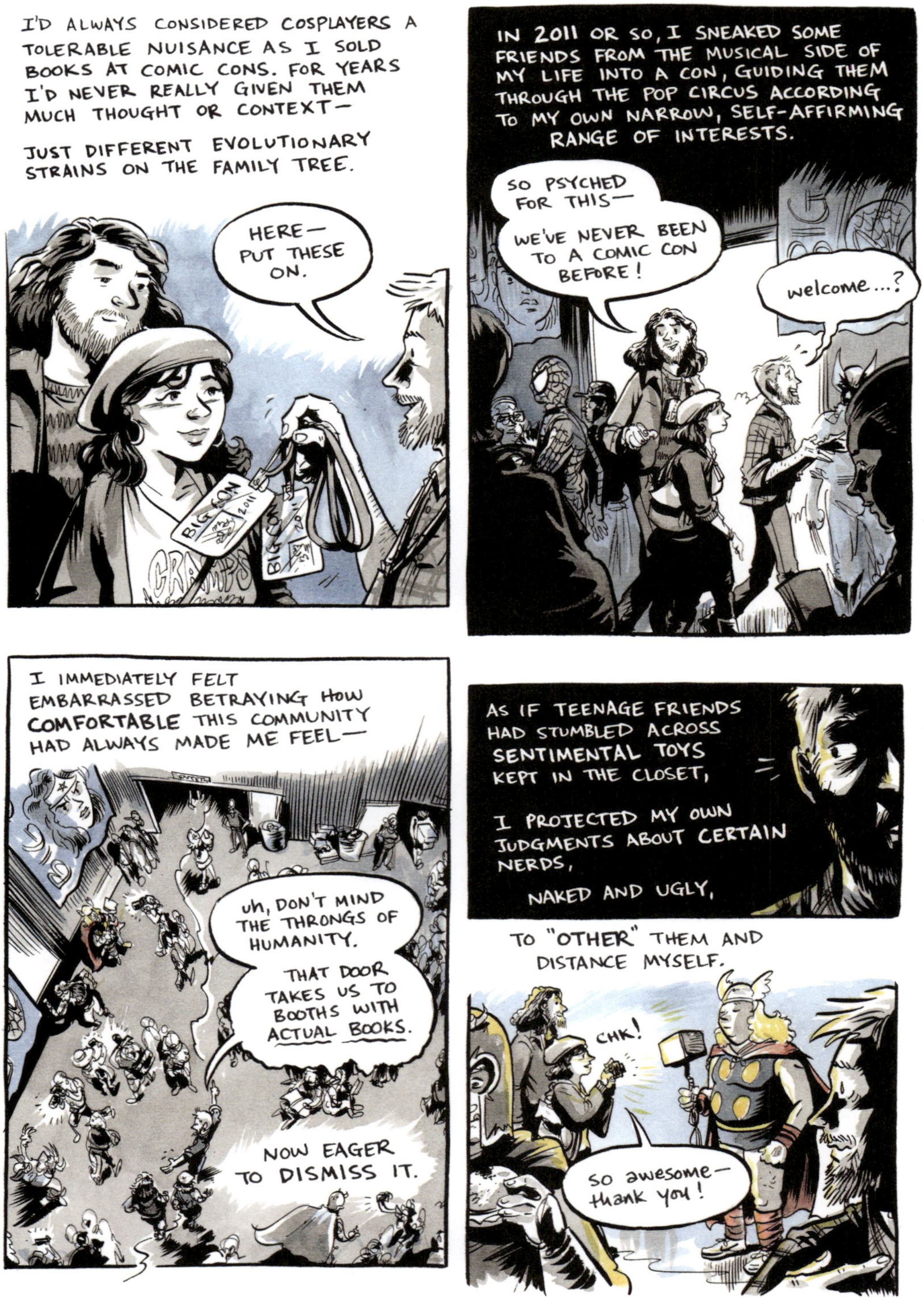
I'D ALWAYS CONSIDERED COSPLAYERS A TOLERABLE NUISANCE AS I SOLD BOOKS AT COMIC CONS. FOR YEARS I'D NEVER REALLY GIVEN THEM MUCH THOUGHT OR CONTEXT—
JUST DIFFERENT EVOLUTIONARY STRAINS ON THE FAMILY TREE.
HERE— PUT THESE ON.
BIG CON 2011
BIG CON 2011
IN 2011 OR SO, I SNEAKED SOME FRIENDS FROM THE MUSICAL SIDE OF MY LIFE INTO A CON, GUIDING THEM THROUGH THE POP CIRCUS ACCORDING TO MY OWN NARROW, SELF-AFFIRMING RANGE OF INTERESTS.
SO PSYCHED FOR THIS—
WE'VE NEVER BEEN TO A COMIC CON BEFORE!
welcome...?
I IMMEDIATELY FELT EMBARRASSED BETRAYING HOW COMFORTABLE THIS COMMUNITY HAD ALWAYS MADE ME FEEL—
uh, DON'T MIND THE THRONGS OF HUMANITY.
THAT DOOR TAKES US TO BOOTHS WITH ACTUAL BOOKS.
NOW EAGER TO DISMISS IT.
AS IF TEENAGE FRIENDS HAD STUMBLED ACROSS SENTIMENTAL TOYS KEPT IN THE CLOSET,
I PROJECTED MY OWN JUDGMENTS ABOUT CERTAIN NERDS,
NAKED AND UGLY,
TO "OTHER" THEM AND DISTANCE MYSELF.
CHK!
So awesome— thank you!

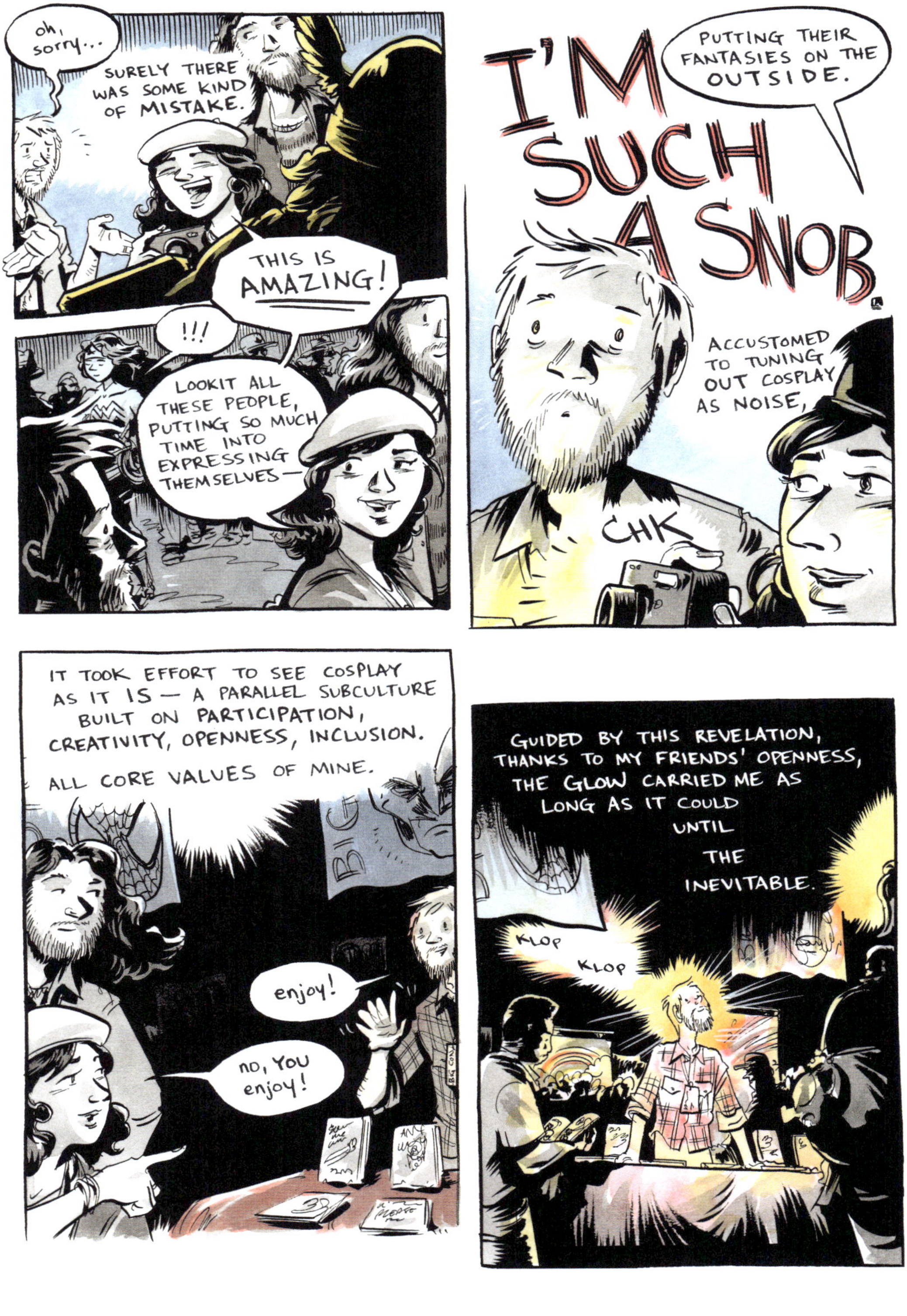
oh, sorry...
SURELY THERE WAS SOME KIND OF MISTAKE.
THIS IS AMAZING!
!!!
LOOKIT ALL THESE PEOPLE, PUTTING SO MUCH TIME INTO EXPRESSING THEMSELVES—
PUTTING THEIR FANTASIES ON THE OUTSIDE.
I'M SUCH A SNOB
ACCUSTOMED TO TUNING OUT COSPLAY AS NOISE,
CHK
IT TOOK EFFORT TO SEE COSPLAY AS IT IS— A PARALLEL SUBCULTURE BUILT ON PARTICIPATION, CREATIVITY, OPENNESS, INCLUSION.
ALL CORE VALUES OF MINE.
enjoy!
no, YOU enjoy!
GUIDED BY THIS REVELATION, THANKS TO MY FRIENDS' OPENNESS, THE GLOW CARRIED ME AS LONG AS IT COULD
UNTIL
THE
INEVITABLE.
KLOP
KLOP

KLOP KLOP

YEP, IT'S

KLOP KLOP

THAT GUY.

SELF-SATISFIED, LIKE A 13-YEAR-OLD WEARING A SLAYER SHIRT TO CHURCH, ACCOMPANIED BY LESSER VILLAINS AND MOUTH BREATHERS,

KLOP KLOP

SWADDLED IN THE MYTH OF (WHAT I PRAY IS) SOME MEDIA PROPERTY. (HEINLEIN? DICK? TARANTINO? DOES THAT MAKE IT ANY BETTER?)

IT TAKES A MINUTE TO PROCESS— I MEAN, I KNOW WHAT'S HAPPENING, JUST LIKE I ALREADY KNOW HOW THIS IS GONNA PLAY OUT.

SO DOES HE.

I JUST NEED TO GO OVER AND ASK HIM.

EVEN JUST HAND-WRINGING, THOUGH, I'M RELIEVED TO SEE I'M NOT ALONE—

THIS IS REAL, IT IS WEIRD, AND OTHERS SEE IT, TOO.

EXCUSE ME—

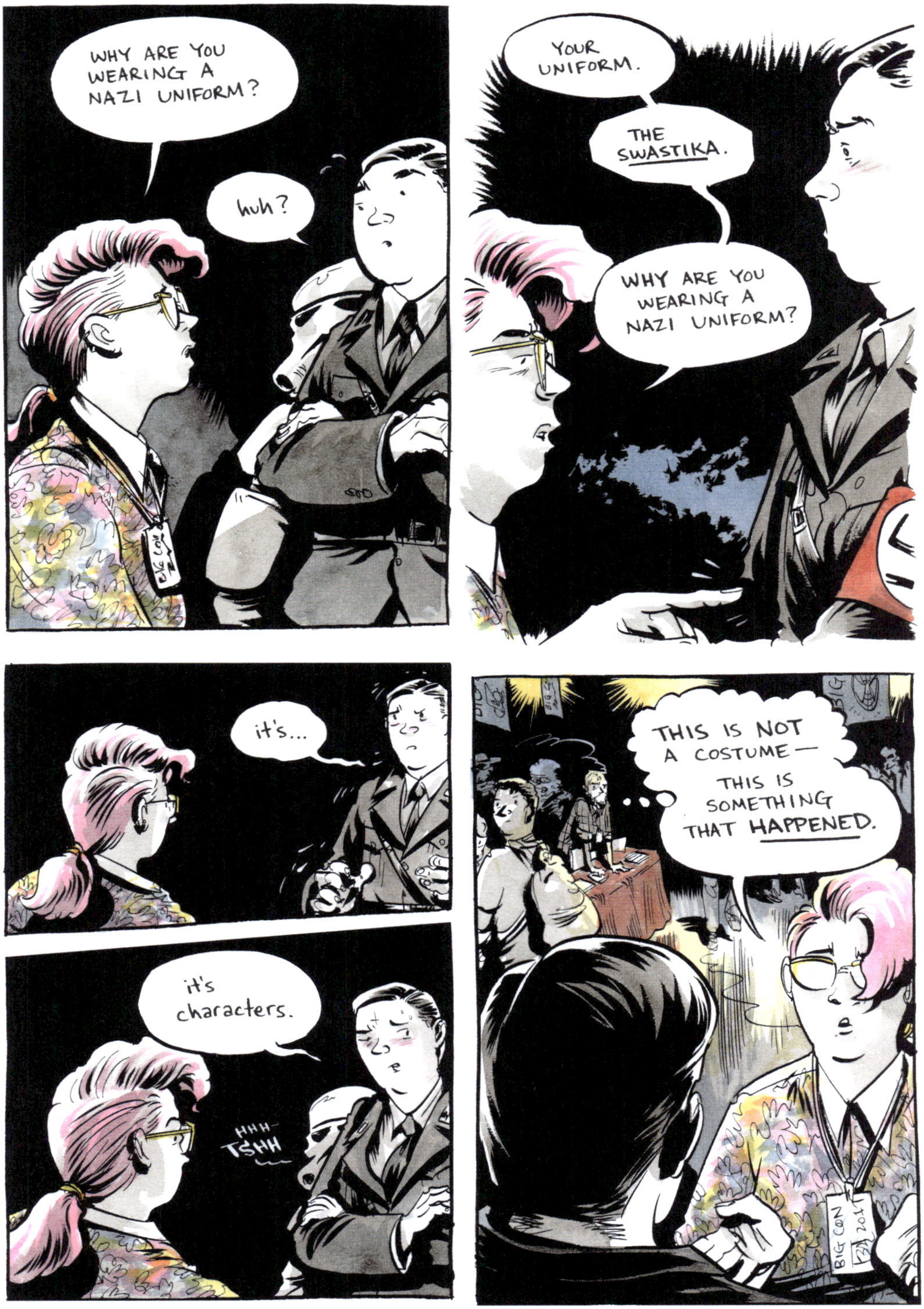
WHY ARE YOU WEARING A NAZI UNIFORM?
huh?
YOUR UNIFORM.
THE SWASTIKA.
WHY ARE YOU WEARING A NAZI UNIFORM?
it's...
it's characters.
HHH-TSHH
THIS IS NOT A COSTUME— THIS IS SOMETHING THAT HAPPENED.

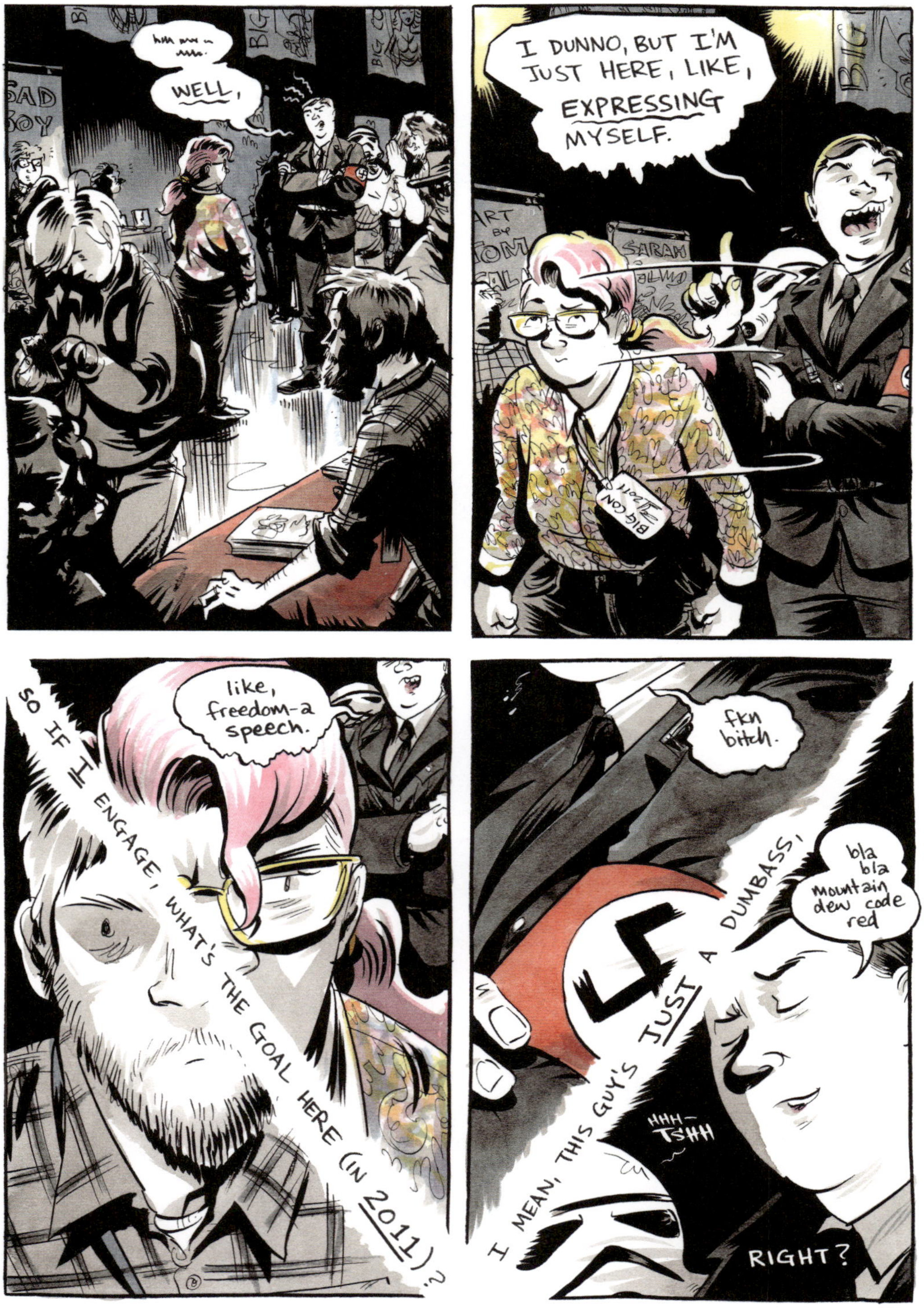
WELL,
I DUNNO, BUT I'M JUST HERE, LIKE, EXPRESSING MYSELF.
like, freedom-a speech.
SO IF I ENGAGE, WHAT'S THE GOAL HERE (IN 2011)?
fkn bitch.
I MEAN, THIS GUY'S JUST A DUMBASS,
bla bla Mountain dew code red
HHH-TSHH
RIGHT?

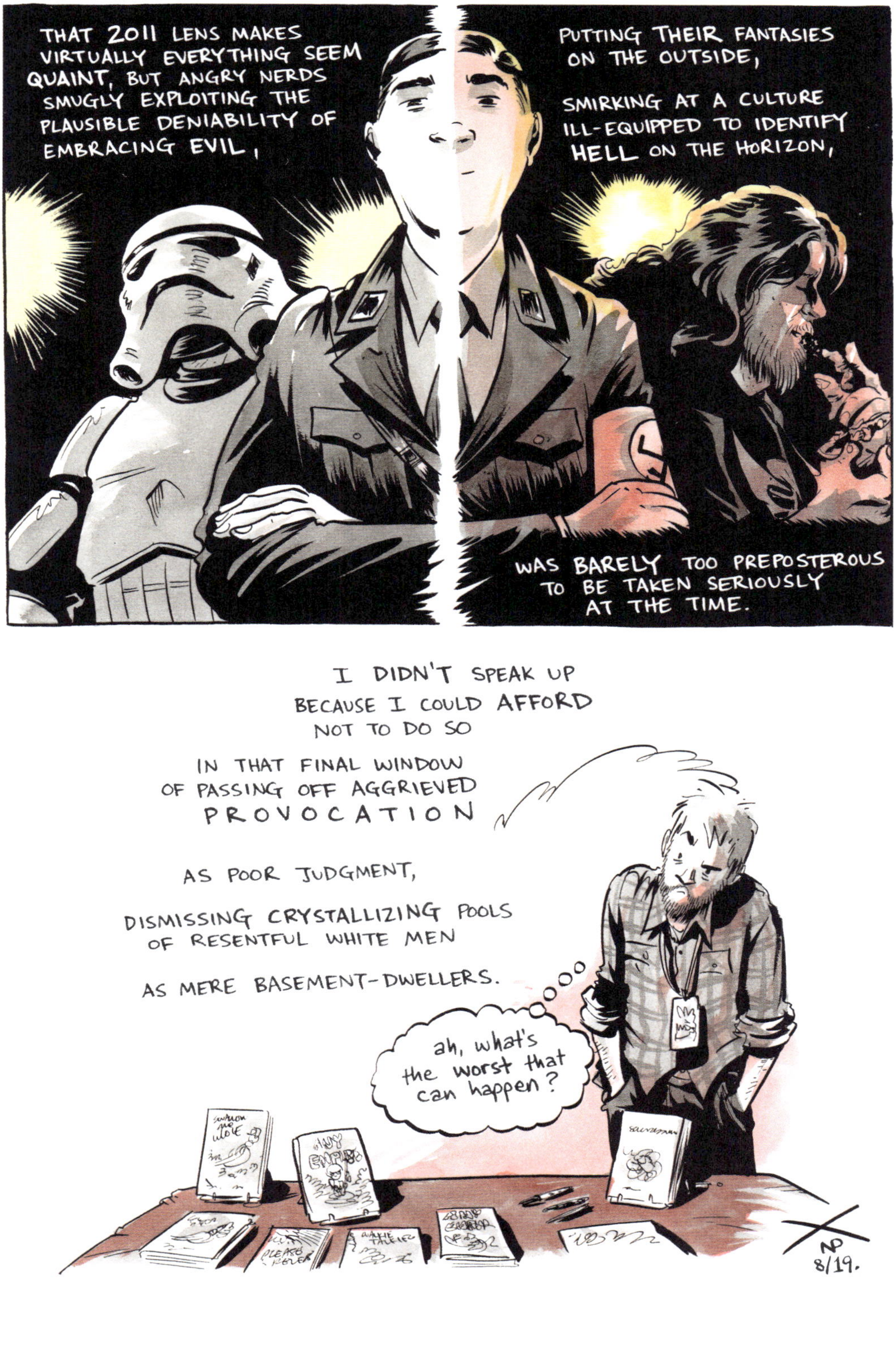
THAT 2011 LENS MAKES VIRTUALLY EVERYTHING SEEM QUAINT, BUT ANGRY NERDS SMUGLY EXPLOITING THE PLAUSIBLE DENIABILITY OF EMBRACING EVIL,
PUTTING THEIR FANTASIES ON THE OUTSIDE,
SMIRKING AT A CULTURE ILL-EQUIPPED TO IDENTIFY HELL ON THE HORIZON,
WAS BARELY TOO PREPOSTEROUS TO BE TAKEN SERIOUSLY AT THE TIME.
I DIDN'T SPEAK UP BECAUSE I COULD AFFORD NOT TO DO SO
IN THAT FINAL WINDOW OF PASSING OFF AGGRIEVED PROVOCATION
AS POOR JUDGMENT,
DISMISSING CRYSTALLIZING POOLS OF RESENTFUL WHITE MEN
AS MERE BASEMENT-DWELLERS.
ah, what's the worst that can happen?
NP 8/19.

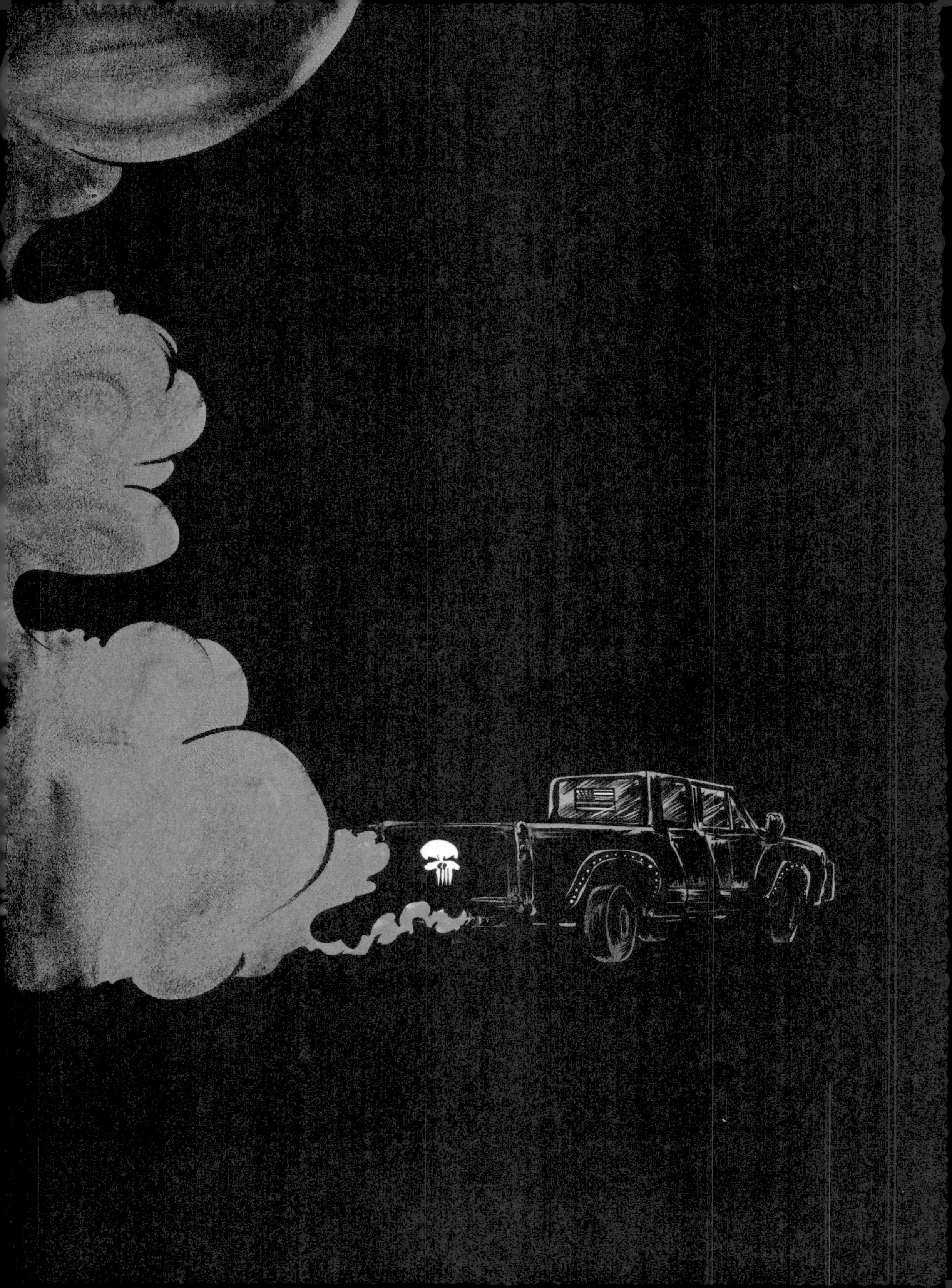

5
ABOUT FACE

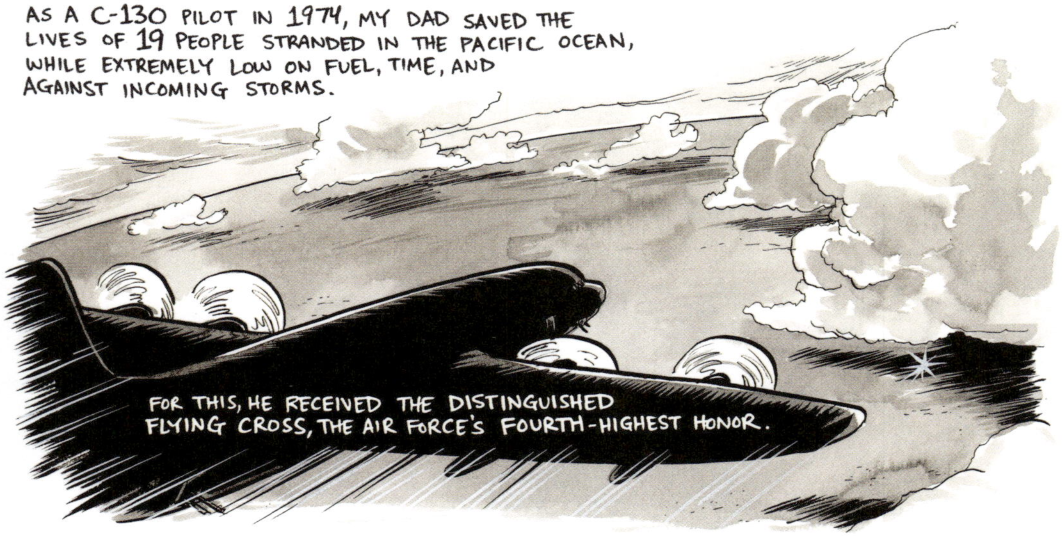
AS A C-130 PILOT IN 1974, MY DAD SAVED THE LIVES OF 19 PEOPLE STRANDED IN THE PACIFIC OCEAN, WHILE EXTREMELY LOW ON FUEL, TIME, AND AGAINST INCOMING STORMS.
FOR THIS, HE RECEIVED THE DISTINGUISHED FLYING CROSS, THE AIR FORCE'S FOURTH-HIGHEST HONOR.

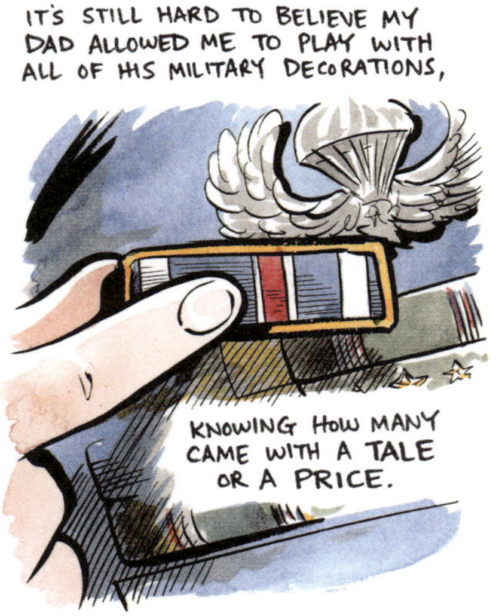
IT'S STILL HARD TO BELIEVE MY DAD ALLOWED ME TO PLAY WITH ALL OF HIS MILITARY DECORATIONS,
KNOWING HOW MANY CAME WITH A TALE OR A PRICE.

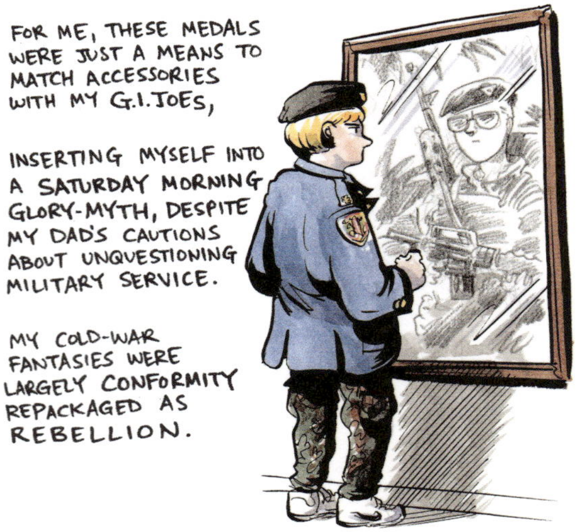
FOR ME, THESE MEDALS WERE JUST A MEANS TO MATCH ACCESSORIES WITH MY G.I.JOES,
INSERTING MYSELF INTO A SATURDAY MORNING GLORY-MYTH, DESPITE MY DAD'S CAUTIONS ABOUT UNQUESTIONING MILITARY SERVICE.
MY COLD-WAR FANTASIES WERE LARGELY CONFORMITY REPACKAGED AS REBELLION.

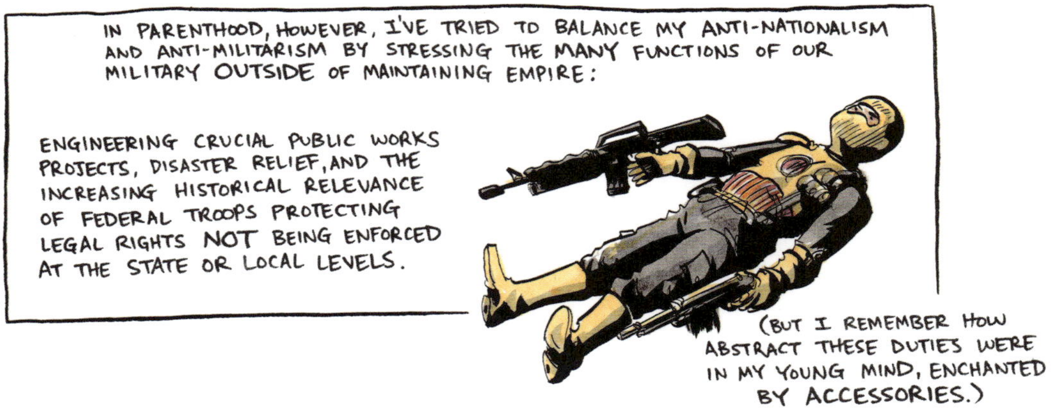
IN PARENTHOOD, HOWEVER, I'VE TRIED TO BALANCE MY ANTI-NATIONALISM AND ANTI-MILITARISM BY STRESSING THE MANY FUNCTIONS OF OUR MILITARY OUTSIDE OF MAINTAINING EMPIRE:
ENGINEERING CRUCIAL PUBLIC WORKS PROJECTS, DISASTER RELIEF, AND THE INCREASING HISTORICAL RELEVANCE OF FEDERAL TROOPS PROTECTING LEGAL RIGHTS NOT BEING ENFORCED AT THE STATE OR LOCAL LEVELS.
(BUT I REMEMBER HOW ABSTRACT THESE DUTIES WERE IN MY YOUNG MIND, ENCHANTED BY ACCESSORIES.)

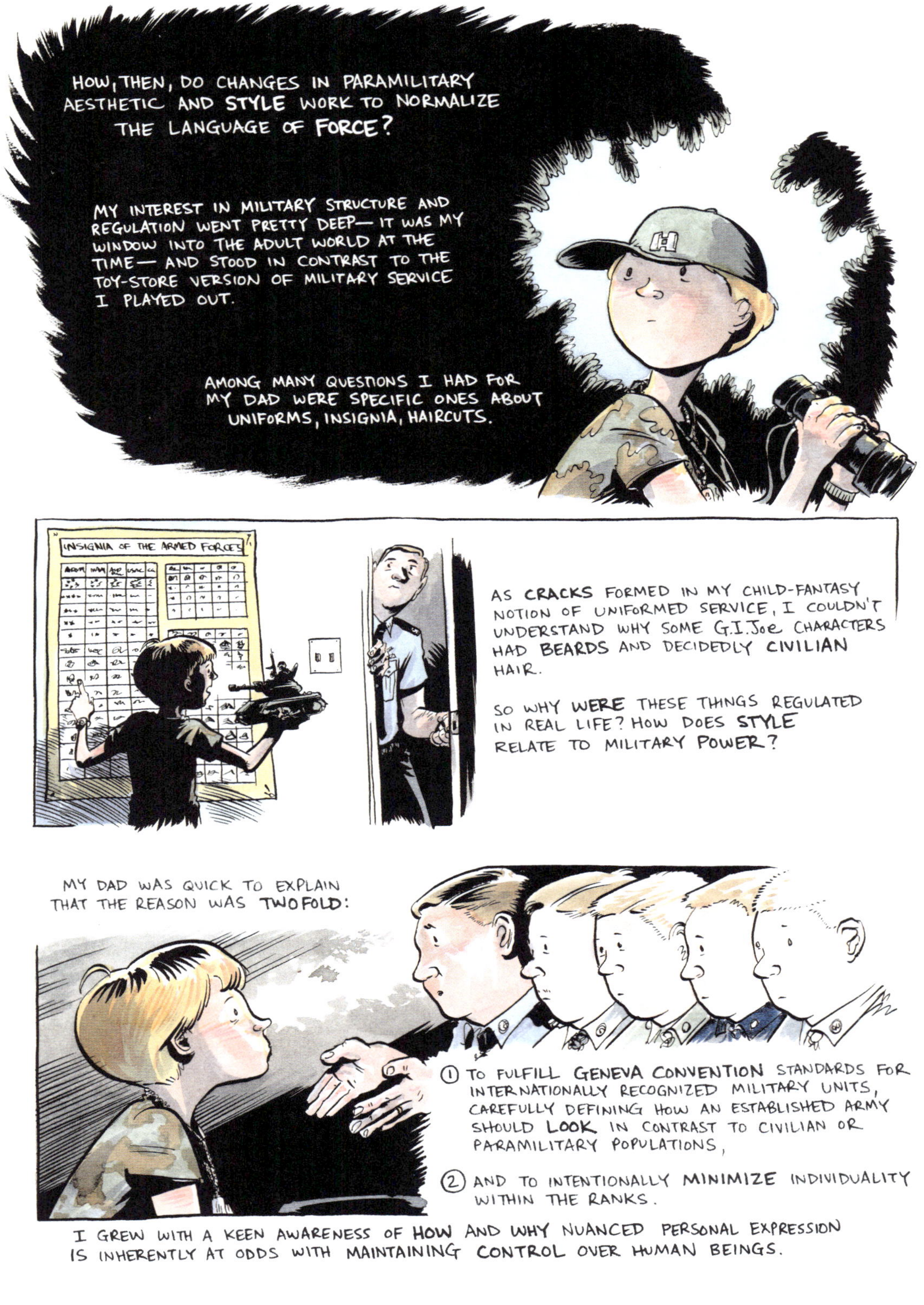
HOW, THEN, DO CHANGES IN PARAMILITARY AESTHETIC AND STYLE WORK TO NORMALIZE THE LANGUAGE OF FORCE?
MY INTEREST IN MILITARY STRUCTURE AND REGULATION WENT PRETTY DEEP— IT WAS MY WINDOW INTO THE ADULT WORLD AT THE TIME— AND STOOD IN CONTRAST TO THE TOY-STORE VERSION OF MILITARY SERVICE I PLAYED OUT.
AMONG MANY QUESTIONS I HAD FOR MY DAD WERE SPECIFIC ONES ABOUT UNIFORMS, INSIGNIA, HAIRCUTS.
INSIGNIA OF THE ARMED FORCES
AS CRACKS FORMED IN MY CHILD-FANTASY NOTION OF UNIFORMED SERVICE, I COULDN'T UNDERSTAND WHY SOME G.I. Joe CHARACTERS HAD BEARDS AND DECIDEDLY CIVILIAN HAIR.
SO WHY WERE THESE THINGS REGULATED IN REAL LIFE? HOW DOES STYLE RELATE TO MILITARY POWER?
MY DAD WAS QUICK TO EXPLAIN THAT THE REASON WAS TWOFOLD:
① TO FULFILL GENEVA CONVENTION STANDARDS FOR INTERNATIONALLY RECOGNIZED MILITARY UNITS, CAREFULLY DEFINING HOW AN ESTABLISHED ARMY SHOULD LOOK IN CONTRAST TO CIVILIAN OR PARAMILITARY POPULATIONS,
② AND TO INTENTIONALLY MINIMIZE INDIVIDUALITY WITHIN THE RANKS.
I GREW WITH A KEEN AWARENESS OF HOW AND WHY NUANCED PERSONAL EXPRESSION IS INHERENTLY AT ODDS WITH MAINTAINING CONTROL OVER HUMAN BEINGS.

THAT STYLISTIC **UNIFORMITY** INCREASED OVER A SINGLE GENERATION. ACTIVE DUTY PERSONNEL IN THE 21ST CENTURY ALMOST EXCLUSIVELY WEAR COMBAT FATIGUES— EVEN OFFICE WORKERS AND HIGHER-RANKING OFFICERS.

WHILE I READ THIS AS EXTENDING UNIFORMITY TO ITS LOGICAL CONCLUSION, IT'S A STYLISTIC SHIFT THAT SEEMS TO ENTERTAIN A STUNTED CHILD'S **PLAYACTING** FANTASY.

ACCOMPANYING THIS "FOREVER-WAR" DRESS STANDARD IS THE ADOPTION OF A DISTINCTLY **PARAMILITARY** AESTHETIC, MOST STRIKINGLY VISIBLE IN THE PRESENCE OF **FACIAL HAIR**, TRICKLING DOWN FROM ALLOWANCES MADE FOR SPECIAL FORCES (AND ACCOMPANYING PRIVATE MERCENARY UNITS, WHICH OFTEN OUT-NUMBER ACTUAL MILITARY FORCES) FOR OPERATIONS IN THE MIDDLE EAST, CENTRAL ASIA, AND AFRICA.

IT SHOULD BE NOTED THAT MANY AFGHAN VILLAGERS HAVE MADE DISTINCTIONS BETWEEN **BEARDED** AND **SHAVEN** AMERICAN TROOPS—

THE BEARDED VARIETY MORE LIKELY TO ACT OUT **VIOLENCE** AND **ABUSE** OF POWER, ACCORDING TO CIVILIAN ACCOUNTS.

BEARDS, LIKE SUNGLASSES AND HEADGEAR, CAN ACT TO OBSCURE **PERSONAL RECOGNITION** AND MINIMIZE **ACCOUNTABILITY**.

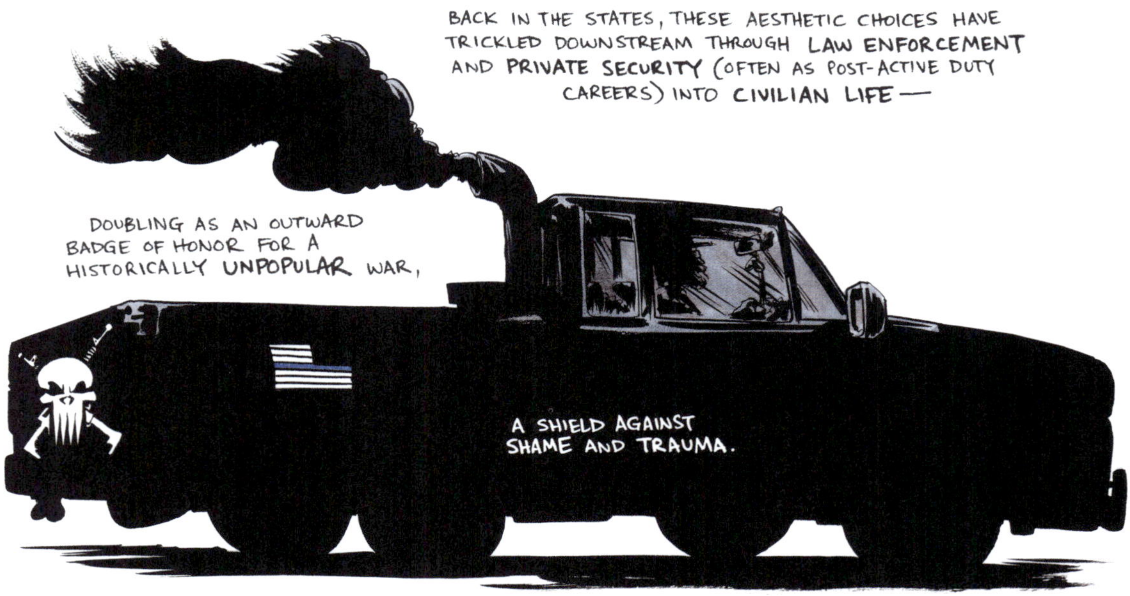
BACK IN THE STATES, THESE AESTHETIC CHOICES HAVE TRICKLED DOWNSTREAM THROUGH LAW ENFORCEMENT AND PRIVATE SECURITY (OFTEN AS POST-ACTIVE DUTY CAREERS) INTO CIVILIAN LIFE—
DOUBLING AS AN OUTWARD BADGE OF HONOR FOR A HISTORICALLY UNPOPULAR WAR,
A SHIELD AGAINST SHAME AND TRAUMA.

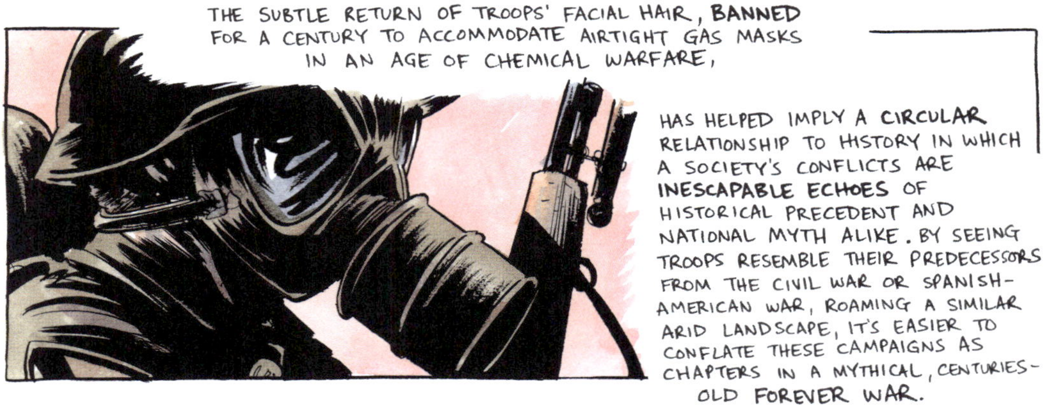
THE SUBTLE RETURN OF TROOPS' FACIAL HAIR, BANNED FOR A CENTURY TO ACCOMMODATE AIRTIGHT GAS MASKS IN AN AGE OF CHEMICAL WARFARE,
HAS HELPED IMPLY A CIRCULAR RELATIONSHIP TO HISTORY IN WHICH A SOCIETY'S CONFLICTS ARE INESCAPABLE ECHOES OF HISTORICAL PRECEDENT AND NATIONAL MYTH ALIKE. BY SEEING TROOPS RESEMBLE THEIR PREDECESSORS FROM THE CIVIL WAR OR SPANISH-AMERICAN WAR, ROAMING A SIMILAR ARID LANDSCAPE, IT'S EASIER TO CONFLATE THESE CAMPAIGNS AS CHAPTERS IN A MYTHICAL, CENTURIES-OLD FOREVER WAR.

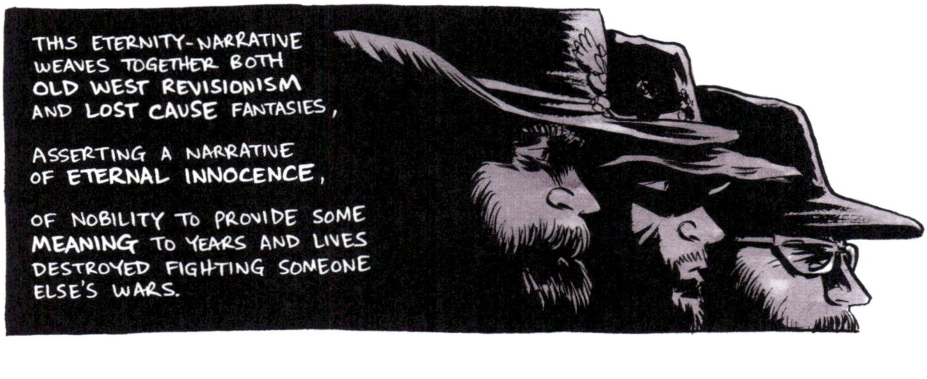
THIS ETERNITY-NARRATIVE WEAVES TOGETHER BOTH OLD WEST REVISIONISM AND LOST CAUSE FANTASIES,
ASSERTING A NARRATIVE OF ETERNAL INNOCENCE,
OF NOBILITY TO PROVIDE SOME MEANING TO YEARS AND LIVES DESTROYED FIGHTING SOMEONE ELSE'S WARS.

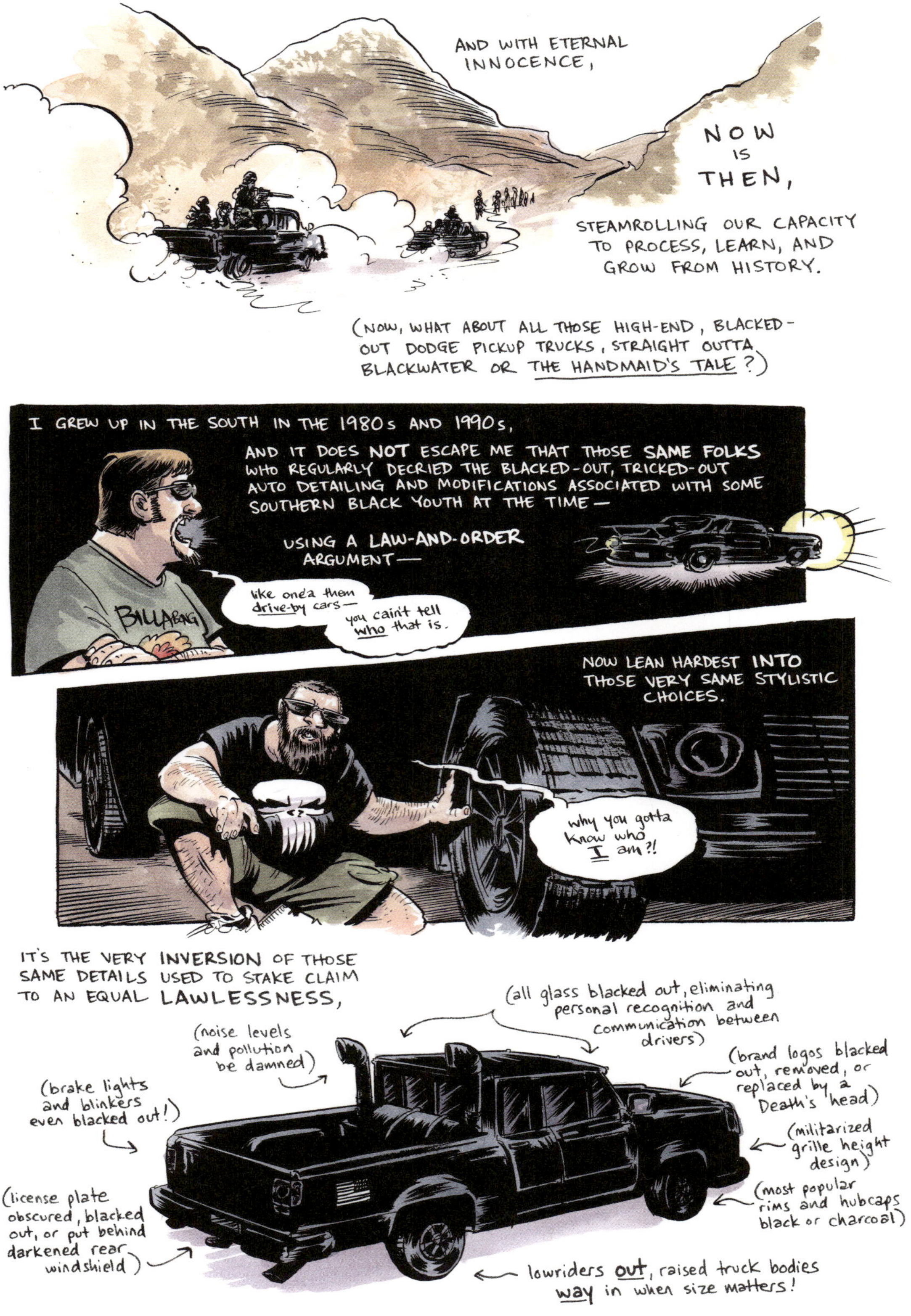
AND WITH ETERNAL INNOCENCE,
NOW IS THEN,
STEAMROLLING OUR CAPACITY TO PROCESS, LEARN, AND GROW FROM HISTORY.
(NOW, WHAT ABOUT ALL THOSE HIGH-END, BLACKED-OUT DODGE PICKUP TRUCKS, STRAIGHT OUTTA BLACKWATER OR THE HANDMAID'S TALE?)
I GREW UP IN THE SOUTH IN THE 1980s AND 1990s,
AND IT DOES NOT ESCAPE ME THAT THOSE SAME FOLKS WHO REGULARLY DECRIED THE BLACKED-OUT, TRICKED-OUT AUTO DETAILING AND MODIFICATIONS ASSOCIATED WITH SOME SOUTHERN BLACK YOUTH AT THE TIME—
USING A LAW-AND-ORDER ARGUMENT—
like one'a them drive-by cars—
you cain't tell who that is.
BILLABONG
NOW LEAN HARDEST INTO THOSE VERY SAME STYLISTIC CHOICES.
why you gotta know who I am?!
IT'S THE VERY INVERSION OF THOSE SAME DETAILS USED TO STAKE CLAIM TO AN EQUAL LAWLESSNESS,
(all glass blacked out, eliminating personal recognition and communication between drivers)
(noise levels and pollution be damned)
(brand logos blacked out, removed, or replaced by a Death's head)
(brake lights and blinkers even blacked out!)
(militarized grille height design)
(most popular rims and hubcaps black or charcoal)
(license plate obscured, blacked out, or put behind darkened rear windshield)
lowriders out, raised truck bodies way in when size matters!

ABOVE THE LAW IN A MYTH OF ETERNAL INNOCENCE.

THE COWBOY,
   THE REBEL,
      THE SOVEREIGN CITIZEN—

TO SOME, AN **ALLOWANCE OF WHITENESS**.

AS CONSUMERS FETISHIZED BIGGER, MORE POWERFUL TOYS, SUVs AND TRUCKS ADOPTED HIGHER GRILLES OF MILITARY DESIGN—

AND PEDESTRIAN DEATHS ROSE DRAMATICALLY IN THE POST-HUMMER ERA.

IN A VEHICULAR DESIGN CONTEXT, SAFETY RARELY CONSIDERS THOSE **OUTSIDE** THE VEHICLE.

~NPCs!

(WHY SHOULD THAT CONCERN A DRIVER WHOSE **ENTIRE** AESTHETIC IS A CHILD'S **REJECTION** OF COMMUNICATION, RECIPROCITY, AND LEGAL ACCOUNTABILITY?)

THE DEPARTMENT OF DEFENSE'S 2019 PB-NSCV MODS FILL IN THE GAPS AS MILITARY TRUCKS EMPLOY G.I. JOE-INSPIRED INTERCHANGEABLE PARTS TO MORE CLOSELY RESEMBLE **CIVILIAN** VEHICLES

(FOR USE IN POTENTIALLY POPULATED FRONTS)—

BUT THIS TOY-STORE MOVE IS ONLY POSSIBLE BY WORKING WITH AUTO MANUFACTURERS WHOSE VEHICLES **ALREADY** MEET CONSUMER DEMAND FOR MILITARIZED VEHICLES, CEMENTING A CYCLICAL DESIGN RELATIONSHIP.

BLOWOUT!

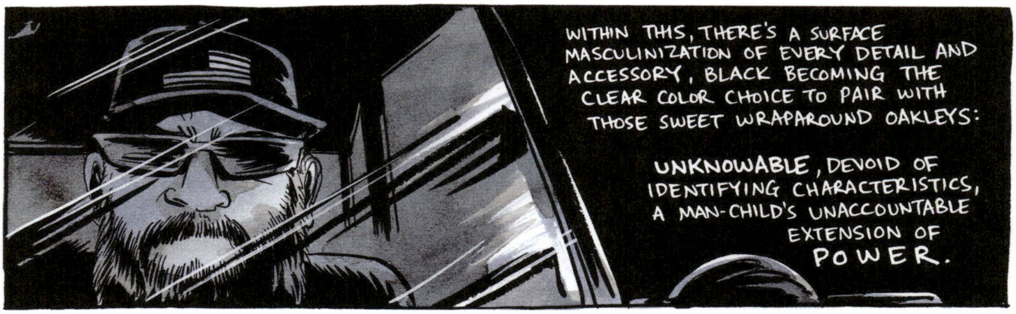
WITHIN THIS, THERE'S A SURFACE MASCULINIZATION OF EVERY DETAIL AND ACCESSORY, BLACK BECOMING THE CLEAR COLOR CHOICE TO PAIR WITH THOSE SWEET WRAPAROUND OAKLEYS:
UNKNOWABLE, DEVOID OF IDENTIFYING CHARACTERISTICS, A MAN-CHILD'S UNACCOUNTABLE EXTENSION OF **POWER**.

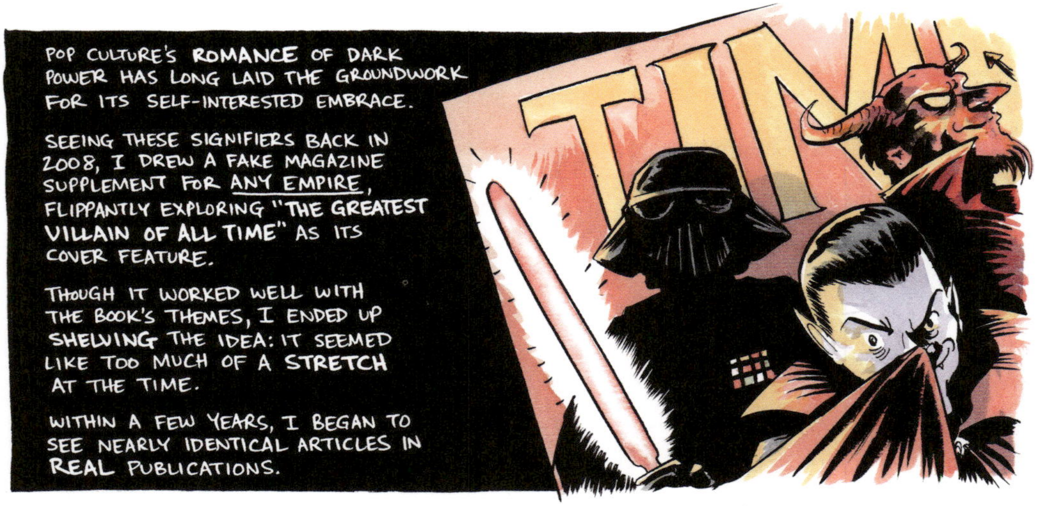
POP CULTURE'S **ROMANCE** OF DARK POWER HAS LONG LAID THE GROUNDWORK FOR ITS SELF-INTERESTED EMBRACE.
SEEING THESE SIGNIFIERS BACK IN 2008, I DREW A FAKE MAGAZINE SUPPLEMENT FOR ANY EMPIRE, FLIPPANTLY EXPLORING **"THE GREATEST VILLAIN OF ALL TIME"** AS ITS COVER FEATURE.
THOUGH IT WORKED WELL WITH THE BOOK'S THEMES, I ENDED UP **SHELVING** THE IDEA: IT SEEMED LIKE TOO MUCH OF A **STRETCH** AT THE TIME.
WITHIN A FEW YEARS, I BEGAN TO SEE NEARLY IDENTICAL ARTICLES IN **REAL** PUBLICATIONS.

AMERICAN FASCIST **STEVE BANNON**'S 2016 UTTERANCE WAS ESPECIALLY TERRIFYING, JUST ONE WEEK AFTER HE MANAGED A SUCCESSFUL PRESIDENTIAL CAMPAIGN RELYING LARGELY ON **TOXIC MASCULINITY**, MISGUIDED **GRIEVANCES**, AND FRONT-AND-CENTER **WHITE NATIONALISM**.

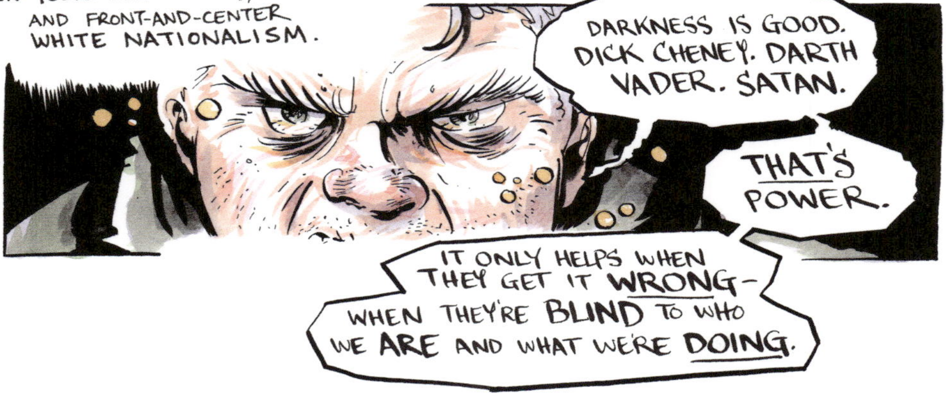
DARKNESS IS GOOD. DICK CHENEY. DARTH VADER. SATAN.
THAT'S POWER.
IT ONLY HELPS WHEN THEY GET IT **WRONG**— WHEN THEY'RE **BLIND** TO WHO WE **ARE** AND WHAT WE'RE **DOING**.

PRESS COVERAGE UNIVERSALLY ATTRIBUTED **"THEY"** TO MEAN LIBERALS AND THE MEDIA, BUT THAT VICTORY IS **EQUALLY** DUE TO EXPLOITING THE **RACISM** AND **IGNORANCE** OF THOSE WHITE AMERICANS EASILY DUPED BY ASSURANCES OF MAINTAINING THOSE DEEP **ALLOWANCES** OF **WHITENESS**.

UNDEAD VILLAINS IN <u>DRACULA</u> HAVE A SEXY ALLURE IN PROSE, BUT ALSO ILLUMINATE THE OVERARCHING PRINCIPLE GOVERNING **WHY** SOME PEOPLE RESPOND TO **POWER**:

THE SEDUCTION OF RELINQUISHING **AGENCY**,

"don't worry—"

OF NOT HAVING THE **BURDEN** OF MAKING ONE'S **OWN CHOICES**, OF CONFORMITY DISGUISED AS REBELLION,

"You'll never doubt again, baby."

CHOMP

THE COMFORTING OBLIVION OF **"JUST FOLLOWING ORDERS."**

(JUST ASK SOMEONE IN UNIFORM ABOUT THAT PRESSURE.)

THIS BRINGS US TO ARCHETYPAL MARVEL ANTIHERO **PUNISHER**'s SKULL LOGO AND ITS RELATIONSHIP WITH— AND **COUNTER TO**— THE CONCEPTS OF **RULE OF LAW** AND OF A FUNCTIONING SOCIETY ITSELF.

INTERESTINGLY ENOUGH, THE **JOLLY ROGER**'S ROOTS WERE **NOT** IN ROGUE PIRATES ON THE SEAS,

BUT AS A SYMBOL OF THE **PRIVATEERS**, A LOOSE COLONIAL PARAMILITARY ORGANIZATION GIVEN **LICENSE TO PLUNDER** ENEMY SHIPS—

POWER ESTABLISHING ITSELF AS **BEYOND** GOOD AND EVIL, BUT A DECLARATION OF POWER FOREMOST.

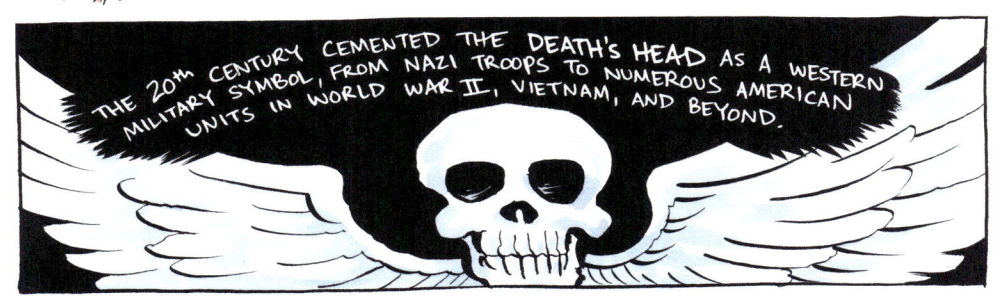

THE 20th CENTURY CEMENTED THE **DEATH'S HEAD** AS A WESTERN MILITARY SYMBOL, FROM NAZI TROOPS TO NUMEROUS AMERICAN UNITS IN WORLD WAR II, VIETNAM, AND BEYOND.

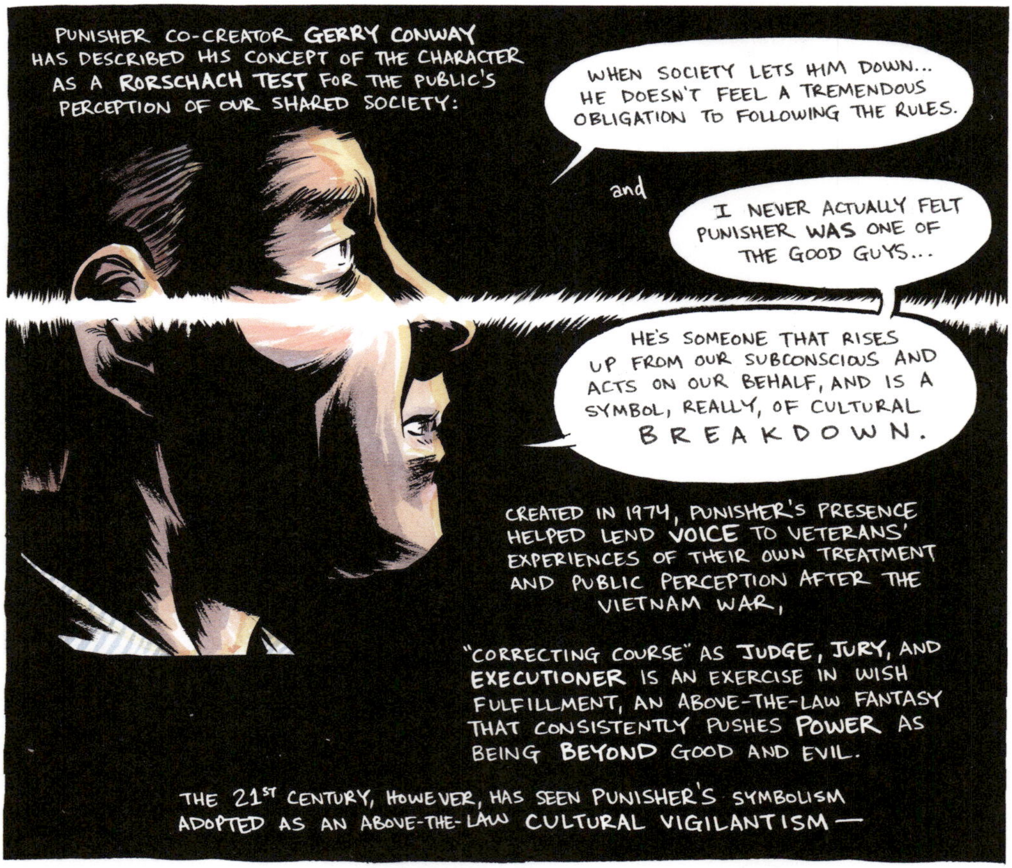
PUNISHER CO-CREATOR GERRY CONWAY HAS DESCRIBED HIS CONCEPT OF THE CHARACTER AS A RORSCHACH TEST FOR THE PUBLIC'S PERCEPTION OF OUR SHARED SOCIETY:
WHEN SOCIETY LETS HIM DOWN... HE DOESN'T FEEL A TREMENDOUS OBLIGATION TO FOLLOWING THE RULES.
and
I NEVER ACTUALLY FELT PUNISHER WAS ONE OF THE GOOD GUYS...
HE'S SOMEONE THAT RISES UP FROM OUR SUBCONSCIOUS AND ACTS ON OUR BEHALF, AND IS A SYMBOL, REALLY, OF CULTURAL BREAKDOWN.
CREATED IN 1974, PUNISHER'S PRESENCE HELPED LEND VOICE TO VETERANS' EXPERIENCES OF THEIR OWN TREATMENT AND PUBLIC PERCEPTION AFTER THE VIETNAM WAR,
"CORRECTING COURSE" AS JUDGE, JURY, AND EXECUTIONER IS AN EXERCISE IN WISH FULFILLMENT, AN ABOVE-THE-LAW FANTASY THAT CONSISTENTLY PUSHES POWER AS BEING BEYOND GOOD AND EVIL.
THE 21ST CENTURY, HOWEVER, HAS SEEN PUNISHER'S SYMBOLISM ADOPTED AS AN ABOVE-THE-LAW CULTURAL VIGILANTISM—

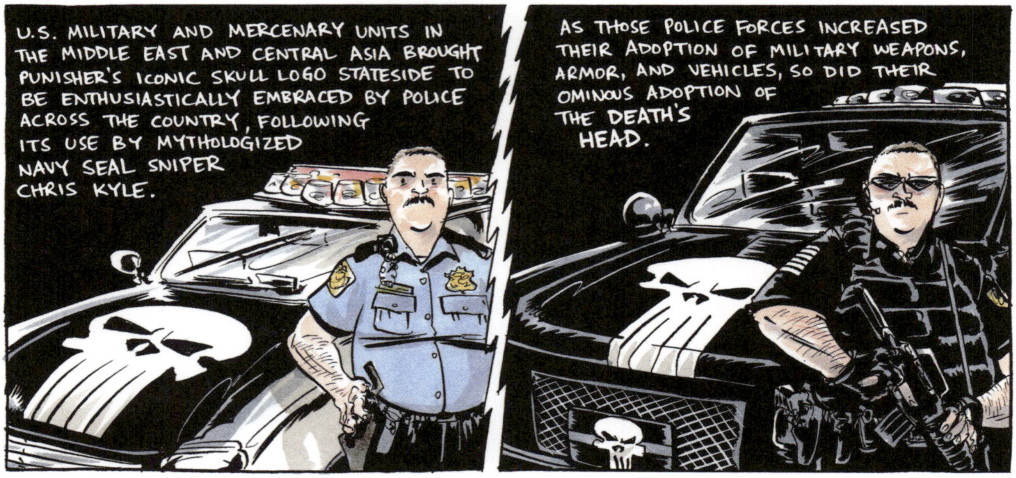
U.S. MILITARY AND MERCENARY UNITS IN THE MIDDLE EAST AND CENTRAL ASIA BROUGHT PUNISHER'S ICONIC SKULL LOGO STATESIDE TO BE ENTHUSIASTICALLY EMBRACED BY POLICE ACROSS THE COUNTRY, FOLLOWING ITS USE BY MYTHOLOGIZED NAVY SEAL SNIPER CHRIS KYLE.
AS THOSE POLICE FORCES INCREASED THEIR ADOPTION OF MILITARY WEAPONS, ARMOR, AND VEHICLES, SO DID THEIR OMINOUS ADOPTION OF THE DEATH'S HEAD.

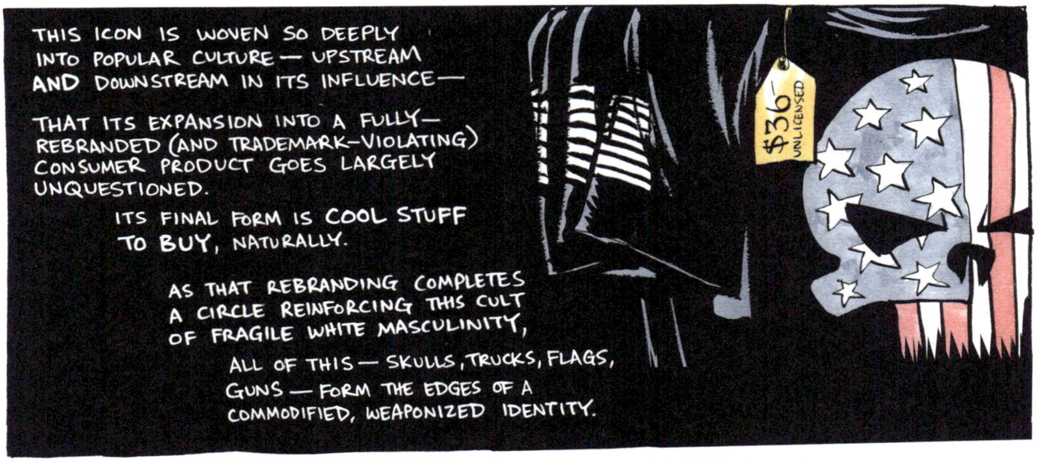
THIS ICON IS WOVEN SO DEEPLY INTO POPULAR CULTURE— UPSTREAM AND DOWNSTREAM IN ITS INFLUENCE—
THAT ITS EXPANSION INTO A FULLY-REBRANDED (AND TRADEMARK-VIOLATING) CONSUMER PRODUCT GOES LARGELY UNQUESTIONED.
ITS FINAL FORM IS COOL STUFF TO BUY, NATURALLY.
AS THAT REBRANDING COMPLETES A CIRCLE REINFORCING THIS CULT OF FRAGILE WHITE MASCULINITY,
ALL OF THIS— SKULLS, TRUCKS, FLAGS, GUNS— FORM THE EDGES OF A COMMODIFIED, WEAPONIZED IDENTITY.
$36 UNLICENSED

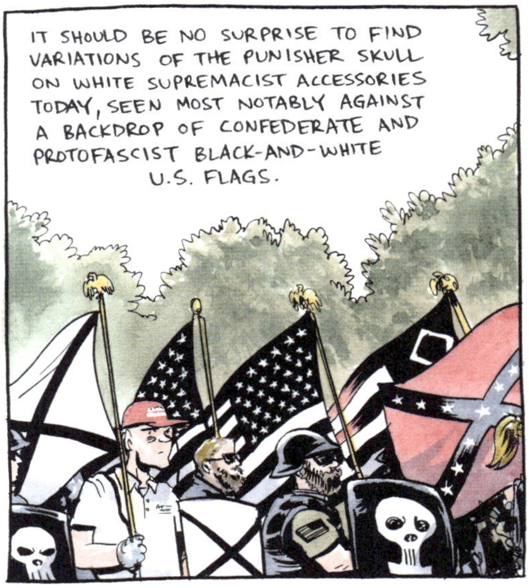
IT SHOULD BE NO SURPRISE TO FIND VARIATIONS OF THE PUNISHER SKULL ON WHITE SUPREMACIST ACCESSORIES TODAY, SEEN MOST NOTABLY AGAINST A BACKDROP OF CONFEDERATE AND PROTOFASCIST BLACK-AND-WHITE U.S. FLAGS.

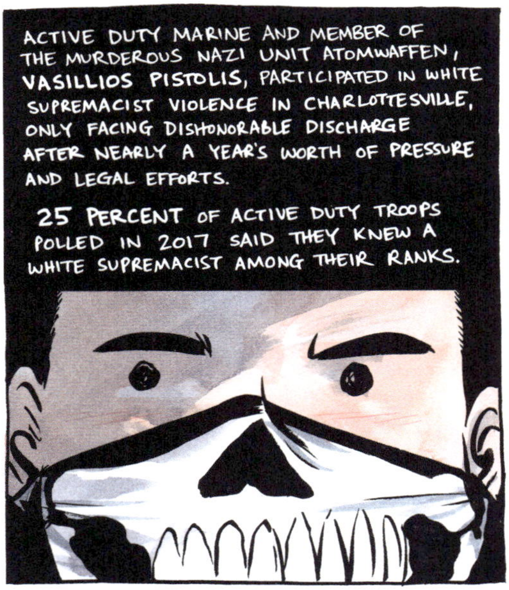
ACTIVE DUTY MARINE AND MEMBER OF THE MURDEROUS NAZI UNIT ATOMWAFFEN, VASILLIOS PISTOLIS, PARTICIPATED IN WHITE SUPREMACIST VIOLENCE IN CHARLOTTESVILLE, ONLY FACING DISHONORABLE DISCHARGE AFTER NEARLY A YEAR'S WORTH OF PRESSURE AND LEGAL EFFORTS.
25 PERCENT OF ACTIVE DUTY TROOPS POLLED IN 2017 SAID THEY KNEW A WHITE SUPREMACIST AMONG THEIR RANKS.

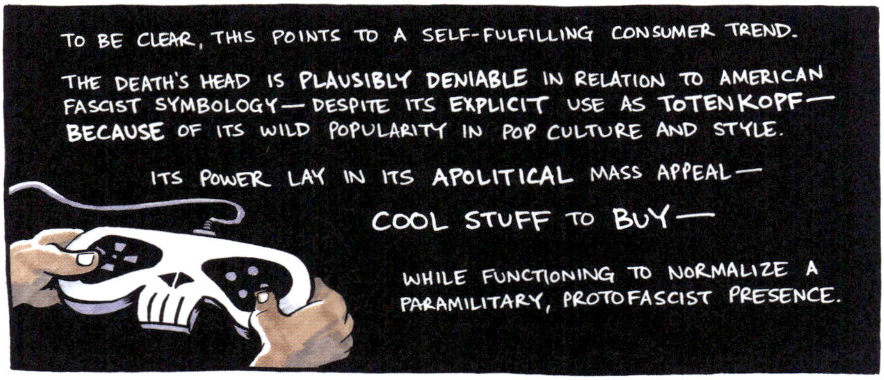
TO BE CLEAR, THIS POINTS TO A SELF-FULFILLING CONSUMER TREND.
THE DEATH'S HEAD IS PLAUSIBLY DENIABLE IN RELATION TO AMERICAN FASCIST SYMBOLOGY— DESPITE ITS EXPLICIT USE AS TOTENKOPF— BECAUSE OF ITS WILD POPULARITY IN POP CULTURE AND STYLE.
ITS POWER LAY IN ITS APOLITICAL MASS APPEAL—
COOL STUFF TO BUY—
WHILE FUNCTIONING TO NORMALIZE A PARAMILITARY, PROTOFASCIST PRESENCE.

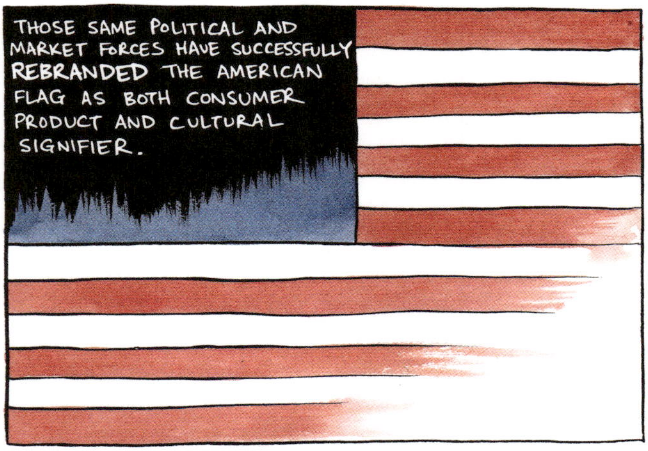
THOSE SAME POLITICAL AND MARKET FORCES HAVE SUCCESSFULLY REBRANDED THE AMERICAN FLAG AS BOTH CONSUMER PRODUCT AND CULTURAL SIGNIFIER.

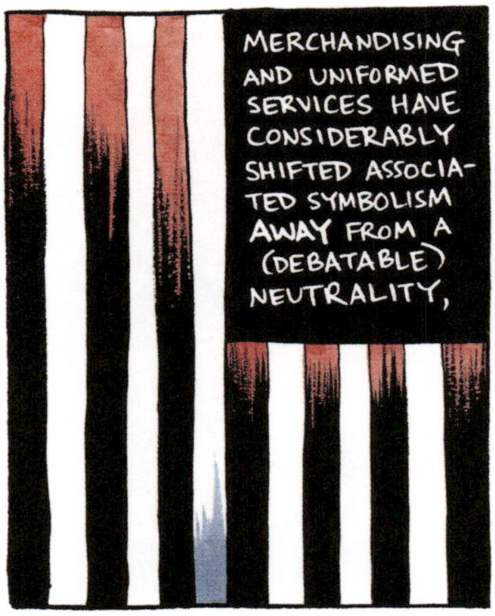
MERCHANDISING AND UNIFORMED SERVICES HAVE CONSIDERABLY SHIFTED ASSOCIATED SYMBOLISM AWAY FROM A (DEBATABLE) NEUTRALITY,

TOWARD A FULLY MASCULINIZED, MILITARIZED ICON EAGER TO MAKE WAY FOR AN **AUTHORITARIAN** FUTURE.

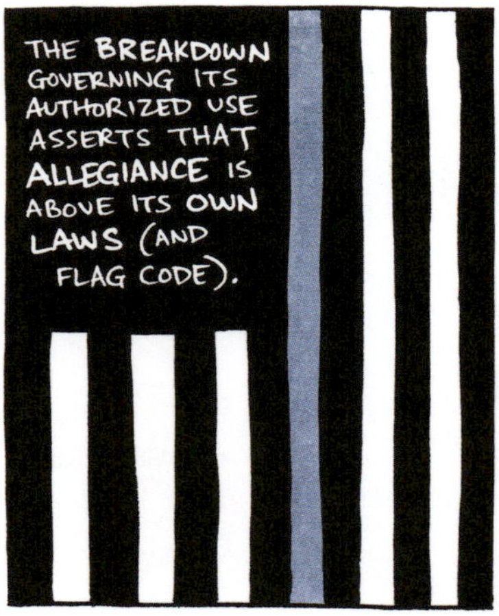
THE BREAKDOWN GOVERNING ITS AUTHORIZED USE ASSERTS THAT ALLEGIANCE IS ABOVE ITS OWN LAWS (AND FLAG CODE).

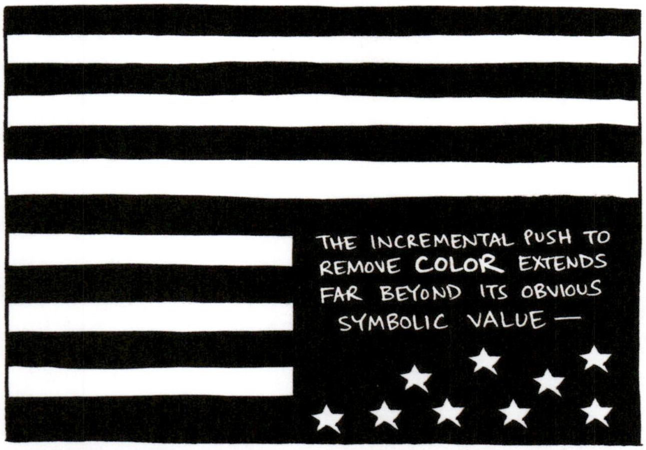
THE INCREMENTAL PUSH TO REMOVE COLOR EXTENDS FAR BEYOND ITS OBVIOUS SYMBOLIC VALUE —

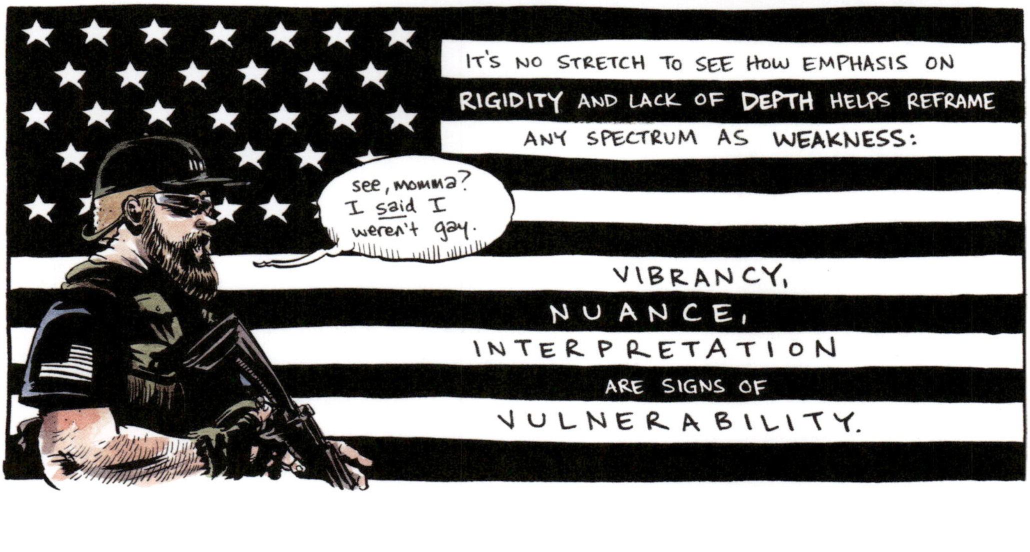
IT'S NO STRETCH TO SEE HOW EMPHASIS ON RIGIDITY AND LACK OF DEPTH HELPS REFRAME ANY SPECTRUM AS WEAKNESS:
see, momma? I said I weren't gay.
VIBRANCY,
NUANCE,
INTERPRETATION
ARE SIGNS OF
VULNERABILITY.

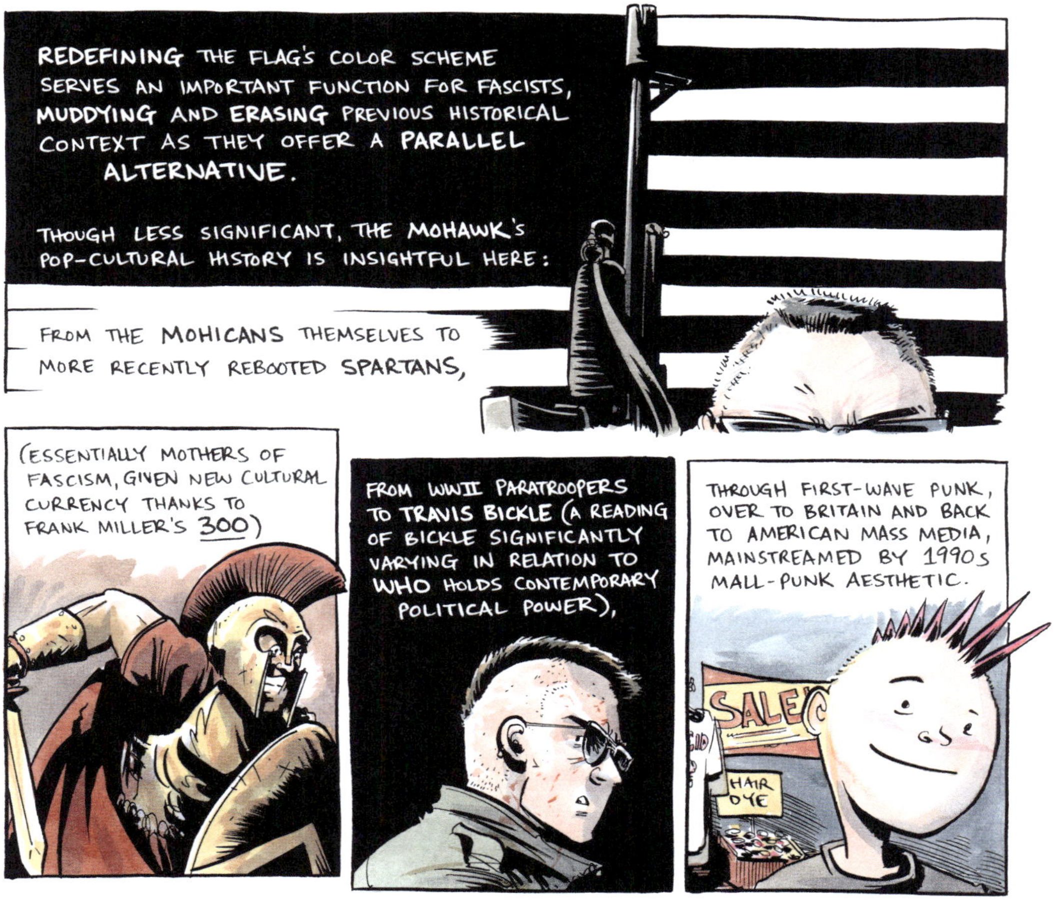
REDEFINING THE FLAG'S COLOR SCHEME SERVES AN IMPORTANT FUNCTION FOR FASCISTS, MUDDYING AND ERASING PREVIOUS HISTORICAL CONTEXT AS THEY OFFER A PARALLEL ALTERNATIVE.
THOUGH LESS SIGNIFICANT, THE MOHAWK'S POP-CULTURAL HISTORY IS INSIGHTFUL HERE:
FROM THE MOHICANS THEMSELVES TO MORE RECENTLY REBOOTED SPARTANS,
(ESSENTIALLY MOTHERS OF FASCISM, GIVEN NEW CULTURAL CURRENCY THANKS TO FRANK MILLER'S 300)
FROM WWII PARATROOPERS TO TRAVIS BICKLE (A READING OF BICKLE SIGNIFICANTLY VARYING IN RELATION TO WHO HOLDS CONTEMPORARY POLITICAL POWER),
THROUGH FIRST-WAVE PUNK, OVER TO BRITAIN AND BACK TO AMERICAN MASS MEDIA, MAINSTREAMED BY 1990s MALL-PUNK AESTHETIC.
SALE
HAIR DYE

WHEN THOSE SAME MALL PUNKS HEADED OFF TO **WAR** IN THE 2000S, THEY ALSO **SHRUGGED OFF** PUNK'S CORE **ANTI-WAR, ANTI-NATIONALIST,** AND **ANTICONFORMIST** BELIEFS, BUT HELD ON TO THE HAIRSTYLE — ITS OWN SHIELD AGAINST SHAME AND TRAUMA. BY THE MID-00S, THE MOHAWK HAD BEEN **REPURPOSED** AS A SYMBOL OF MASCULINE FORCE, OF **CONFORMITY** DISGUISED AS **REBELLION.**

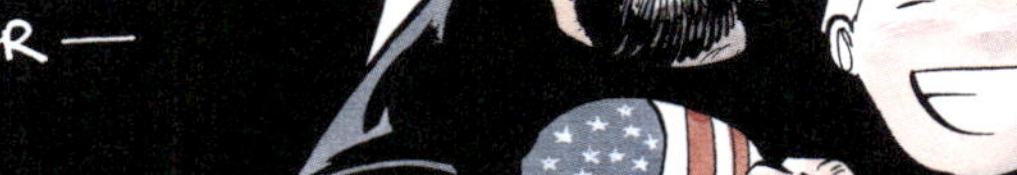

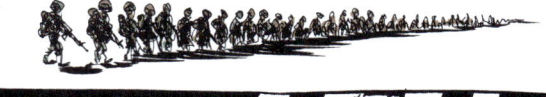

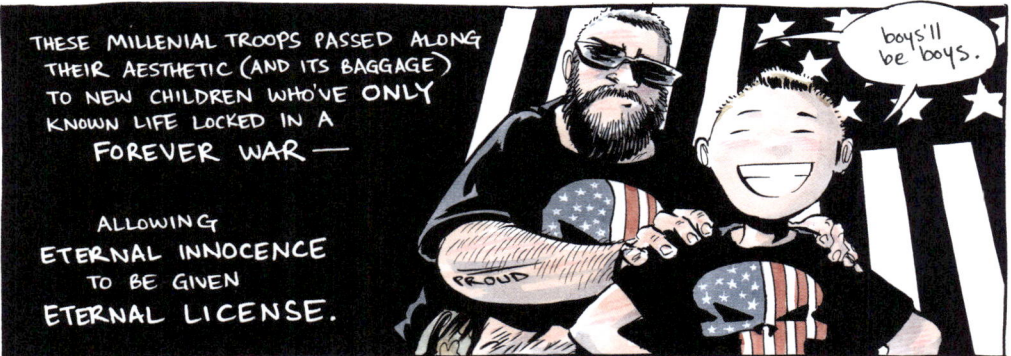

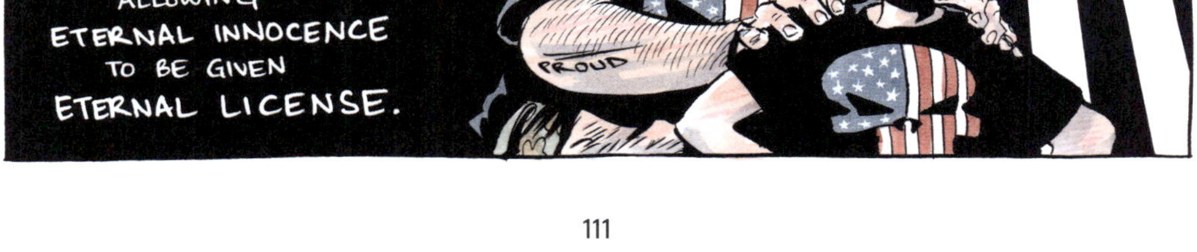
THESE MILLENIAL TROOPS PASSED ALONG THEIR AESTHETIC (AND ITS BAGGAGE) TO NEW CHILDREN WHO'VE ONLY KNOWN LIFE LOCKED IN A FOREVER WAR —
ALLOWING ETERNAL INNOCENCE TO BE GIVEN ETERNAL LICENSE.
boys'll be boys.
PROUD

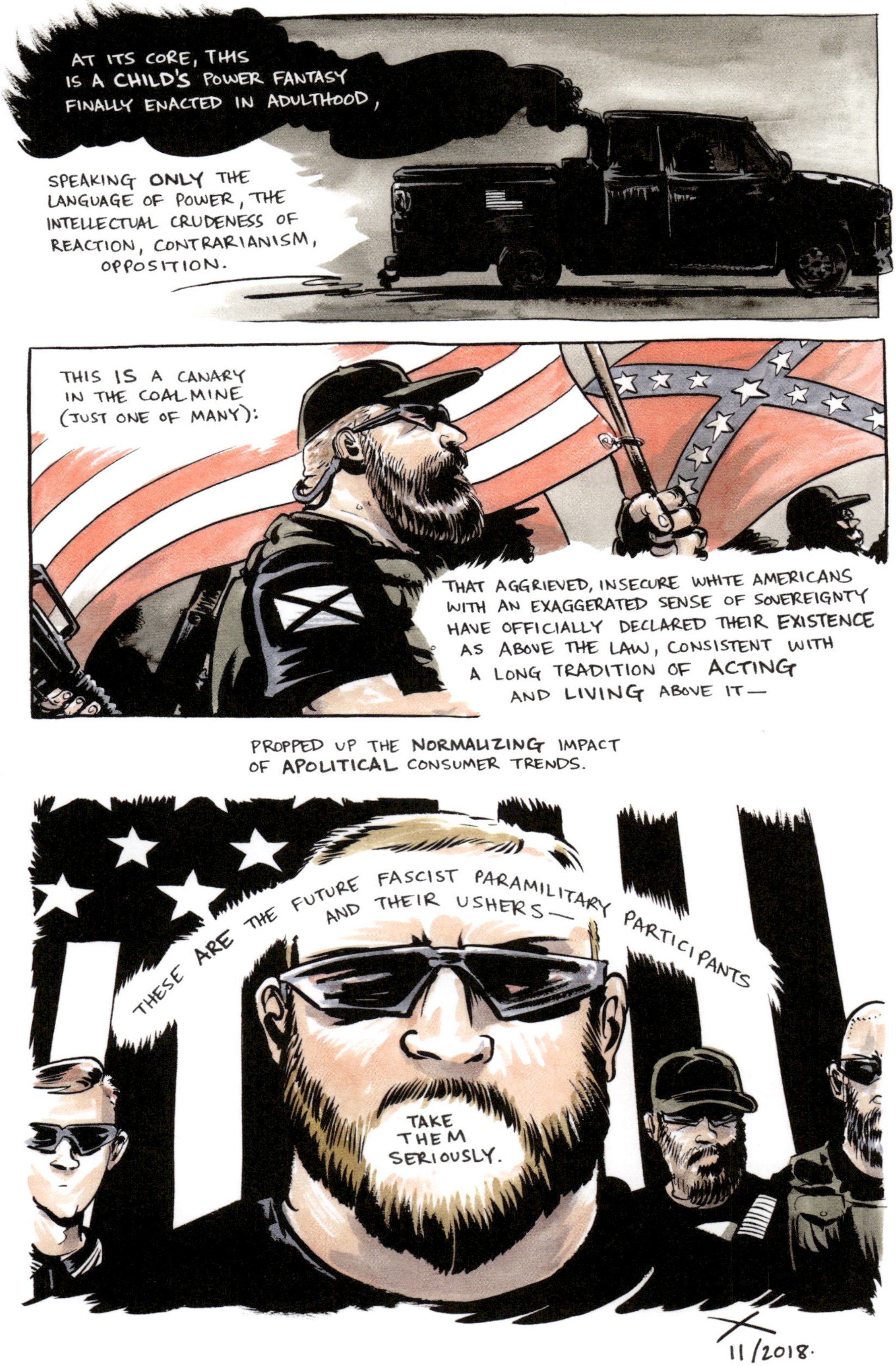
AT ITS CORE, THIS IS A CHILD'S POWER FANTASY FINALLY ENACTED IN ADULTHOOD,
SPEAKING ONLY THE LANGUAGE OF POWER, THE INTELLECTUAL CRUDENESS OF REACTION, CONTRARIANISM, OPPOSITION.
THIS IS A CANARY IN THE COALMINE (JUST ONE OF MANY):
THAT AGGRIEVED, INSECURE WHITE AMERICANS WITH AN EXAGGERATED SENSE OF SOVEREIGNTY HAVE OFFICIALLY DECLARED THEIR EXISTENCE AS ABOVE THE LAW, CONSISTENT WITH A LONG TRADITION OF ACTING AND LIVING ABOVE IT—
PROPPED UP THE NORMALIZING IMPACT OF APOLITICAL CONSUMER TRENDS.
THESE ARE THE FUTURE FASCIST PARAMILITARY PARTICIPANTS AND THEIR USHERS—
TAKE THEM SERIOUSLY.
11/2018.

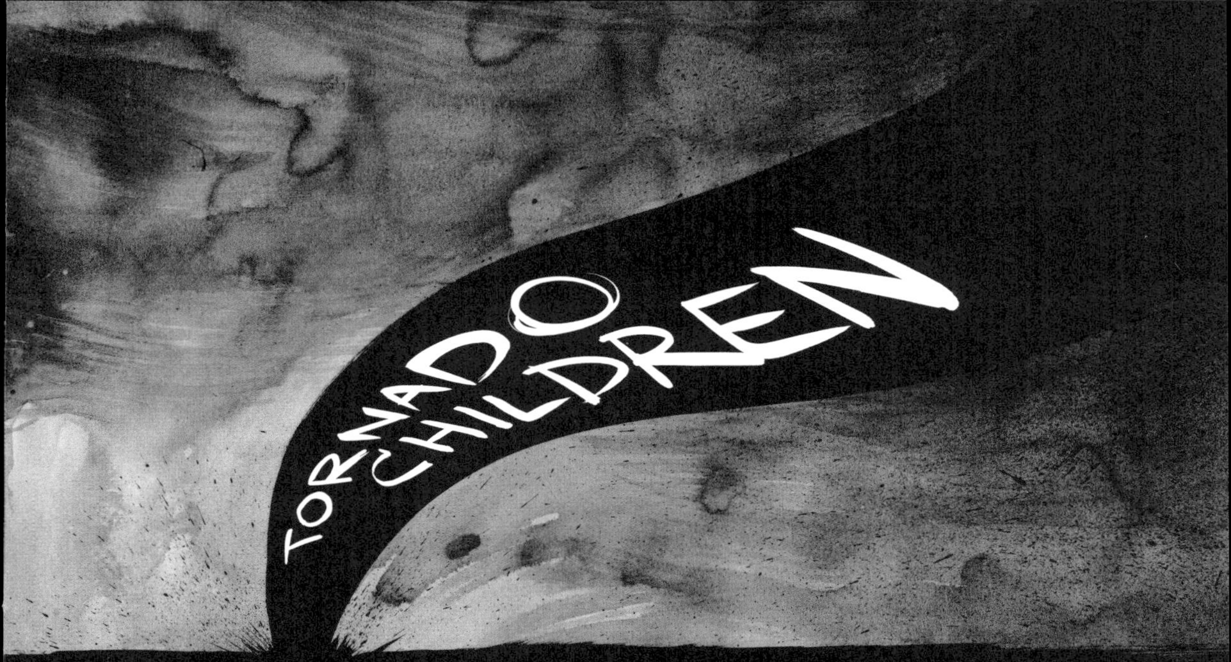

6 TORNADO CHILDREN

NO MATTER HOW FAR AWAY
WE SAW IT COMING,

WE'LL ALL BE LIVING 2020
FOR DECADES.

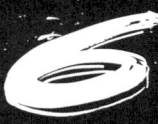

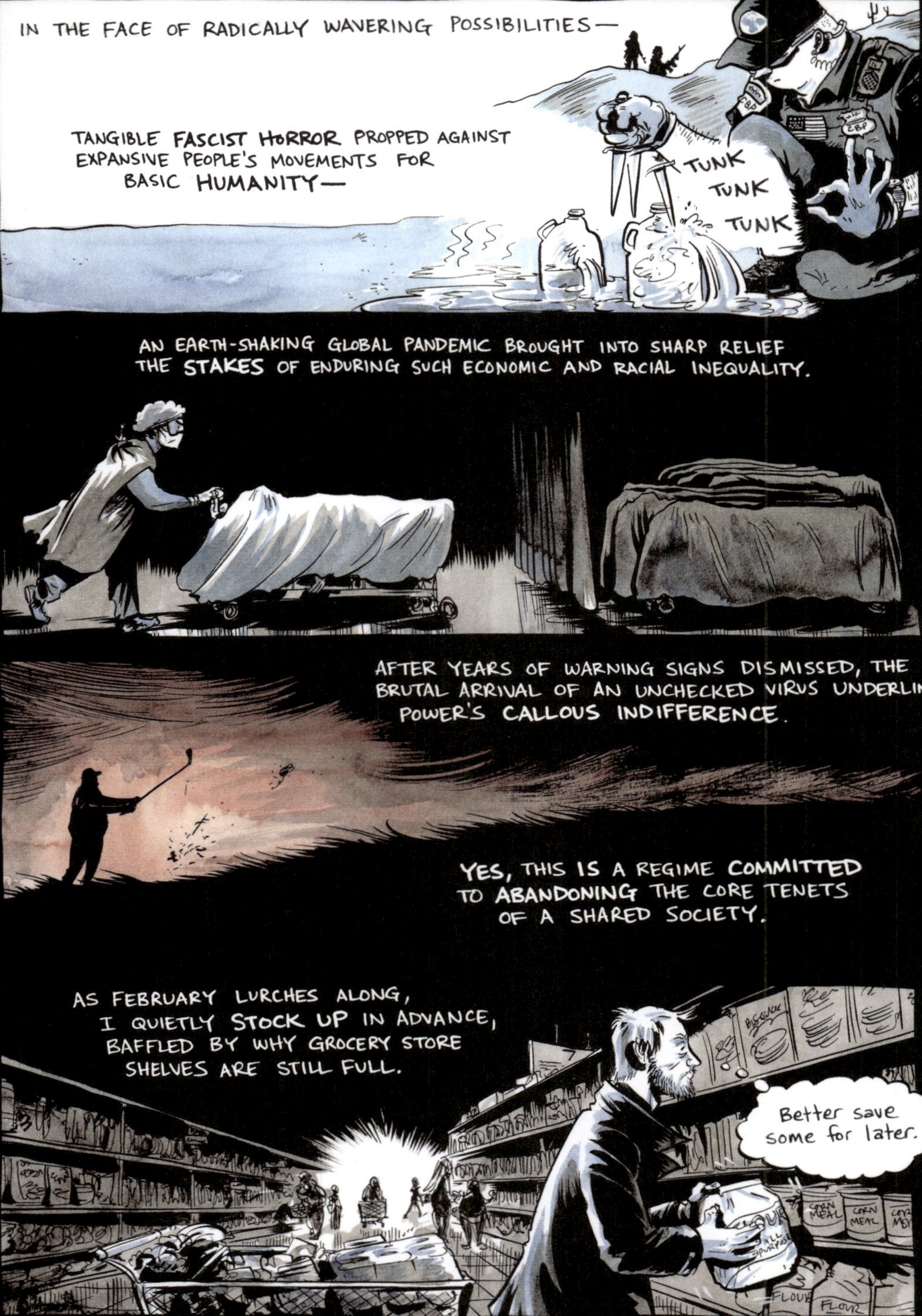
IN THE FACE OF RADICALLY WAVERING POSSIBILITIES—
TANGIBLE FASCIST HORROR PROPPED AGAINST EXPANSIVE PEOPLE'S MOVEMENTS FOR BASIC HUMANITY—
TUNK
TUNK
TUNK
AN EARTH-SHAKING GLOBAL PANDEMIC BROUGHT INTO SHARP RELIEF THE STAKES OF ENDURING SUCH ECONOMIC AND RACIAL INEQUALITY.
AFTER YEARS OF WARNING SIGNS DISMISSED, THE BRUTAL ARRIVAL OF AN UNCHECKED VIRUS UNDERLINES POWER'S CALLOUS INDIFFERENCE.
YES, THIS IS A REGIME COMMITTED TO ABANDONING THE CORE TENETS OF A SHARED SOCIETY.
AS FEBRUARY LURCHES ALONG, I QUIETLY STOCK UP IN ADVANCE, BAFFLED BY WHY GROCERY STORE SHELVES ARE STILL FULL.
Better save some for later.

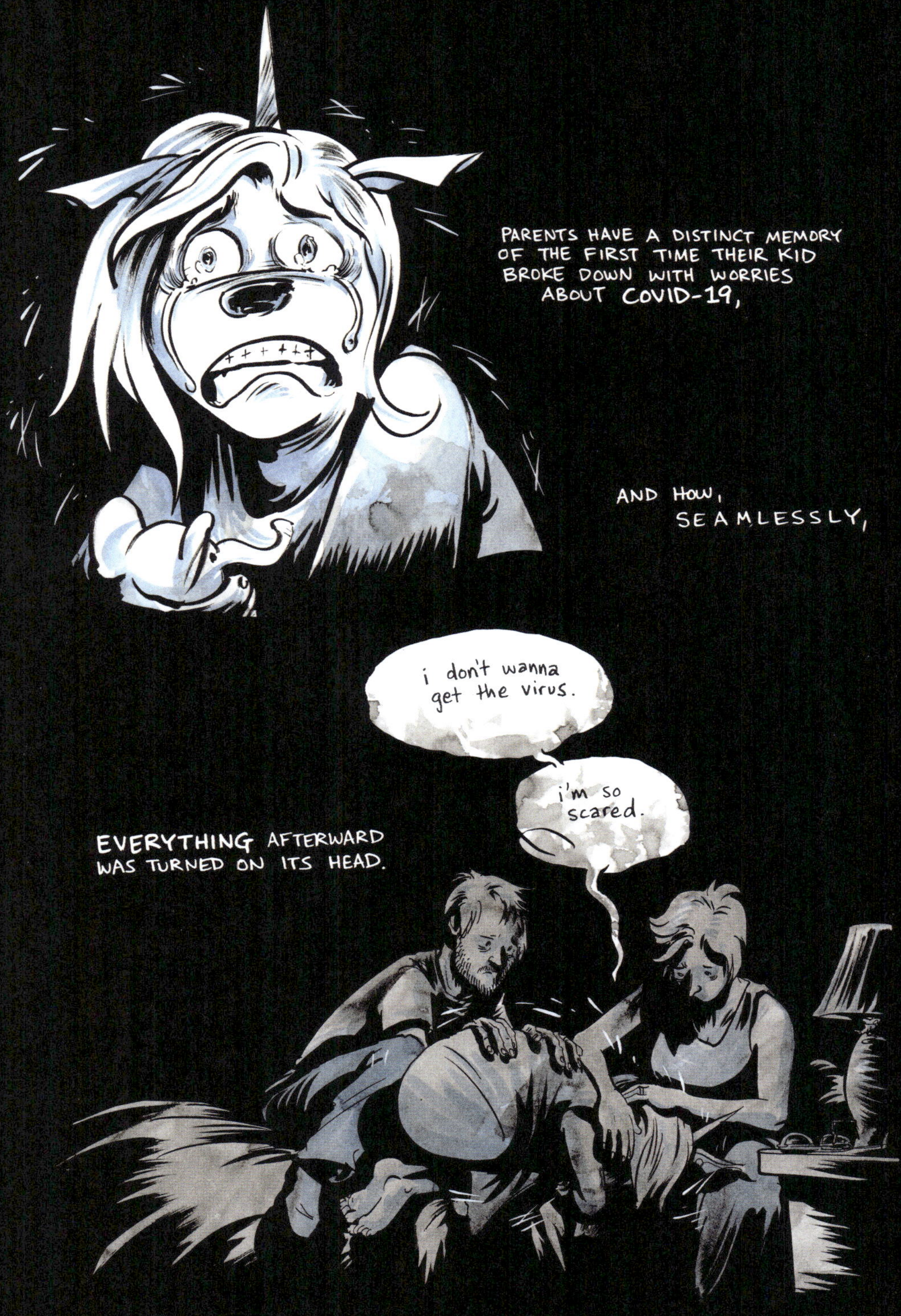
PARENTS HAVE A DISTINCT MEMORY OF THE FIRST TIME THEIR KID BROKE DOWN WITH WORRIES ABOUT COVID-19,
AND HOW, SEAMLESSLY,
EVERYTHING AFTERWARD WAS TURNED ON ITS HEAD.
i don't wanna get the virus.
i'm so scared.

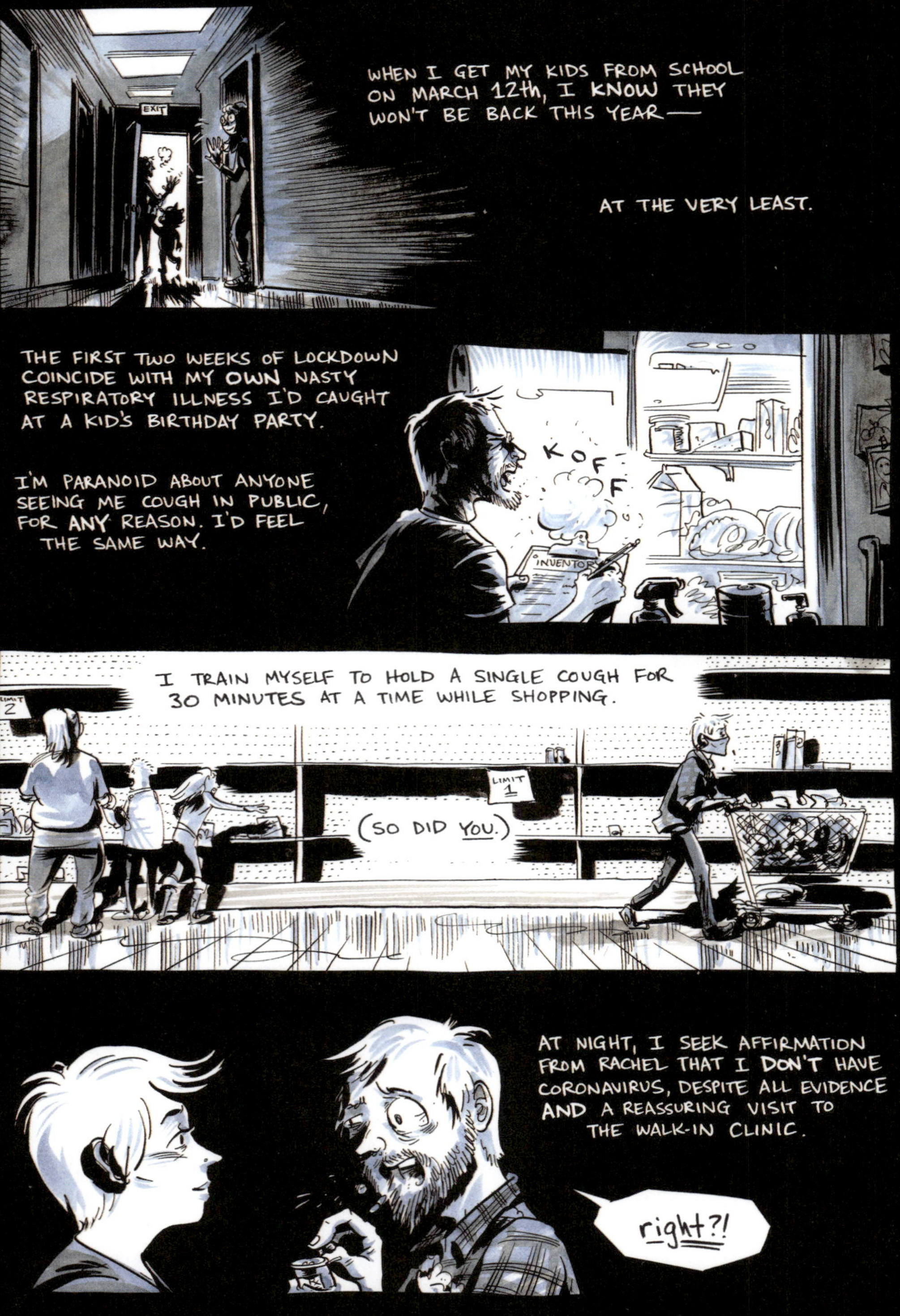
WHEN I GET MY KIDS FROM SCHOOL ON MARCH 12th, I KNOW THEY WON'T BE BACK THIS YEAR—
EXIT
AT THE VERY LEAST.
THE FIRST TWO WEEKS OF LOCKDOWN COINCIDE WITH MY OWN NASTY RESPIRATORY ILLNESS I'D CAUGHT AT A KID'S BIRTHDAY PARTY.
I'M PARANOID ABOUT ANYONE SEEING ME COUGH IN PUBLIC, FOR ANY REASON. I'D FEEL THE SAME WAY.
KOFF
INVENTOR
I TRAIN MYSELF TO HOLD A SINGLE COUGH FOR 30 MINUTES AT A TIME WHILE SHOPPING.
LIMIT 2
LIMIT 1
(SO DID YOU.)
AT NIGHT, I SEEK AFFIRMATION FROM RACHEL THAT I DON'T HAVE CORONAVIRUS, DESPITE ALL EVIDENCE AND A REASSURING VISIT TO THE WALK-IN CLINIC.
right?!

I SHAVE CLEAN AGAIN, APPLYING WHAT I LEARNED ABOUT MASKS AND BEARDS WHILE RESEARCHING CHAPTER 5.

KEEP EVERYONE BUSY AND COOL. HIDE ADULT TERROR AND DEPRESSION FROM THE KIDS. FIND KINDER TONES FOR OUR VIGILANCE.

GLITTER SLIME!

♪ SAVE SOME GLUE FOR LAAATERR! ♪

ON DAY 9, I'M DESPERATE FOR UNEARNED HOPE AFTER SEEING A TOUGH GUY LEAVING THE GROCERY STORE WITH A 4-PACK OF TOILET PAPER.

He's... listening!

Everyone's following through—

we're... gonna make it through this!?

SQUEEZE SQUEEZE

HUFF HUFF

THAT NIGHT BRINGS MY FIRST PANIC ATTACK IN 12 YEARS.

HYPERVIGILANCE HAS ITS LIMITS.

THE BODY SAYS NO.

I RECOVER IN THE DARK RELIEF THAT I'M NOT HAVING A HEART ATTACK.

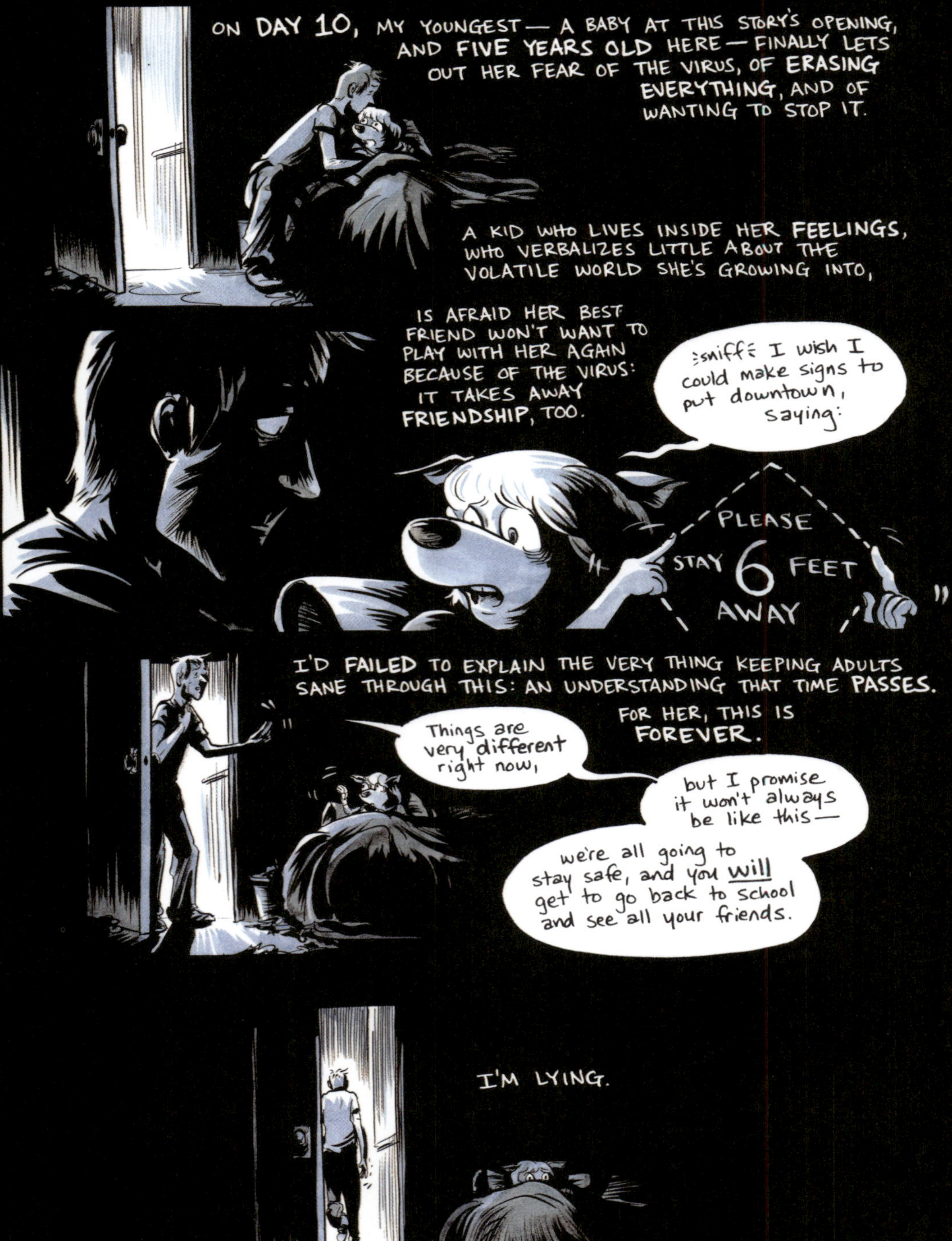
ON DAY 10, MY YOUNGEST— A BABY AT THIS STORY'S OPENING, AND FIVE YEARS OLD HERE— FINALLY LETS OUT HER FEAR OF THE VIRUS, OF ERASING EVERYTHING, AND OF WANTING TO STOP IT.
A KID WHO LIVES INSIDE HER FEELINGS, WHO VERBALIZES LITTLE ABOUT THE VOLATILE WORLD SHE'S GROWING INTO,
IS AFRAID HER BEST FRIEND WON'T WANT TO PLAY WITH HER AGAIN BECAUSE OF THE VIRUS: IT TAKES AWAY FRIENDSHIP, TOO.
sniff I wish I could make signs to put downtown, saying:
"PLEASE STAY 6 FEET AWAY"
I'D FAILED TO EXPLAIN THE VERY THING KEEPING ADULTS SANE THROUGH THIS: AN UNDERSTANDING THAT TIME PASSES.
FOR HER, THIS IS FOREVER.
Things are very different right now,
but I promise it won't always be like this—
we're all going to stay safe, and you will get to go back to school and see all your friends.
I'M LYING.

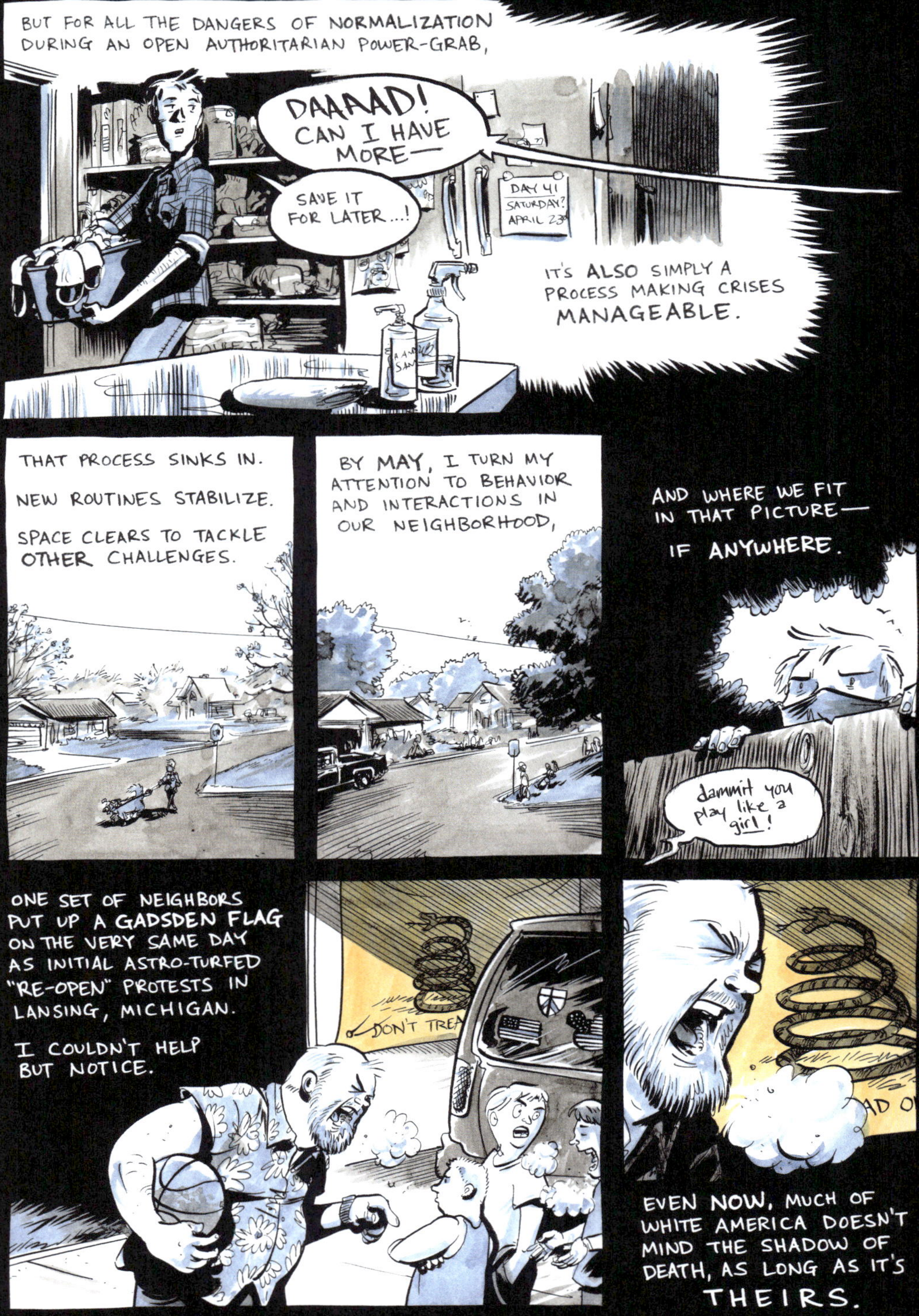
BUT FOR ALL THE DANGERS OF NORMALIZATION DURING AN OPEN AUTHORITARIAN POWER-GRAB,
DAAAAD! CAN I HAVE MORE—
SAVE IT FOR LATER...!
DAY 41 SATURDAY? APRIL 23rd
IT'S ALSO SIMPLY A PROCESS MAKING CRISES MANAGEABLE.
THAT PROCESS SINKS IN.
NEW ROUTINES STABILIZE.
SPACE CLEARS TO TACKLE OTHER CHALLENGES.
BY MAY, I TURN MY ATTENTION TO BEHAVIOR AND INTERACTIONS IN OUR NEIGHBORHOOD,
AND WHERE WE FIT IN THAT PICTURE—
IF ANYWHERE.
dammit you play like a girl!
ONE SET OF NEIGHBORS PUT UP A GADSDEN FLAG ON THE VERY SAME DAY AS INITIAL ASTRO-TURFED "RE-OPEN" PROTESTS IN LANSING, MICHIGAN.
I COULDN'T HELP BUT NOTICE.
DON'T TREA
EVEN NOW, MUCH OF WHITE AMERICA DOESN'T MIND THE SHADOW OF DEATH, AS LONG AS IT'S THEIRS.

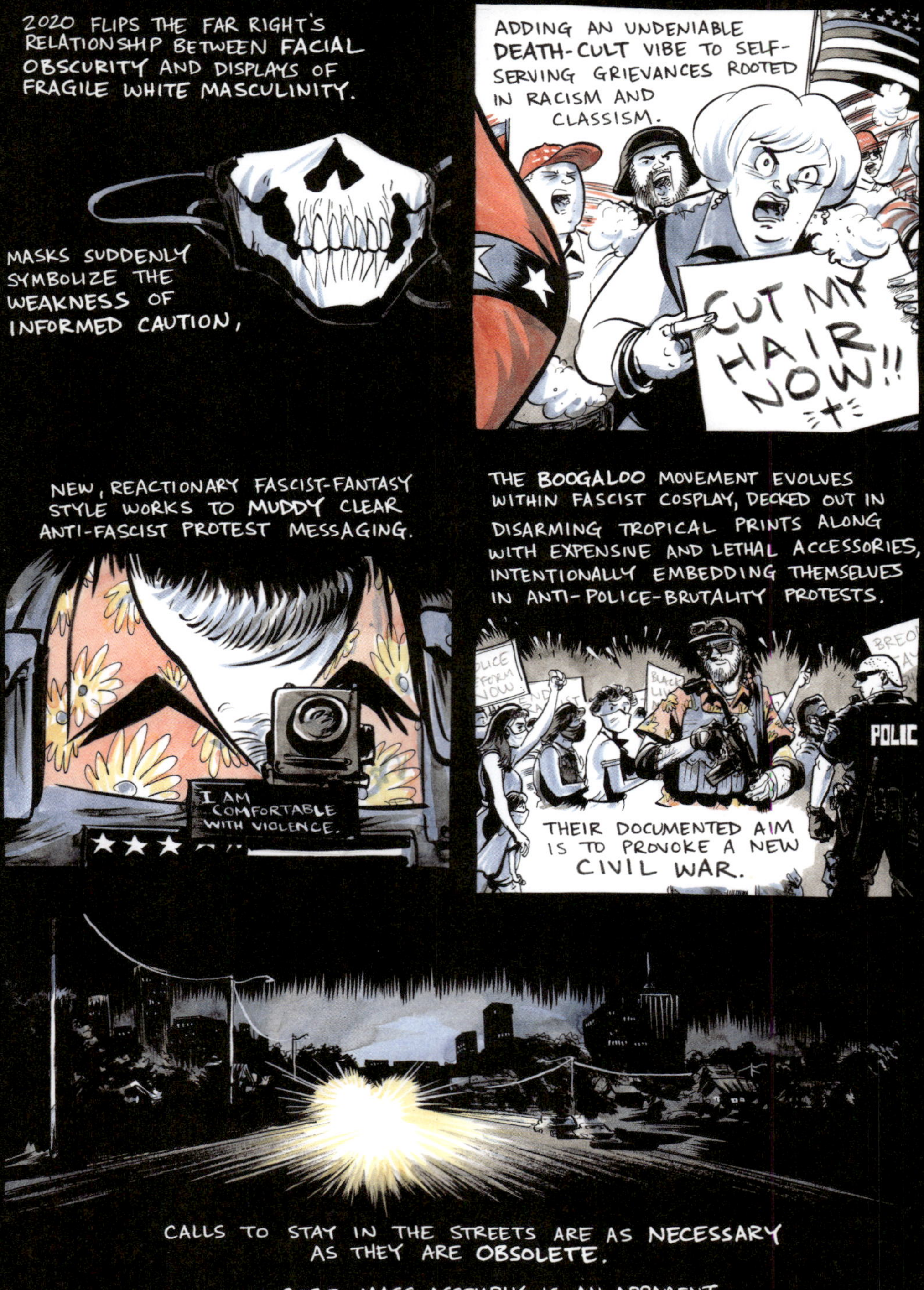
2020 FLIPS THE FAR RIGHT'S RELATIONSHIP BETWEEN **FACIAL OBSCURITY** AND DISPLAYS OF **FRAGILE WHITE MASCULINITY.**
MASKS SUDDENLY SYMBOLIZE THE **WEAKNESS** OF **INFORMED CAUTION,**
ADDING AN UNDENIABLE **DEATH-CULT** VIBE TO SELF-SERVING GRIEVANCES ROOTED IN RACISM AND CLASSISM.
CUT MY HAIR NOW!!
NEW, REACTIONARY FASCIST-FANTASY STYLE WORKS TO **MUDDY** CLEAR ANTI-FASCIST PROTEST MESSAGING.
I AM COMFORTABLE WITH VIOLENCE.
THE **BOOGALOO** MOVEMENT EVOLVES WITHIN FASCIST COSPLAY, DECKED OUT IN DISARMING TROPICAL PRINTS ALONG WITH EXPENSIVE AND LETHAL ACCESSORIES, INTENTIONALLY EMBEDDING THEMSELVES IN ANTI-POLICE-BRUTALITY PROTESTS.
POLIC
THEIR DOCUMENTED AIM IS TO PROVOKE A NEW CIVIL WAR.
CALLS TO STAY IN THE STREETS ARE AS **NECESSARY** AS THEY ARE **OBSOLETE.**
IN 2020, MASS ASSEMBLY IS AN APPARENT **DEATH WISH** OF ITS OWN.

THE OVERTON WINDOW WORKS OVERTIME TO ACCOMMODATE EXPLICITLY NAZI IDEAS, WEDGING QUESTIONS INTO THE NATIONAL CONVERSATION:

WHO'S DISPOSABLE?

WHO'S A BURDEN?

WHO'S A SACRIFICIAL HERO?

WHO'S SIMPLY A SACRIFICE?

MONTHS OF PAINFUL QUIET ON AMERICAN STREETS SHIELD THE HORROR OF HUNDREDS OF THOUSANDS OF PRIVATE COVID DEATHS—

AND VERY PUBLIC MURDER OF BLACK AMERICANS AT THE HANDS OF POLICE VIRTUALLY IMMUNE TO PROSECUTION.

This certainly isn't the apocalypse-as-promised in the popular imagination.

For myself, every fantasy went THIS way:

An impending catastrophe,

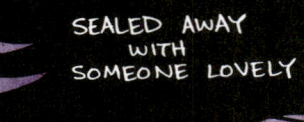

sealed away with someone lovely

watching things disappear.

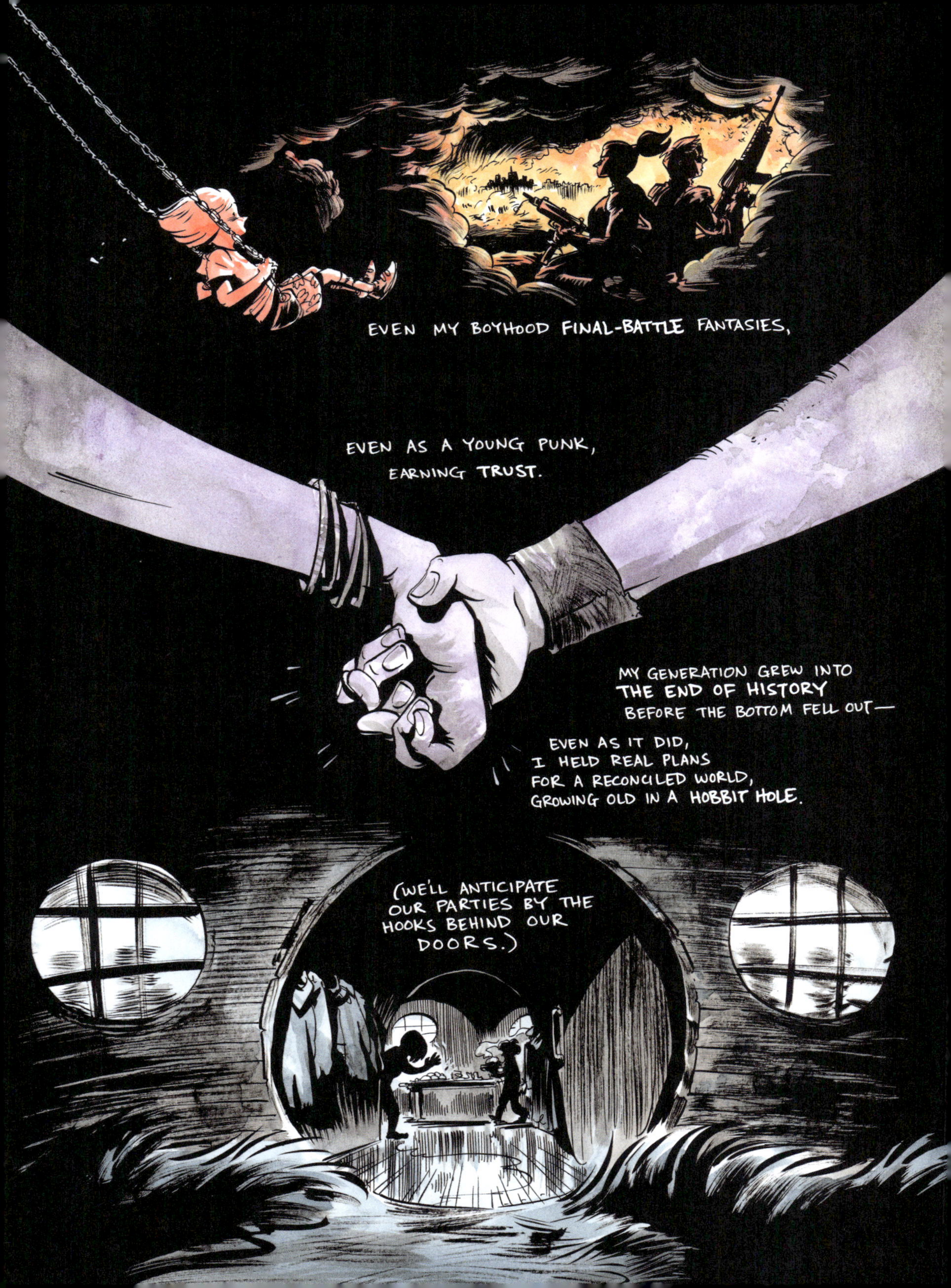
EVEN MY BOYHOOD FINAL-BATTLE FANTASIES,
EVEN AS A YOUNG PUNK, EARNING TRUST.
MY GENERATION GREW INTO THE END OF HISTORY BEFORE THE BOTTOM FELL OUT—
EVEN AS IT DID, I HELD REAL PLANS FOR A RECONCILED WORLD, GROWING OLD IN A HOBBIT HOLE.
(WE'LL ANTICIPATE OUR PARTIES BY THE HOOKS BEHIND OUR DOORS.)

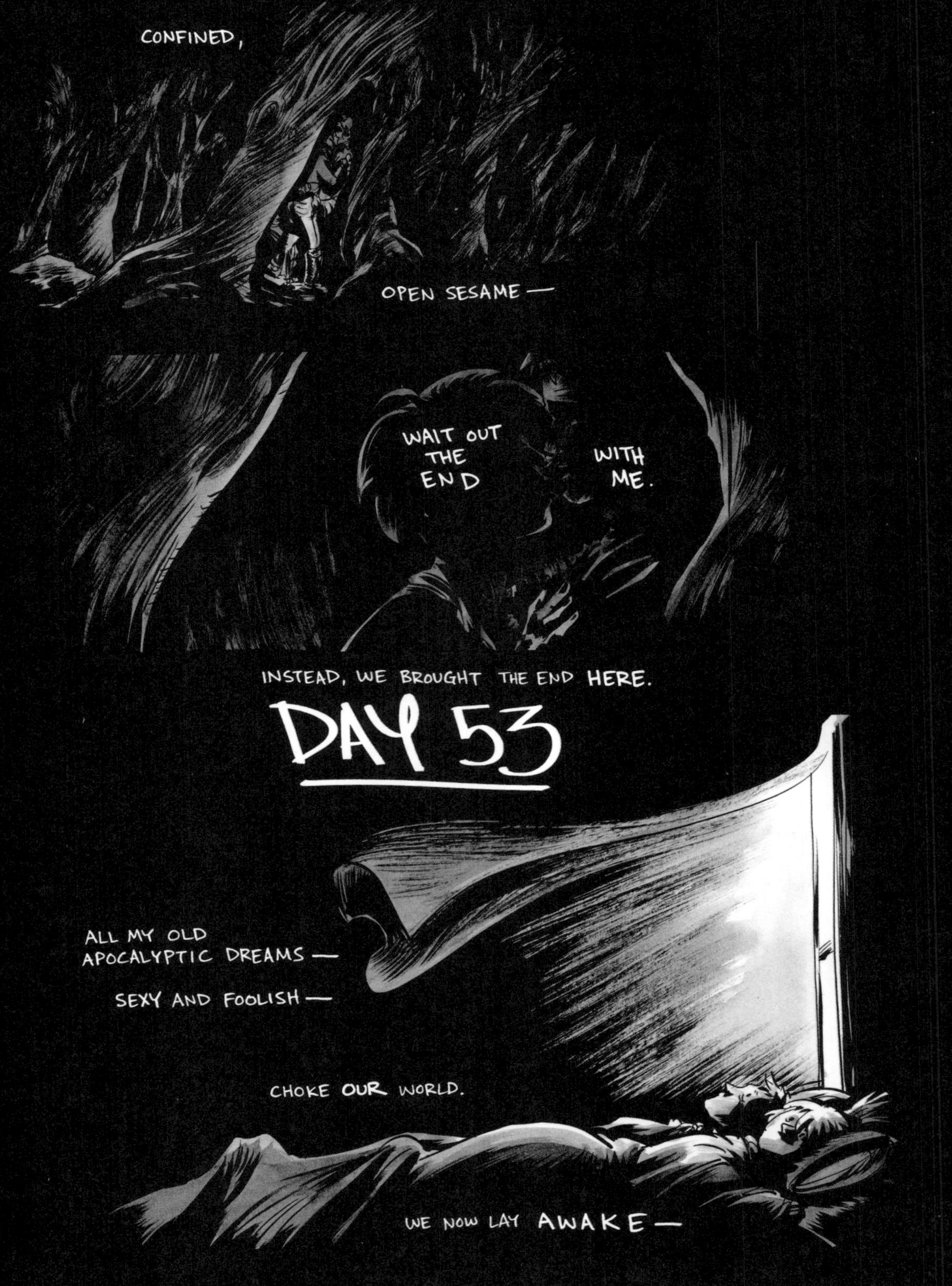
CONFINED,
OPEN SESAME—
WAIT OUT THE END
WITH ME.
INSTEAD, WE BROUGHT THE END HERE.
DAY 53
ALL MY OLD APOCALYPTIC DREAMS—
SEXY AND FOOLISH—
CHOKE OUR WORLD.
WE NOW LAY AWAKE—

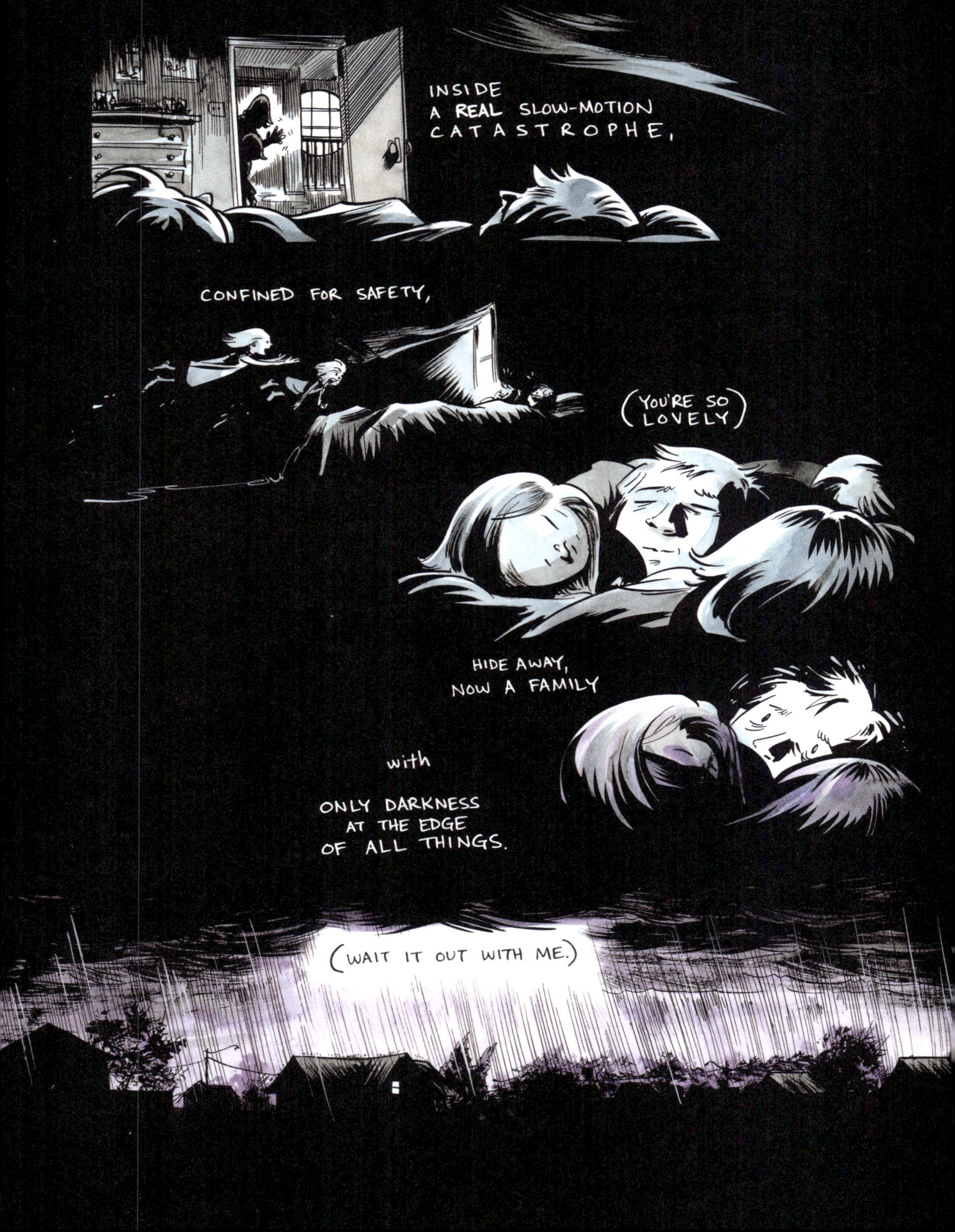
INSIDE A REAL SLOW-MOTION CATASTROPHE,
CONFINED FOR SAFETY,
(YOU'RE SO LOVELY)
HIDE AWAY, NOW A FAMILY
with
ONLY DARKNESS AT THE EDGE OF ALL THINGS.
(WAIT IT OUT WITH ME.)

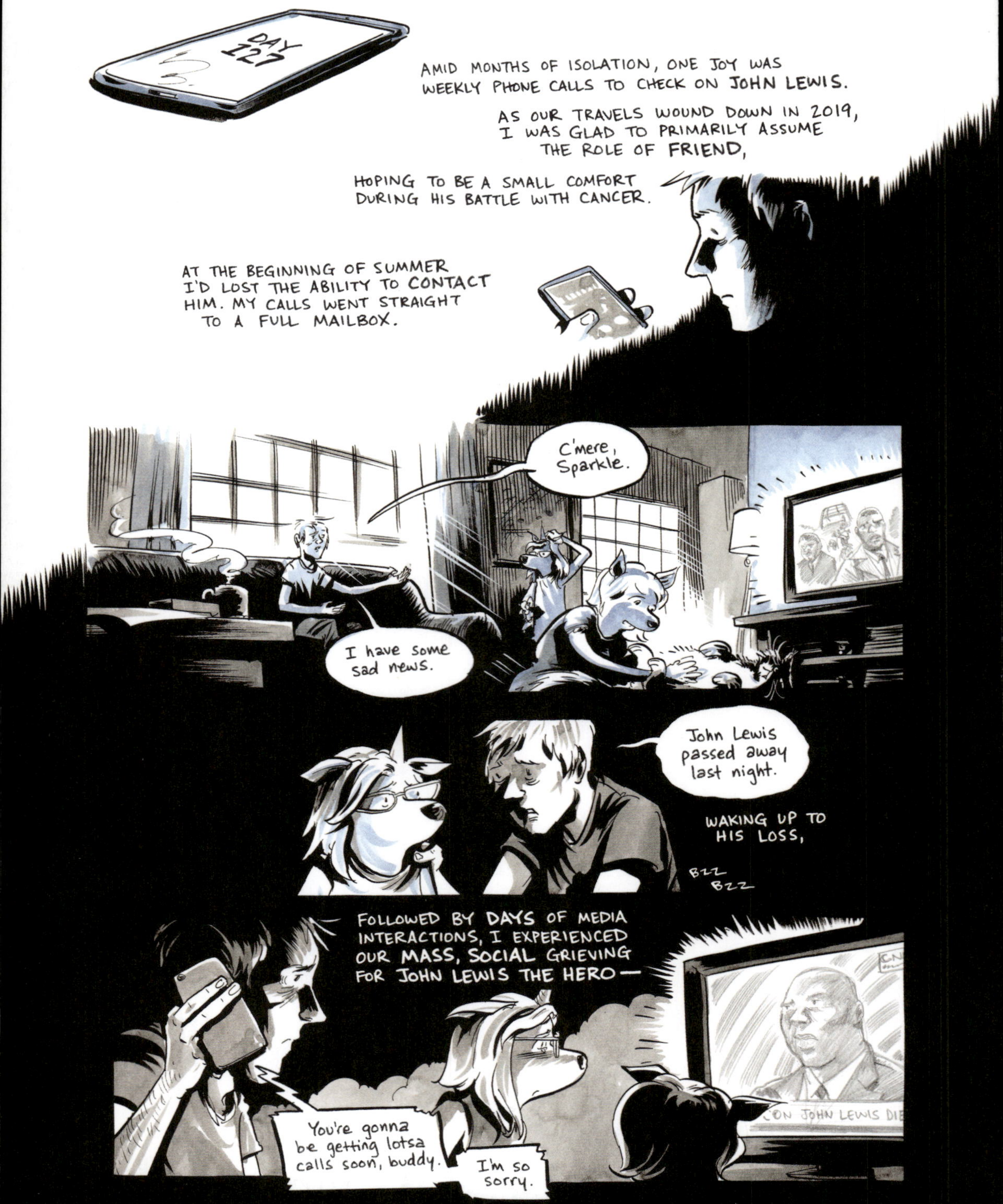
DAY 127
AMID MONTHS OF ISOLATION, ONE JOY WAS WEEKLY PHONE CALLS TO CHECK ON JOHN LEWIS.
AS OUR TRAVELS WOUND DOWN IN 2019, I WAS GLAD TO PRIMARILY ASSUME THE ROLE OF FRIEND,
HOPING TO BE A SMALL COMFORT DURING HIS BATTLE WITH CANCER.
AT THE BEGINNING OF SUMMER I'D LOST THE ABILITY TO CONTACT HIM. MY CALLS WENT STRAIGHT TO A FULL MAILBOX.
C'mere, Sparkle.
I have some sad news.
John Lewis passed away last night.
WAKING UP TO HIS LOSS,
BZZ BZZ
FOLLOWED BY DAYS OF MEDIA INTERACTIONS, I EXPERIENCED OUR MASS, SOCIAL GRIEVING FOR JOHN LEWIS THE HERO—
You're gonna be getting lotsa calls soon, buddy.
I'm so sorry.

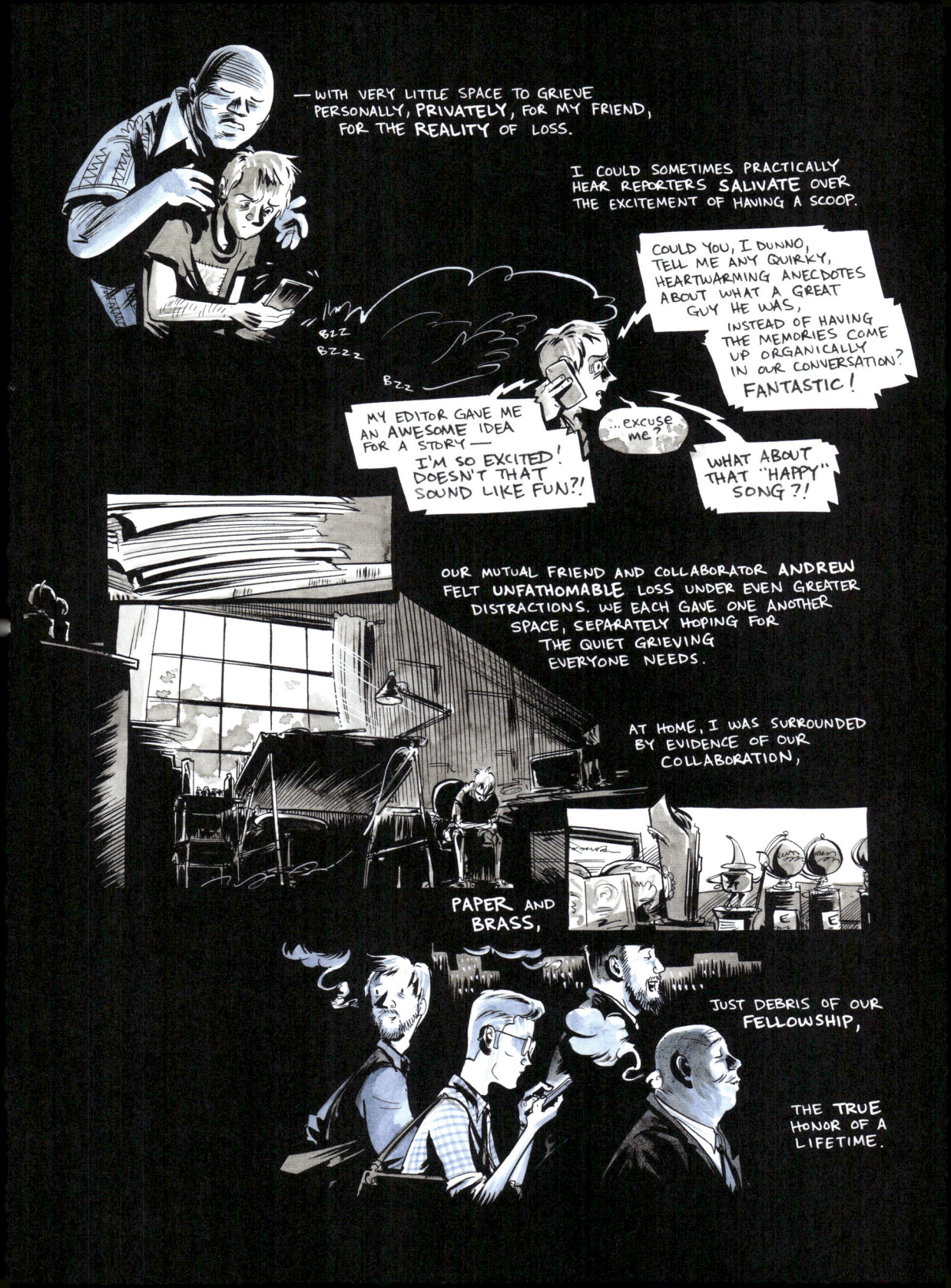

—WITH VERY LITTLE SPACE TO GRIEVE PERSONALLY, PRIVATELY, FOR MY FRIEND, FOR THE REALITY OF LOSS.

I COULD SOMETIMES PRACTICALLY HEAR REPORTERS SALIVATE OVER THE EXCITEMENT OF HAVING A SCOOP.

COULD YOU, I DUNNO, TELL ME ANY QUIRKY, HEARTWARMING ANECDOTES ABOUT WHAT A GREAT GUY HE WAS, INSTEAD OF HAVING THE MEMORIES COME UP ORGANICALLY IN OUR CONVERSATION? FANTASTIC!

MY EDITOR GAVE ME AN AWESOME IDEA FOR A STORY— I'M SO EXCITED! DOESN'T THAT SOUND LIKE FUN?!

...excuse me?

WHAT ABOUT THAT "HAPPY" SONG?!

OUR MUTUAL FRIEND AND COLLABORATOR ANDREW FELT UNFATHOMABLE LOSS UNDER EVEN GREATER DISTRACTIONS. WE EACH GAVE ONE ANOTHER SPACE, SEPARATELY HOPING FOR THE QUIET GRIEVING EVERYONE NEEDS.

AT HOME, I WAS SURROUNDED BY EVIDENCE OF OUR COLLABORATION,

PAPER AND BRASS,

JUST DEBRIS OF OUR FELLOWSHIP,

THE TRUE HONOR OF A LIFETIME.

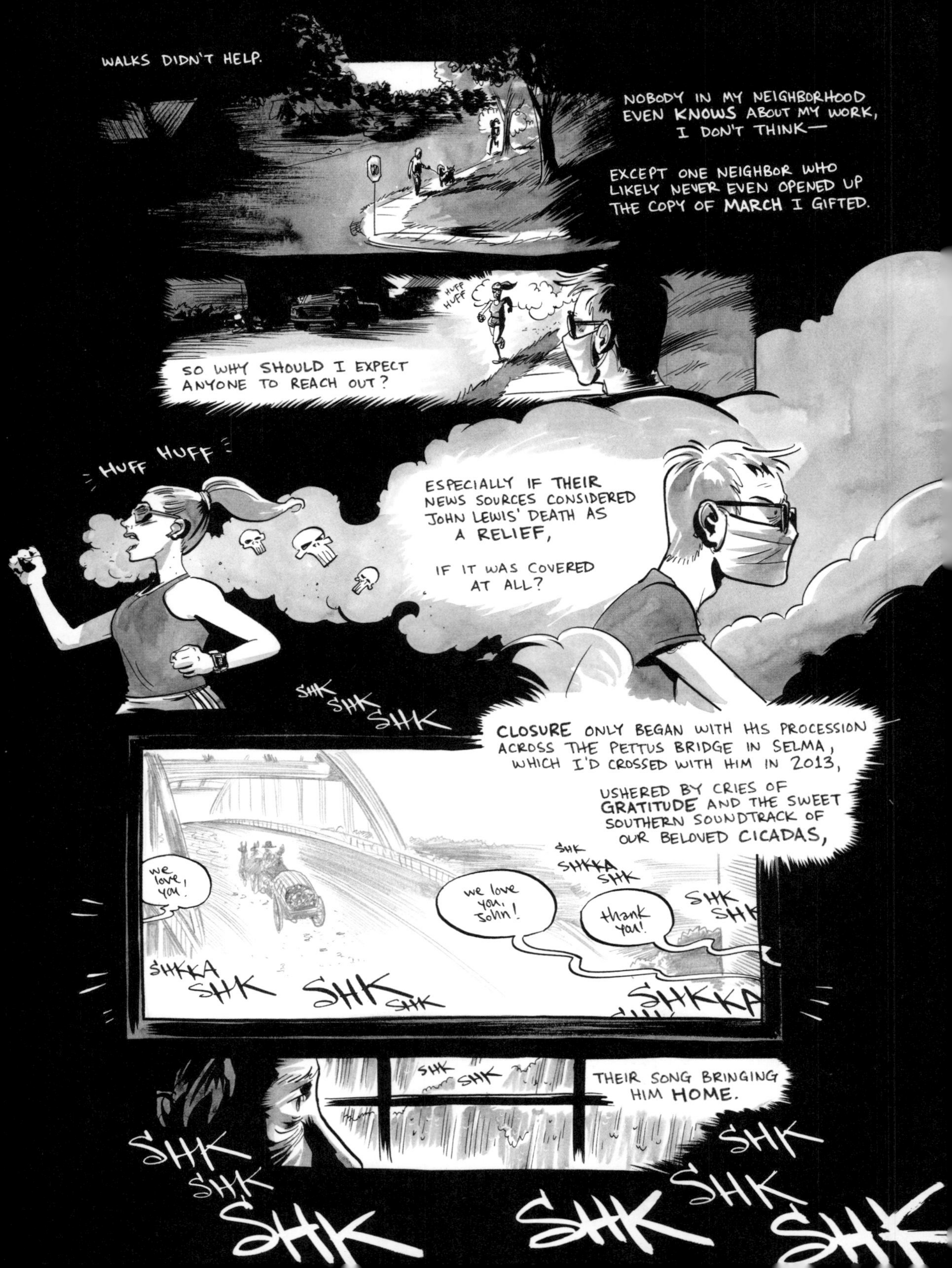
WALKS DIDN'T HELP.
NOBODY IN MY NEIGHBORHOOD EVEN KNOWS ABOUT MY WORK, I DON'T THINK—
EXCEPT ONE NEIGHBOR WHO LIKELY NEVER EVEN OPENED UP THE COPY OF MARCH I GIFTED.
HUFF HUFF
SO WHY SHOULD I EXPECT ANYONE TO REACH OUT?
HUFF HUFF
ESPECIALLY IF THEIR NEWS SOURCES CONSIDERED JOHN LEWIS' DEATH AS A RELIEF,
IF IT WAS COVERED AT ALL?
SHK SHK SHK
CLOSURE ONLY BEGAN WITH HIS PROCESSION ACROSS THE PETTUS BRIDGE IN SELMA, WHICH I'D CROSSED WITH HIM IN 2013,
USHERED BY CRIES OF GRATITUDE AND THE SWEET SOUTHERN SOUNDTRACK OF OUR BELOVED CICADAS,
SHK SHKKA SHK
we love you!
we love you, John!
thank you!
SHK SHK
SHKKA SHK
SHK SHK
SHKKA
SHK SHK
THEIR SONG BRINGING HIM HOME.
SHK SHK SHK
SHK SHK SHK
SHK SHK

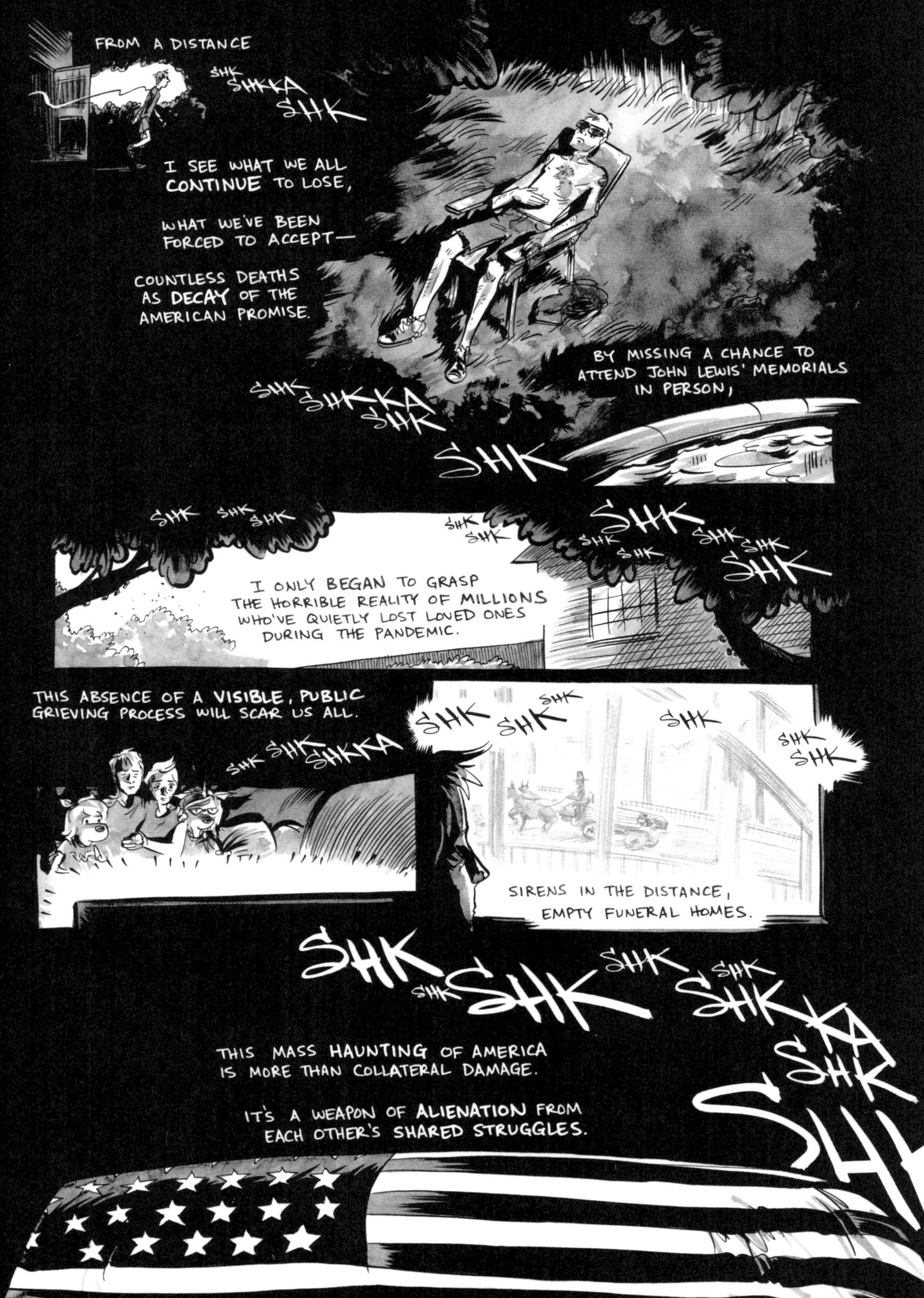
FROM A DISTANCE
SHK SHKKA SHK
I SEE WHAT WE ALL CONTINUE TO LOSE,
WHAT WE'VE BEEN FORCED TO ACCEPT—
COUNTLESS DEATHS AS DECAY OF THE AMERICAN PROMISE.
BY MISSING A CHANCE TO ATTEND JOHN LEWIS' MEMORIALS IN PERSON,
SHK SHKKA SHK
SHK
SHK SHK SHK
SHK SHK
SHK SHK SHK SHK SHK SHK
I ONLY BEGAN TO GRASP THE HORRIBLE REALITY OF MILLIONS WHO'VE QUIETLY LOST LOVED ONES DURING THE PANDEMIC.
THIS ABSENCE OF A VISIBLE, PUBLIC GRIEVING PROCESS WILL SCAR US ALL.
SHK SHK SHKKA
SHK SHK SHK
SHK
SHK SHK
SIRENS IN THE DISTANCE, EMPTY FUNERAL HOMES.
SHK SHK SHK SHK SHK SHKKA SHR
THIS MASS HAUNTING OF AMERICA IS MORE THAN COLLATERAL DAMAGE.
IT'S A WEAPON OF ALIENATION FROM EACH OTHER'S SHARED STRUGGLES.

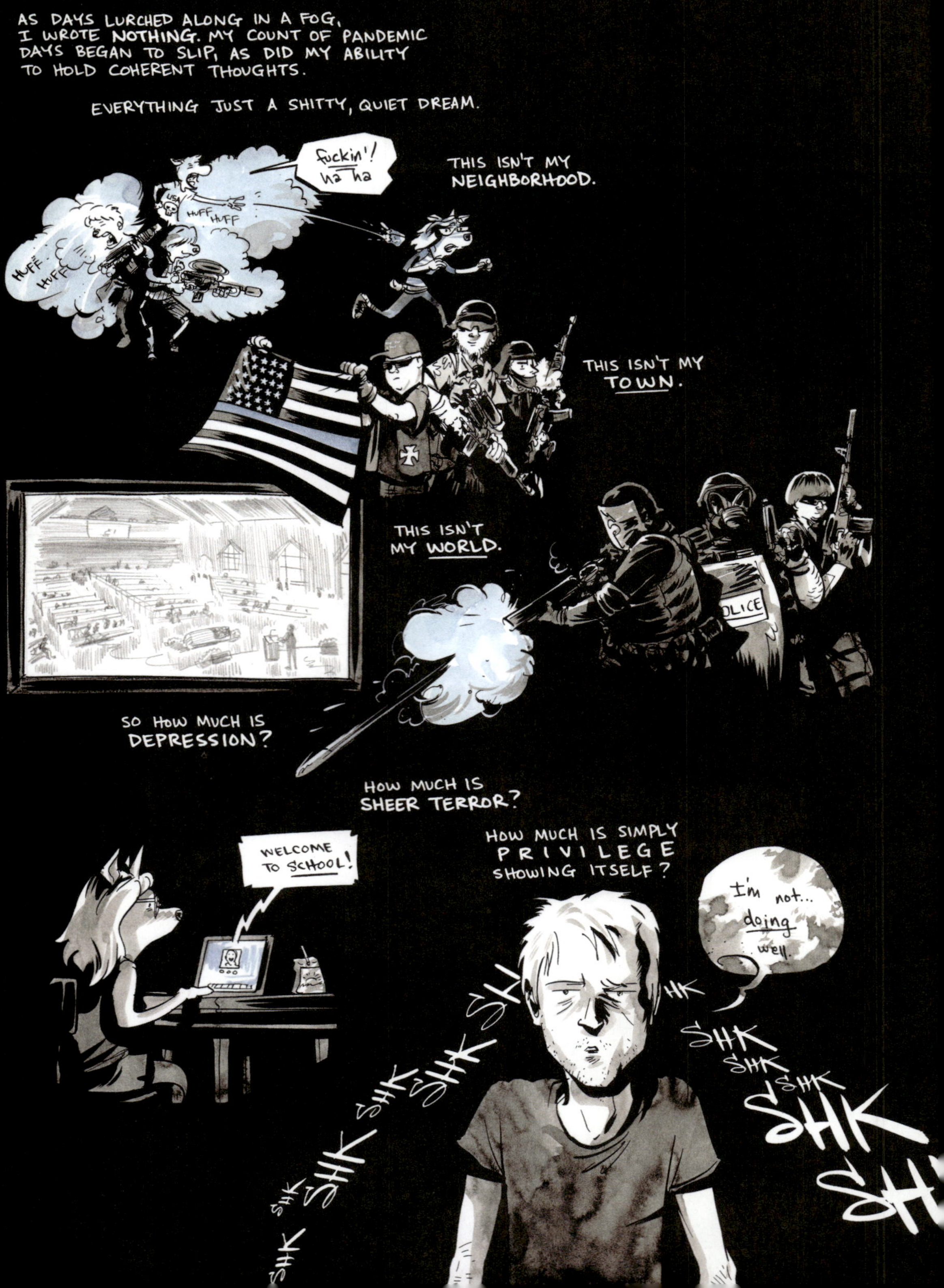
AS DAYS LURCHED ALONG IN A FOG, I WROTE NOTHING. MY COUNT OF PANDEMIC DAYS BEGAN TO SLIP, AS DID MY ABILITY TO HOLD COHERENT THOUGHTS.
EVERYTHING JUST A SHITTY, QUIET DREAM.
fuckin'! ha ha
HUFF HUFF
HUFF HUFF
THIS ISN'T MY NEIGHBORHOOD.
THIS ISN'T MY TOWN.
THIS ISN'T MY WORLD.
OLICE
SO HOW MUCH IS DEPRESSION?
HOW MUCH IS SHEER TERROR?
HOW MUCH IS SIMPLY PRIVILEGE SHOWING ITSELF?
WELCOME TO SCHOOL!
I'm not... doing well.
SHK SHK SHK SHK SHK SHK SHK SH
HK SHK SHK SHK SHK SH

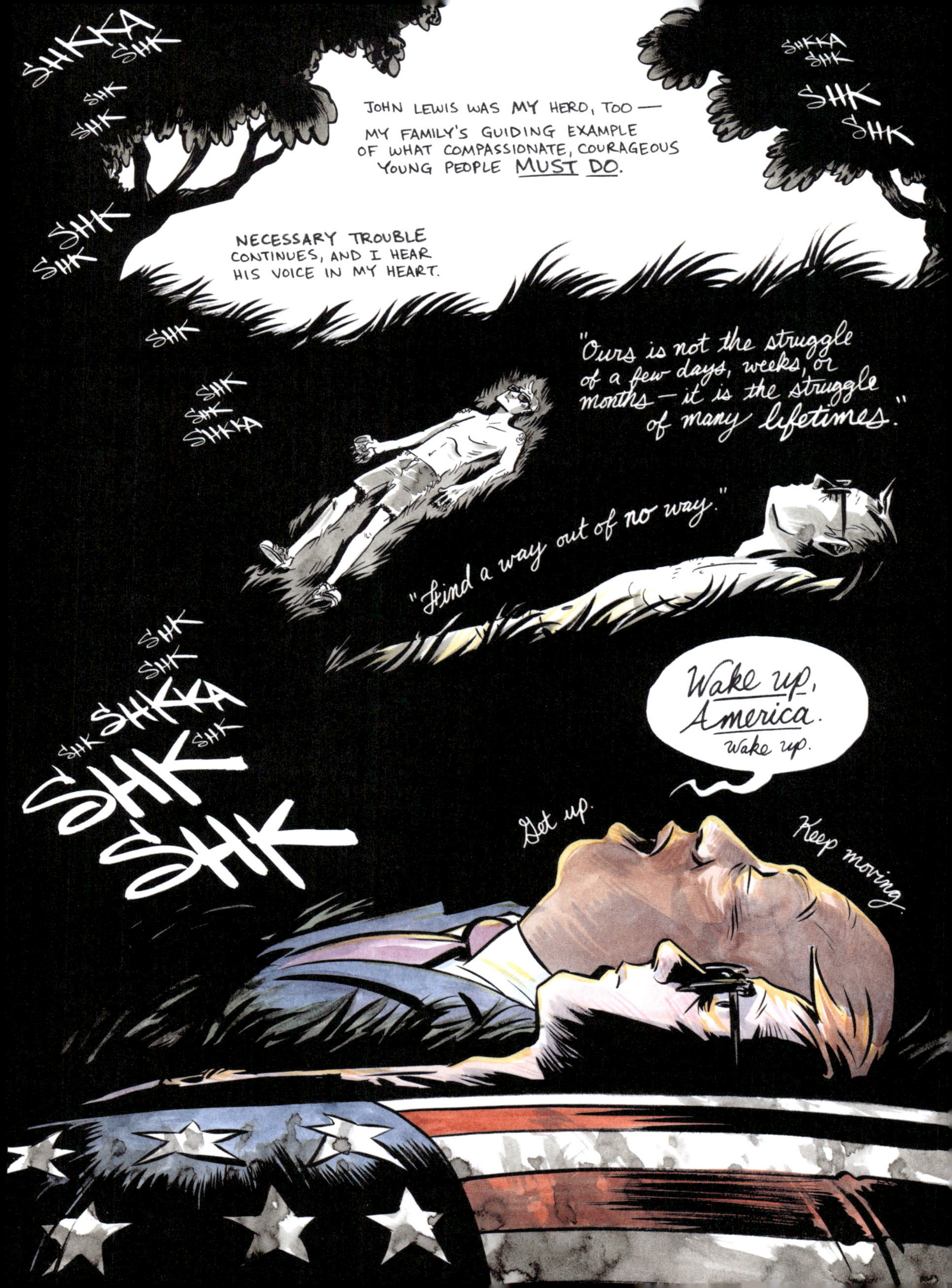
SHKKA SHK
SHK
SHK
SHK
SHK
JOHN LEWIS WAS MY HERO, TOO — MY FAMILY'S GUIDING EXAMPLE OF WHAT COMPASSIONATE, COURAGEOUS YOUNG PEOPLE MUST DO.
SHKKA SHK
SHK
SHK
NECESSARY TROUBLE CONTINUES, AND I HEAR HIS VOICE IN MY HEART.
SHK
SHK
SHK
SHKKA
"Ours is not the struggle of a few days, weeks, or months—it is the struggle of many lifetimes."
"Find a way out of no way."
SHK
SHK
SHKKA
SHK
SHK
SHK
SHK
Wake up, America. Wake up.
Get up.
Keep moving.

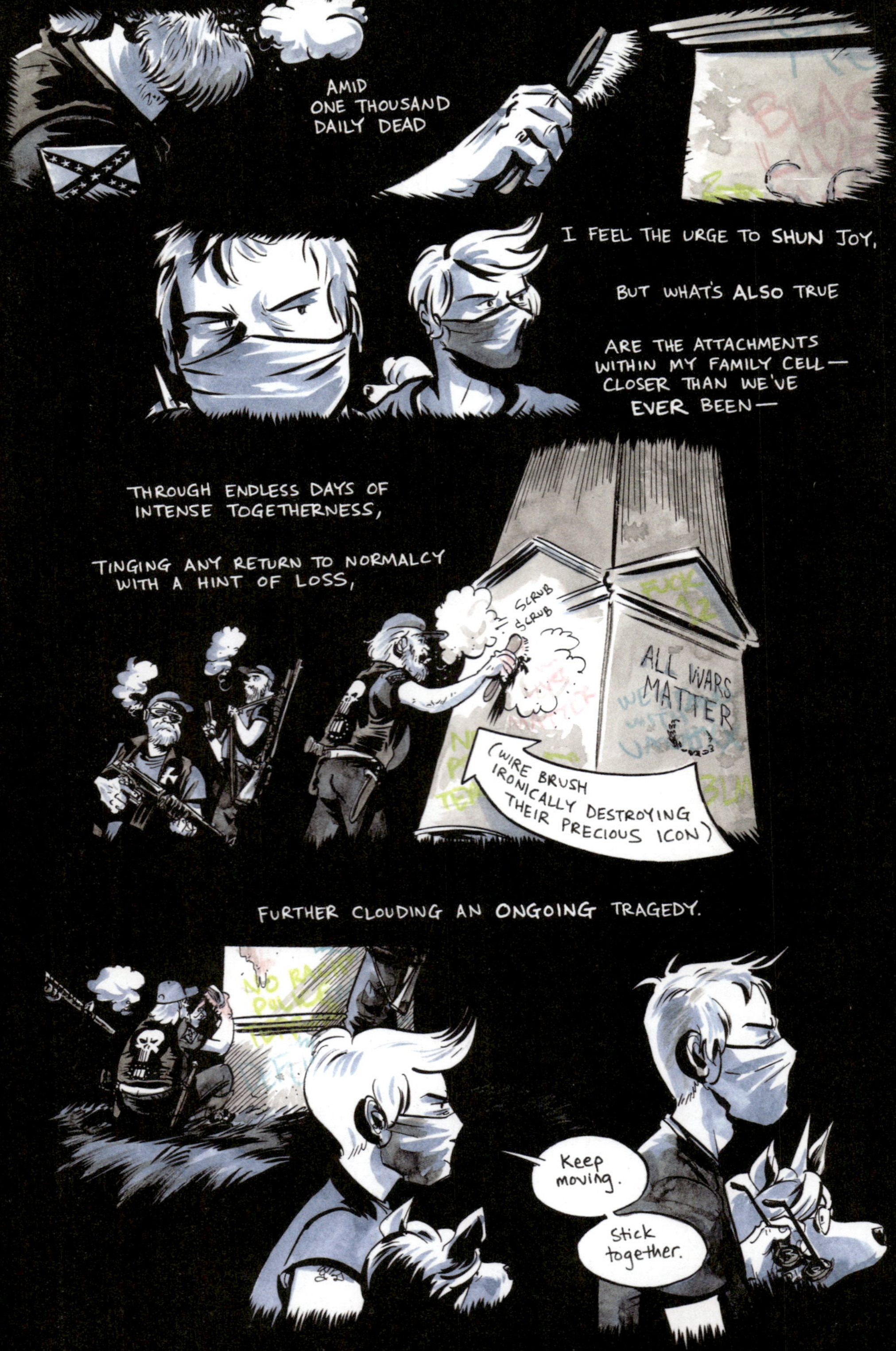
AMID ONE THOUSAND DAILY DEAD
I FEEL THE URGE TO SHUN JOY,
BUT WHAT'S ALSO TRUE
ARE THE ATTACHMENTS WITHIN MY FAMILY CELL— CLOSER THAN WE'VE EVER BEEN—
THROUGH ENDLESS DAYS OF INTENSE TOGETHERNESS,
TINGING ANY RETURN TO NORMALCY WITH A HINT OF LOSS,
SCRUB SCRUB
FUCK 12
ALL WARS MATTER
(WIRE BRUSH IRONICALLY DESTROYING THEIR PRECIOUS ICON)
FURTHER CLOUDING AN ONGOING TRAGEDY.
Keep moving.
Stick together.

POSSIBLE FUTURES SEEM TO **VANISH**.

NEIGHBORS VISIBLY **ABANDON** EFFORTS TO CURB RISK TO OTHERS **OR** THEMSELVES,

LEANING INSTEAD INTO **FANTASY**,
SPITE,
HOLLOW FAITH.

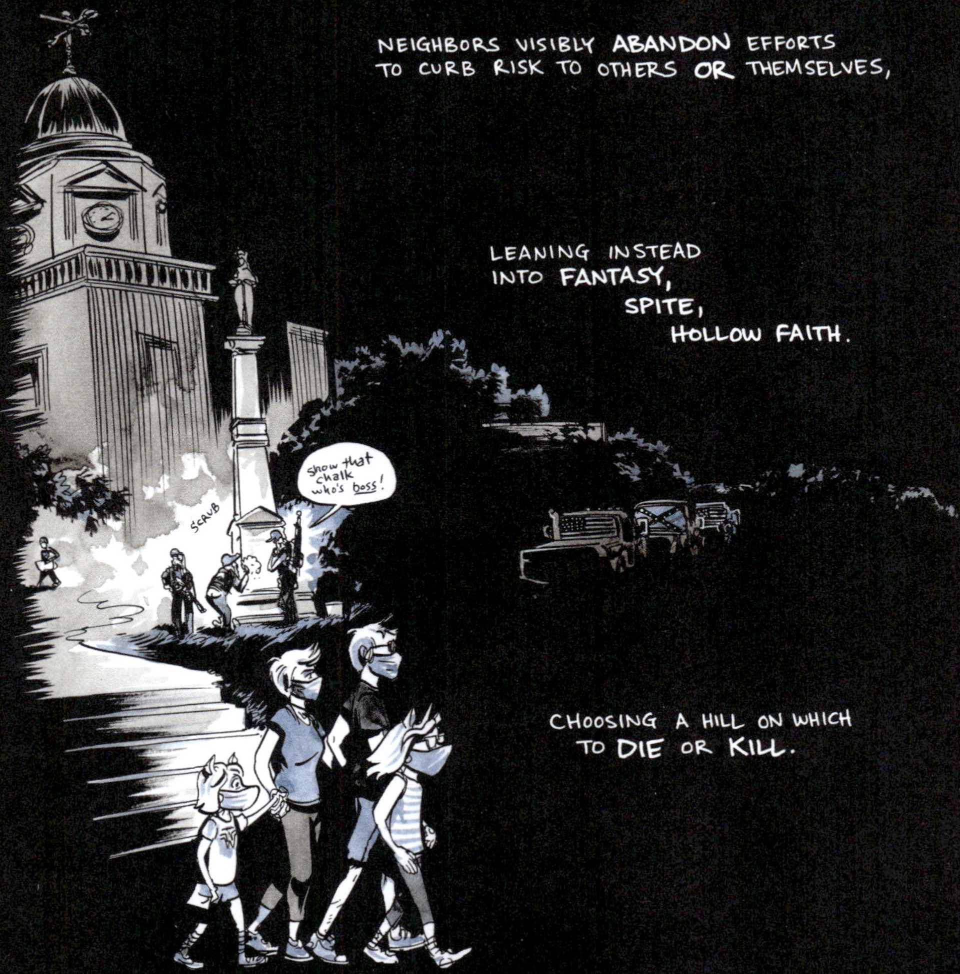
show that chalk who's boss!
SCRUB

CHOOSING A HILL ON WHICH TO **DIE** OR **KILL**.

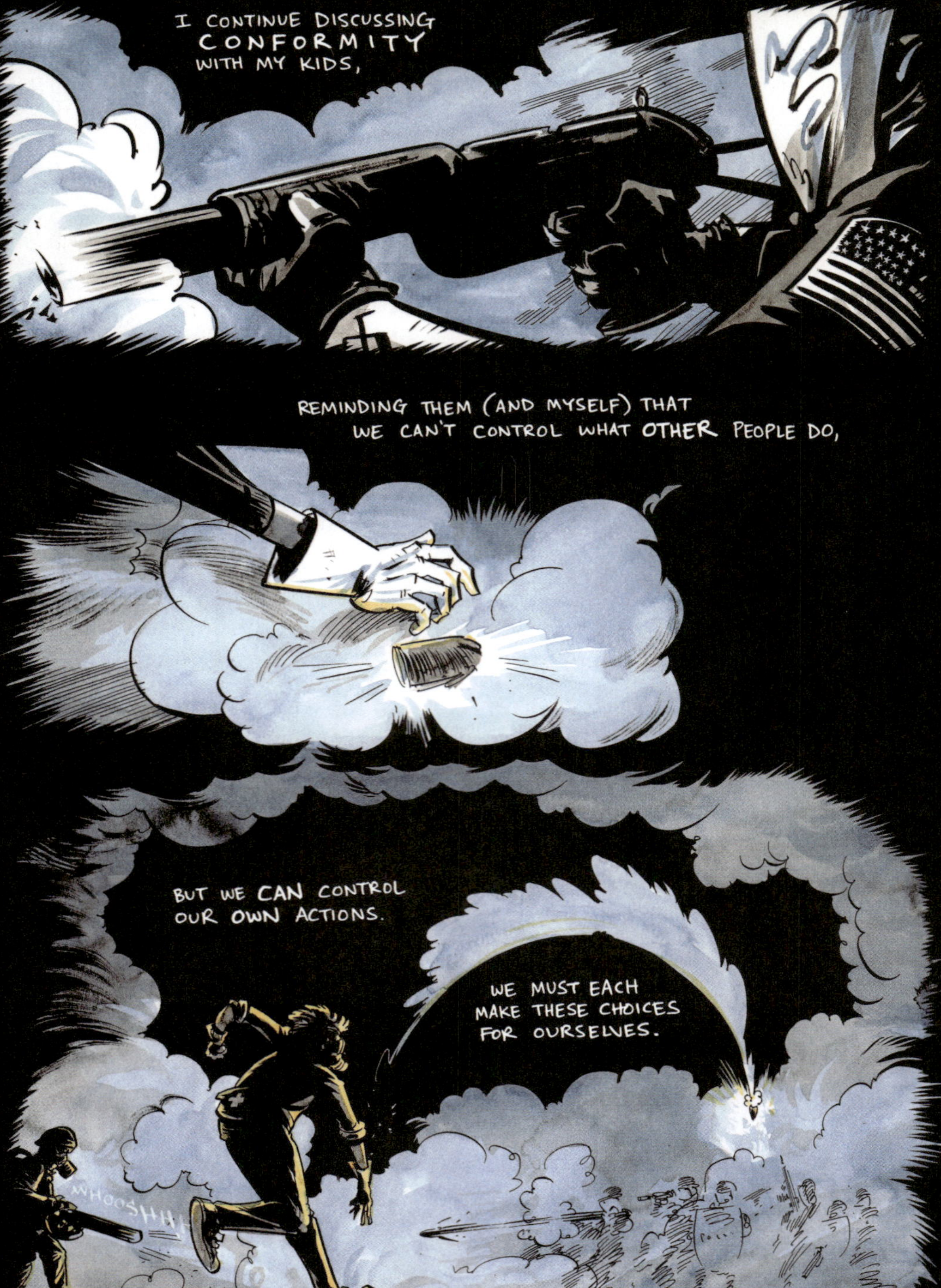
I CONTINUE DISCUSSING CONFORMITY WITH MY KIDS,
REMINDING THEM (AND MYSELF) THAT WE CAN'T CONTROL WHAT OTHER PEOPLE DO,
BUT WE CAN CONTROL OUR OWN ACTIONS.
WE MUST EACH MAKE THESE CHOICES FOR OURSELVES.
WHOOSHH!

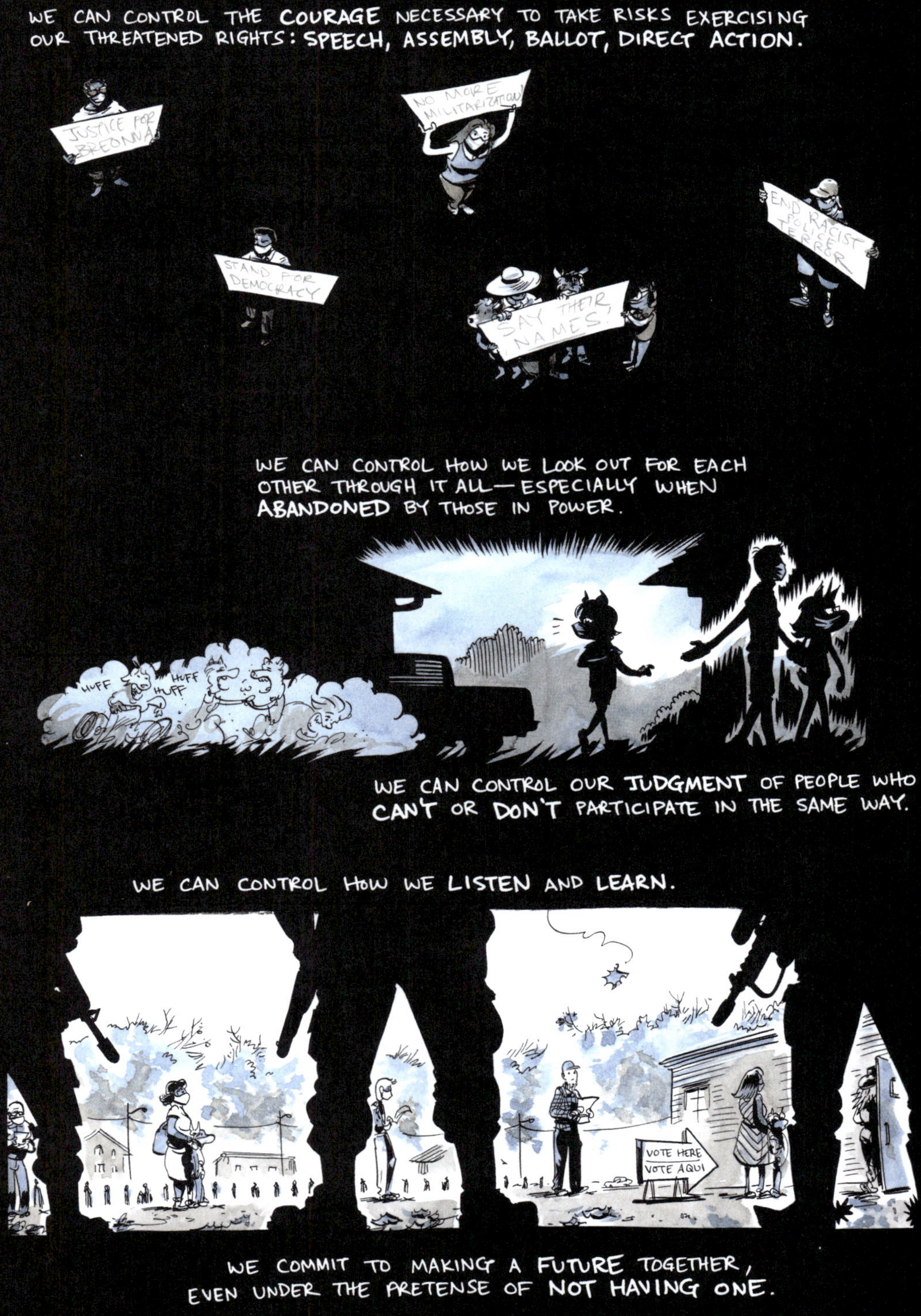
WE CAN CONTROL THE COURAGE NECESSARY TO TAKE RISKS EXERCISING OUR THREATENED RIGHTS: SPEECH, ASSEMBLY, BALLOT, DIRECT ACTION.
JUSTICE FOR BREONNA
NO MORE MILITARIZATION
END RACIST POLICE TERROR
STAND FOR DEMOCRACY
SAY THEIR NAMES!
WE CAN CONTROL HOW WE LOOK OUT FOR EACH OTHER THROUGH IT ALL—ESPECIALLY WHEN ABANDONED BY THOSE IN POWER.
HUFF
HUFF
HUFF
WE CAN CONTROL OUR JUDGMENT OF PEOPLE WHO CAN'T OR DON'T PARTICIPATE IN THE SAME WAY.
WE CAN CONTROL HOW WE LISTEN AND LEARN.
VOTE HERE
VOTE AQUI
WE COMMIT TO MAKING A FUTURE TOGETHER, EVEN UNDER THE PRETENSE OF NOT HAVING ONE.

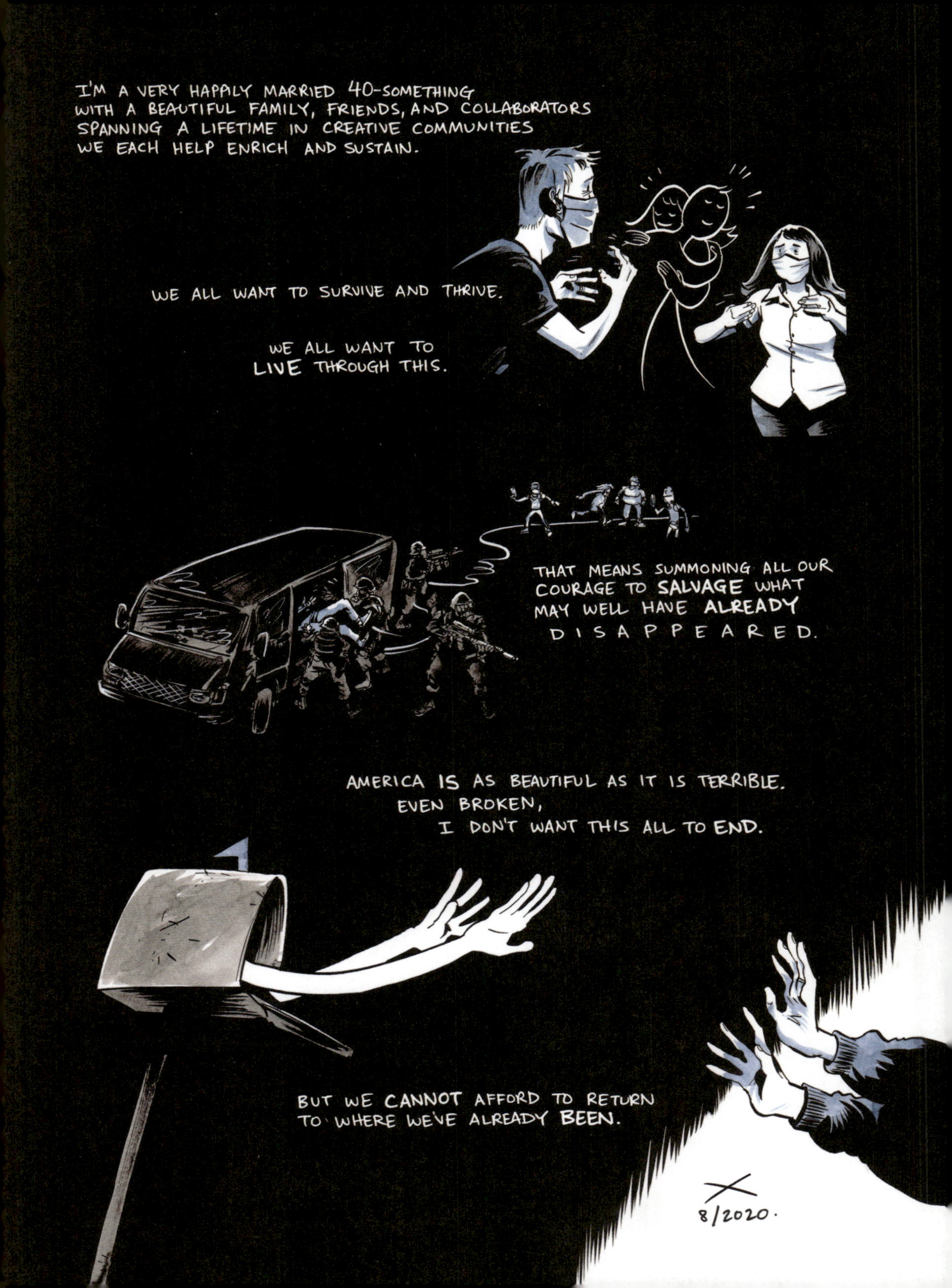
I'M A VERY HAPPILY MARRIED 40-SOMETHING WITH A BEAUTIFUL FAMILY, FRIENDS, AND COLLABORATORS SPANNING A LIFETIME IN CREATIVE COMMUNITIES WE EACH HELP ENRICH AND SUSTAIN.
WE ALL WANT TO SURVIVE AND THRIVE.
WE ALL WANT TO LIVE THROUGH THIS.
THAT MEANS SUMMONING ALL OUR COURAGE TO SALVAGE WHAT MAY WELL HAVE ALREADY DISAPPEARED.
AMERICA IS AS BEAUTIFUL AS IT IS TERRIBLE. EVEN BROKEN, I DON'T WANT THIS ALL TO END.
BUT WE CANNOT AFFORD TO RETURN TO WHERE WE'VE ALREADY BEEN.
8/2020.

7
WINGNUT

138

FACING THESE WARNING SIGNS, MY GENERATION RECKONS WITH OUR PARENTS' DEEPLY INGRAINED ASSUMPTIONS WHICH HAVE BROUGHT THE VERY REAL FEAR OF FASCISM AT OUR DOOR.

MY GENERATION MUST ALSO CONFRONT THE FACT THAT WE SHARE MANY OF THOSE SAME ASSUMPTIONS,

"C'MON, YOU LIKE THIS, REMEMBER?!"

"BUT... IT'S DISGUSTING."

AND THAT OUR CHILDREN WILL BE ABLE TO SMELL THE BULLSHIT MILES AWAY.

WHITE, MIDDLE-CLASS BABY BOOMERS GENERALLY RAISED THEIR KIDS WITH A SENSE OF THE INEVITABILITY OF SOCIAL PROGRESS, OF A WORLD GRADUALLY, CASUALLY BECOMING MORE JUST—

(A STRAIGHT LINE FROM THE DEFEAT OF NAZI GERMANY TO CIVIL RIGHTS FIGUREHEADS SINGLE-HANDEDLY TOPPLING SEGREGATION TO FOLLOWING OUR OWN DREAMS WITH THE HELP OF A FEW STUDENT LOANS)

AS EVIDENCE THAT THE STRUCTURES HOLDING US TOGETHER ACTUALLY WORK.

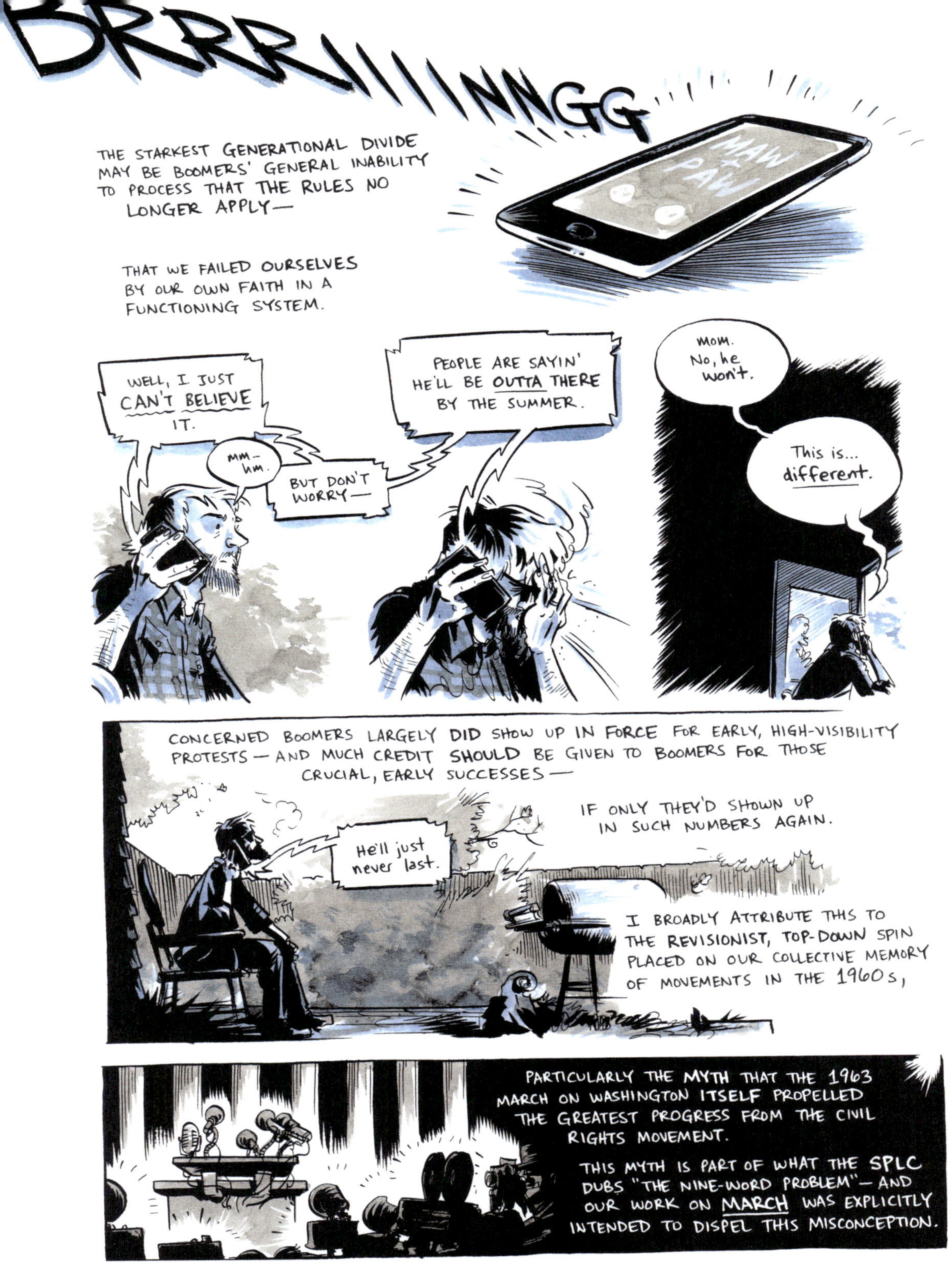
BRRRIIIIINNGG
MAW PAW
THE STARKEST GENERATIONAL DIVIDE MAY BE BOOMERS' GENERAL INABILITY TO PROCESS THAT THE RULES NO LONGER APPLY—
THAT WE FAILED OURSELVES BY OUR OWN FAITH IN A FUNCTIONING SYSTEM.
WELL, I JUST CAN'T BELIEVE IT.
MM-HM.
BUT DON'T WORRY—
PEOPLE ARE SAYIN' HE'LL BE OUTTA THERE BY THE SUMMER.
MOM. No, he won't.
This is... different.
CONCERNED BOOMERS LARGELY DID SHOW UP IN FORCE FOR EARLY, HIGH-VISIBILITY PROTESTS—AND MUCH CREDIT SHOULD BE GIVEN TO BOOMERS FOR THOSE CRUCIAL, EARLY SUCCESSES—
He'll just never last.
IF ONLY THEY'D SHOWN UP IN SUCH NUMBERS AGAIN.
I BROADLY ATTRIBUTE THIS TO THE REVISIONIST, TOP-DOWN SPIN PLACED ON OUR COLLECTIVE MEMORY OF MOVEMENTS IN THE 1960s,
PARTICULARLY THE MYTH THAT THE 1963 MARCH ON WASHINGTON ITSELF PROPELLED THE GREATEST PROGRESS FROM THE CIVIL RIGHTS MOVEMENT.
THIS MYTH IS PART OF WHAT THE SPLC DUBS "THE NINE-WORD PROBLEM"—AND OUR WORK ON MARCH WAS EXPLICITLY INTENDED TO DISPEL THIS MISCONCEPTION.

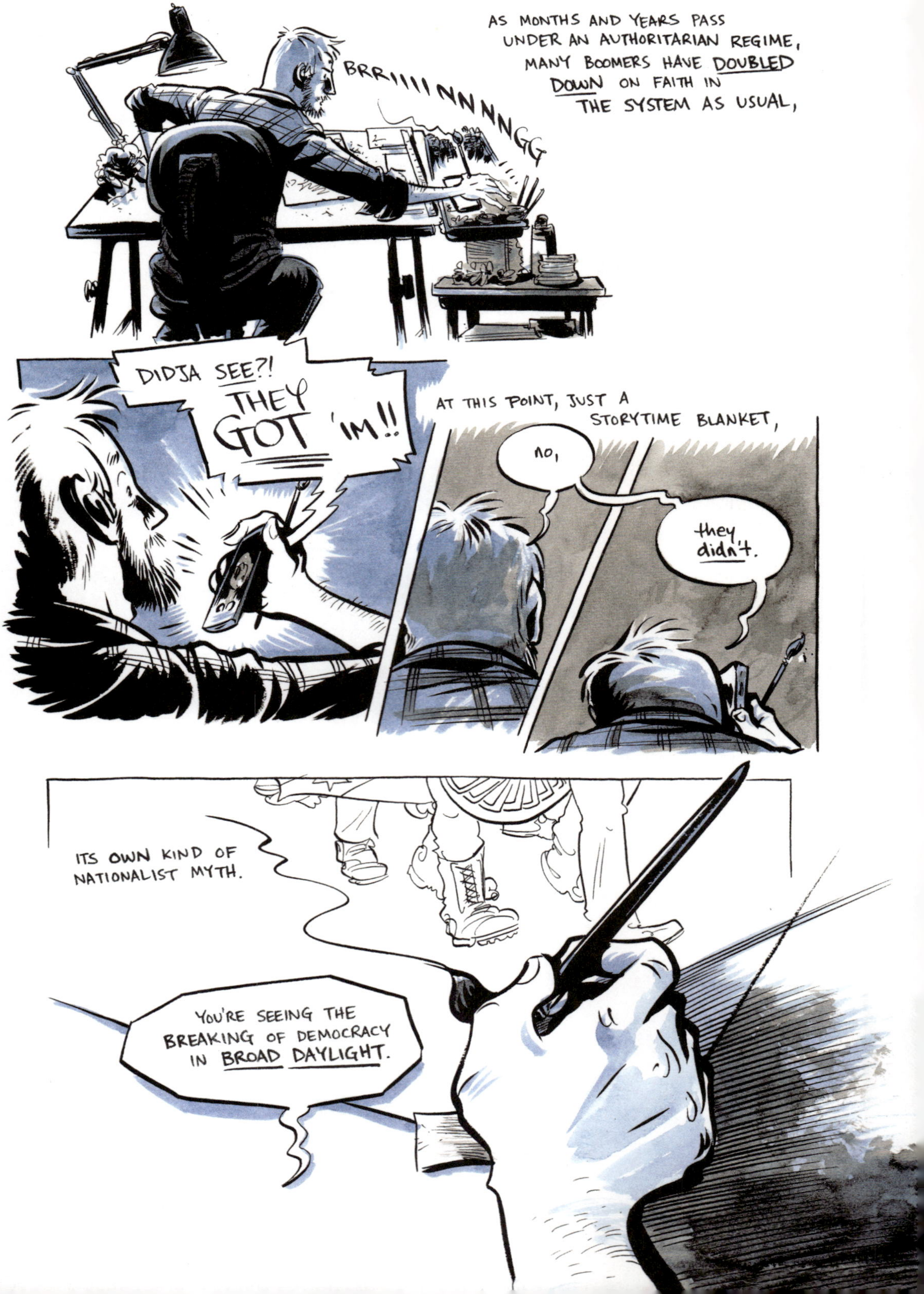
AS MONTHS AND YEARS PASS UNDER AN AUTHORITARIAN REGIME, MANY BOOMERS HAVE DOUBLED DOWN ON FAITH IN THE SYSTEM AS USUAL,
BRRIIIINNNNNGG
DIDJA SEE?! THEY GOT 'IM!!
AT THIS POINT, JUST A STORYTIME BLANKET,
no,
they didn't.
ITS OWN KIND OF NATIONALIST MYTH.
YOU'RE SEEING THE BREAKING OF DEMOCRACY IN BROAD DAYLIGHT.

PERHAPS THE MOST TANGIBLE DANGER POSED BY THESE ERRORS OF FAITH:

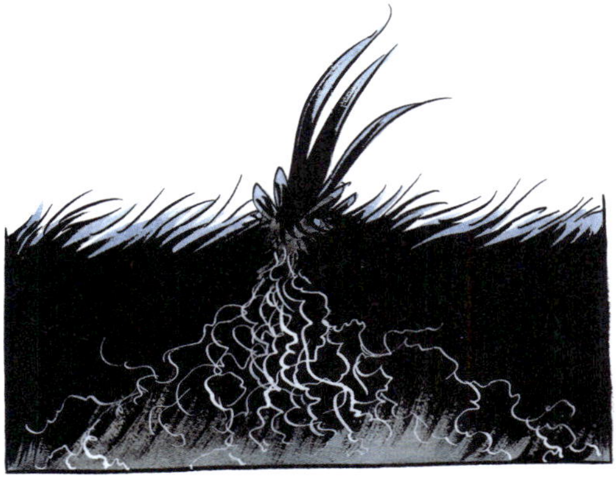

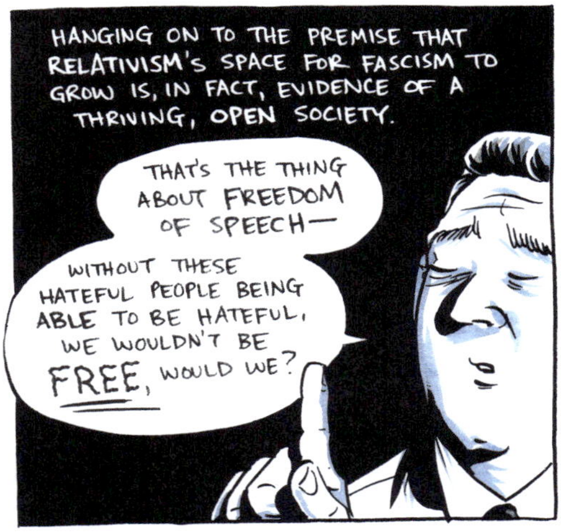
HANGING ON TO THE PREMISE THAT RELATIVISM'S SPACE FOR FASCISM TO GROW IS, IN FACT, EVIDENCE OF A THRIVING, OPEN SOCIETY.
THAT'S THE THING ABOUT FREEDOM OF SPEECH—
WITHOUT THESE HATEFUL PEOPLE BEING ABLE TO BE HATEFUL, WE WOULDN'T BE FREE, WOULD WE?

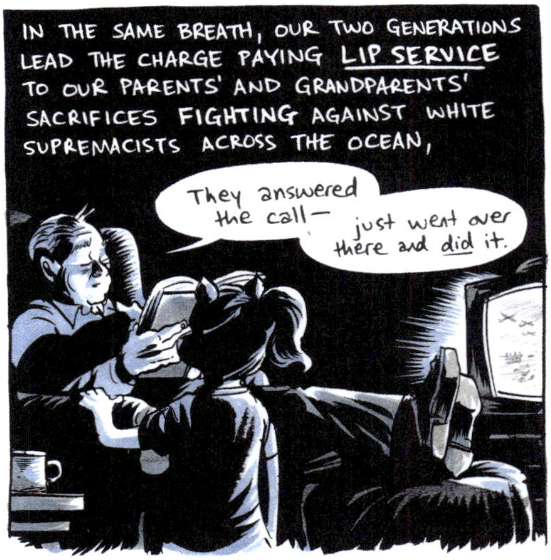
IN THE SAME BREATH, OUR TWO GENERATIONS LEAD THE CHARGE PAYING LIP SERVICE TO OUR PARENTS' AND GRANDPARENTS' SACRIFICES FIGHTING AGAINST WHITE SUPREMACISTS ACROSS THE OCEAN,
They answered the call—
just went over there and did it.

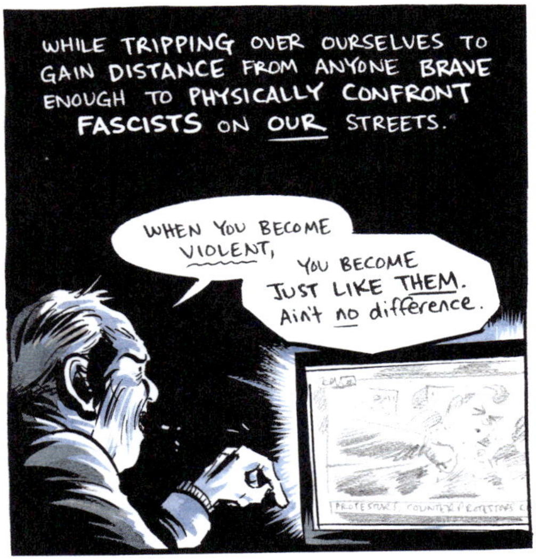
WHILE TRIPPING OVER OURSELVES TO GAIN DISTANCE FROM ANYONE BRAVE ENOUGH TO PHYSICALLY CONFRONT FASCISTS ON OUR STREETS.
WHEN YOU BECOME VIOLENT,
YOU BECOME JUST LIKE THEM. Ain't no difference.

NATIONALIST MYTH REQUIRES EXTERNAL FOES, EVEN WHEN THEIR DOMESTIC COUNTERPARTS POSE AN EXISTENTIAL THREAT TO US ALL.

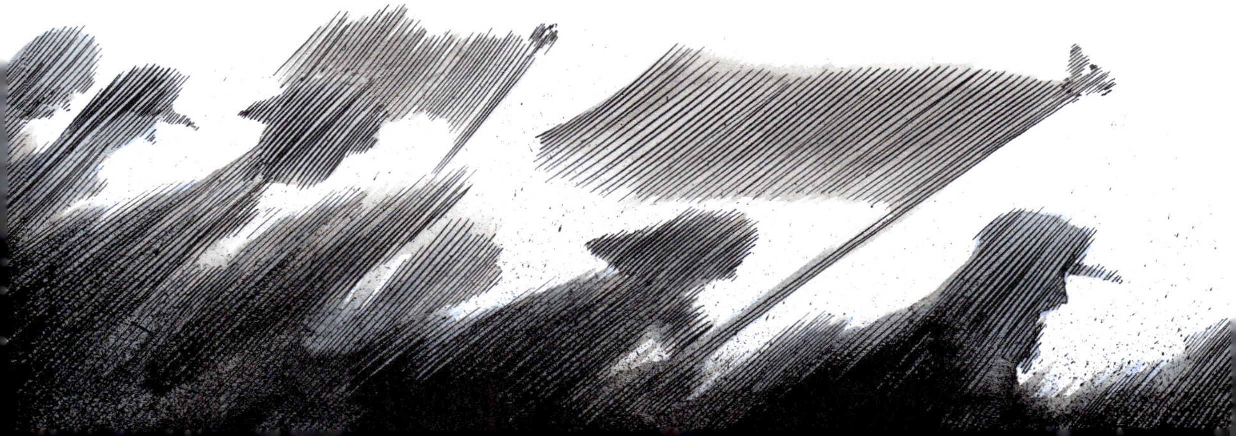

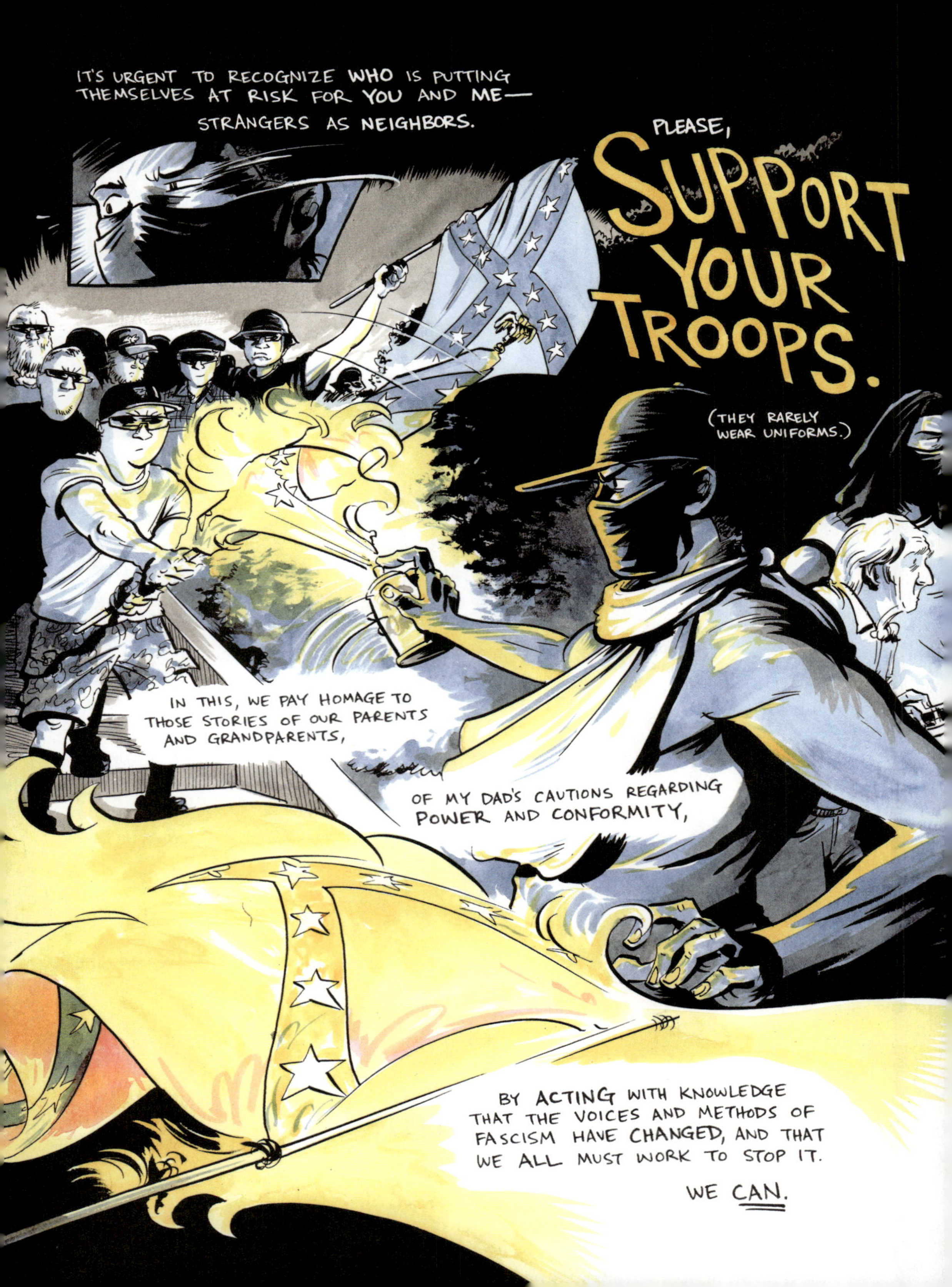
IT'S URGENT TO RECOGNIZE WHO IS PUTTING THEMSELVES AT RISK FOR YOU AND ME—
STRANGERS AS NEIGHBORS.
PLEASE,
SUPPORT YOUR TROOPS.
(THEY RARELY WEAR UNIFORMS.)
IN THIS, WE PAY HOMAGE TO THOSE STORIES OF OUR PARENTS AND GRANDPARENTS,
OF MY DAD'S CAUTIONS REGARDING POWER AND CONFORMITY,
BY ACTING WITH KNOWLEDGE THAT THE VOICES AND METHODS OF FASCISM HAVE CHANGED, AND THAT WE ALL MUST WORK TO STOP IT.
WE CAN.

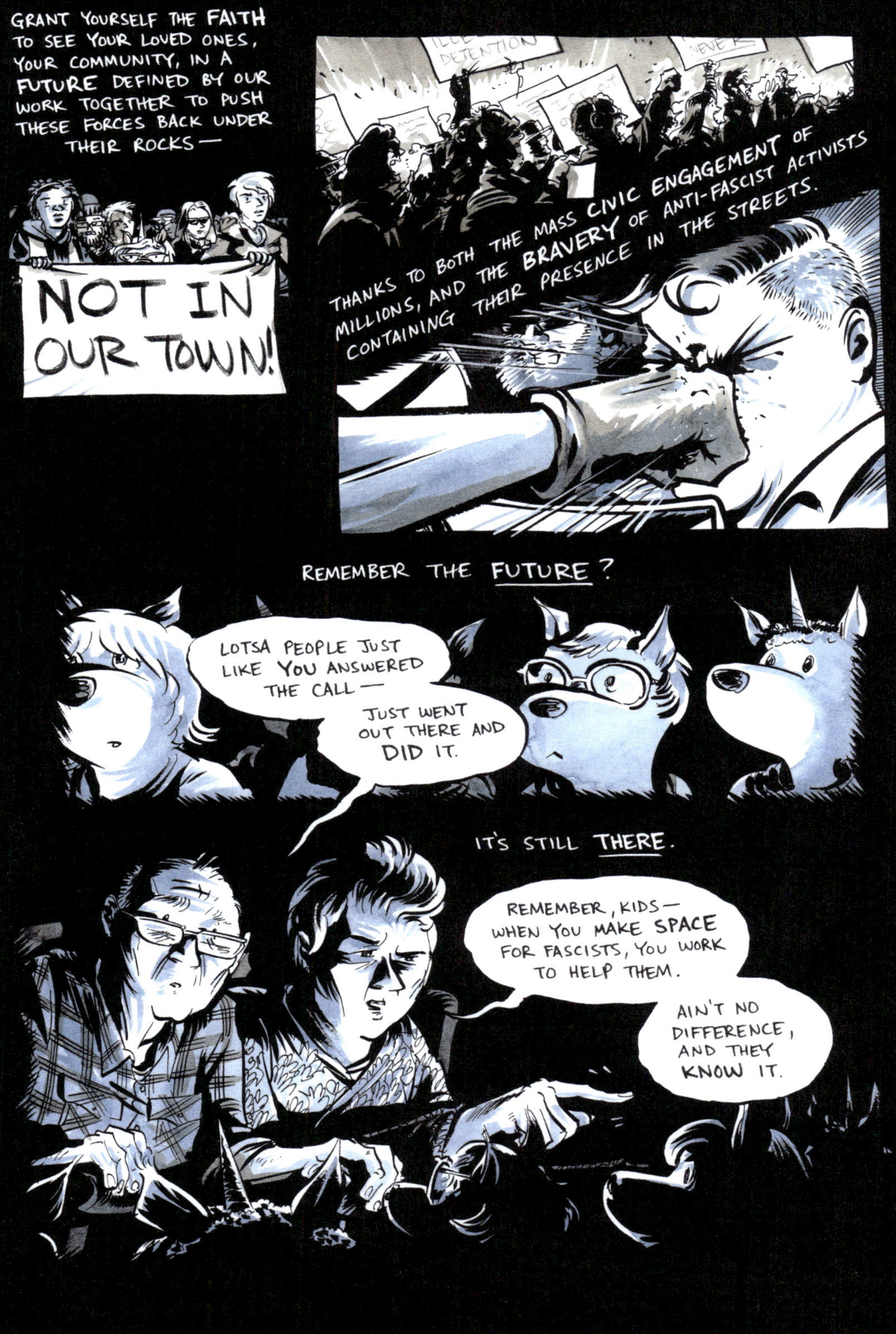
GRANT YOURSELF THE FAITH TO SEE YOUR LOVED ONES, YOUR COMMUNITY, IN A FUTURE DEFINED BY OUR WORK TOGETHER TO PUSH THESE FORCES BACK UNDER THEIR ROCKS—
NOT IN OUR TOWN!
THANKS TO BOTH THE MASS CIVIC ENGAGEMENT OF MILLIONS, AND THE BRAVERY OF ANTI-FASCIST ACTIVISTS CONTAINING THEIR PRESENCE IN THE STREETS.
REMEMBER THE FUTURE?
LOTSA PEOPLE JUST LIKE YOU ANSWERED THE CALL—
JUST WENT OUT THERE AND DID IT.
IT'S STILL THERE.
REMEMBER, KIDS— WHEN YOU MAKE SPACE FOR FASCISTS, YOU WORK TO HELP THEM.
AIN'T NO DIFFERENCE, AND THEY KNOW IT.

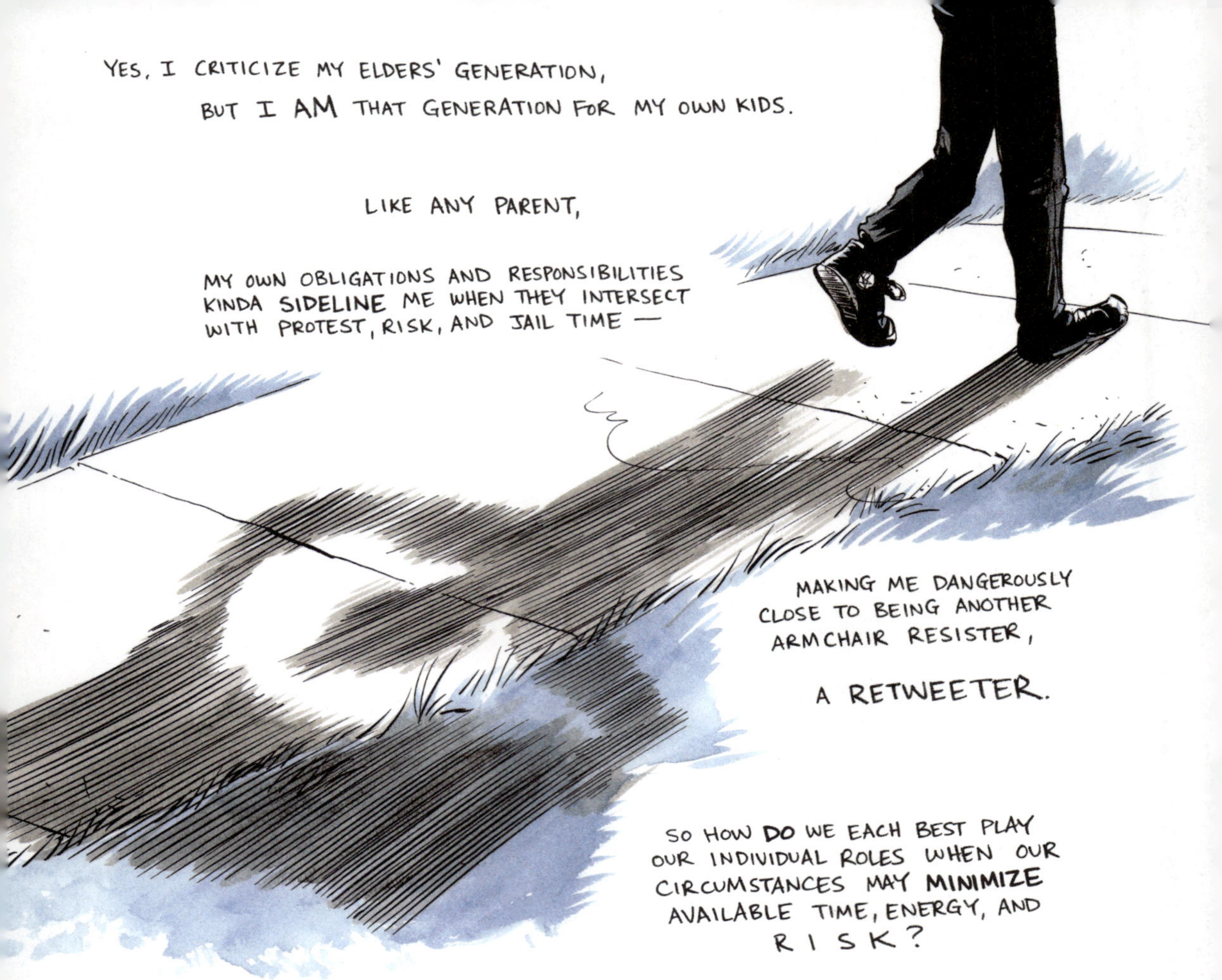
YES, I CRITICIZE MY ELDERS' GENERATION,
BUT I AM THAT GENERATION FOR MY OWN KIDS.
LIKE ANY PARENT,
MY OWN OBLIGATIONS AND RESPONSIBILITIES KINDA SIDELINE ME WHEN THEY INTERSECT WITH PROTEST, RISK, AND JAIL TIME —
MAKING ME DANGEROUSLY CLOSE TO BEING ANOTHER ARMCHAIR RESISTER,
A RETWEETER.
SO HOW DO WE EACH BEST PLAY OUR INDIVIDUAL ROLES WHEN OUR CIRCUMSTANCES MAY MINIMIZE AVAILABLE TIME, ENERGY, AND R I S K?

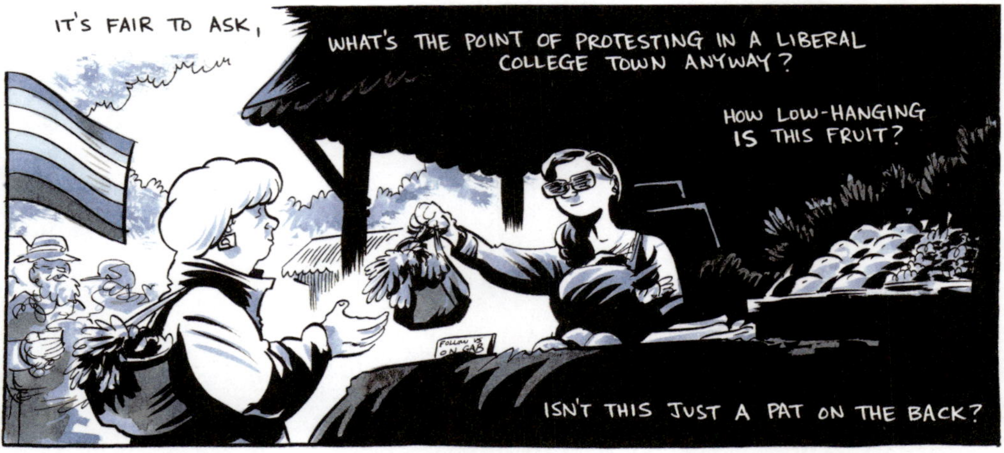
IT'S FAIR TO ASK,
WHAT'S THE POINT OF PROTESTING IN A LIBERAL COLLEGE TOWN ANYWAY?
HOW LOW-HANGING IS THIS FRUIT?
ISN'T THIS JUST A PAT ON THE BACK?

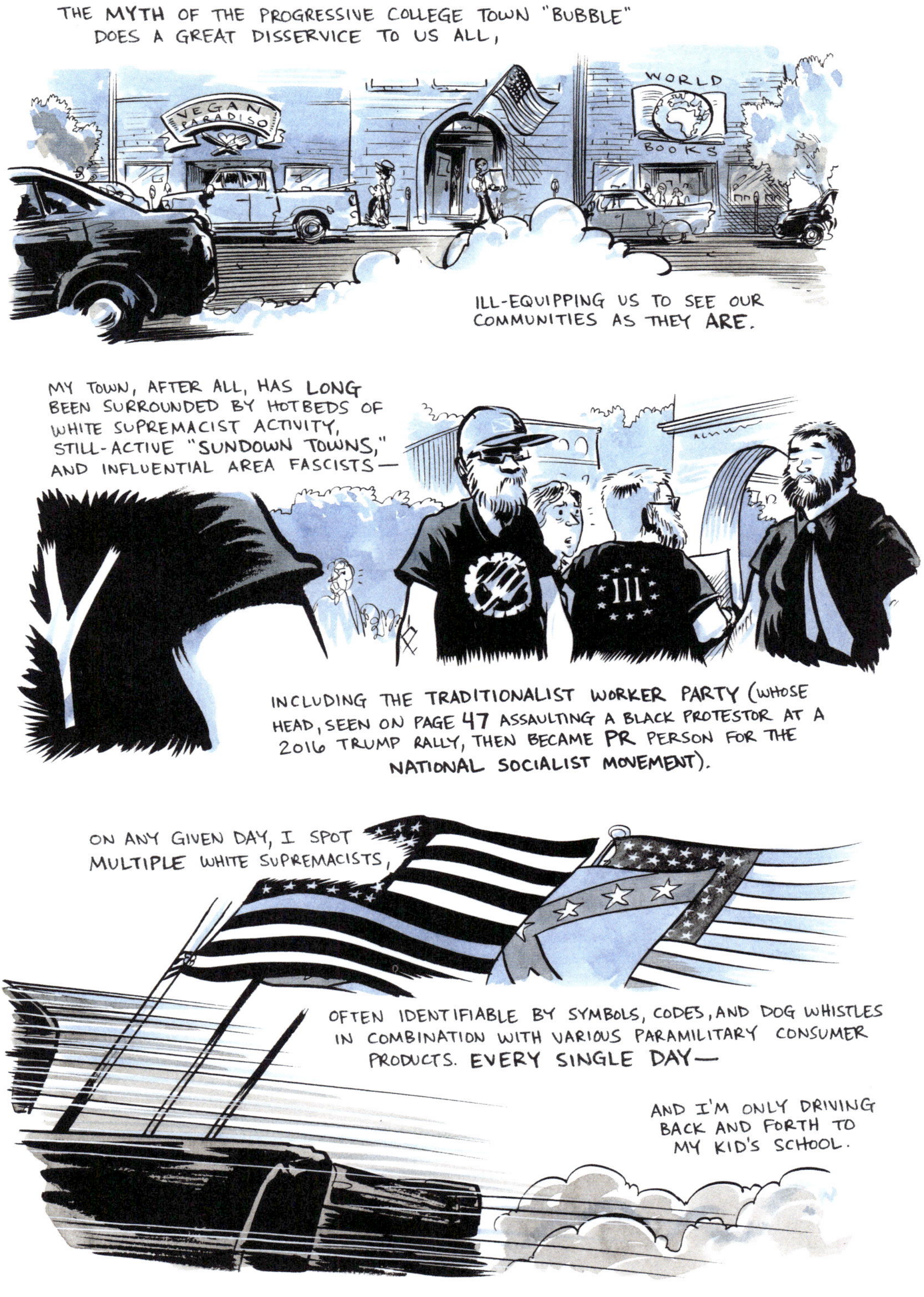
THE MYTH OF THE PROGRESSIVE COLLEGE TOWN "BUBBLE" DOES A GREAT DISSERVICE TO US ALL,
VEGAN PARADISO
WORLD BOOKS
ILL-EQUIPPING US TO SEE OUR COMMUNITIES AS THEY ARE.
MY TOWN, AFTER ALL, HAS LONG BEEN SURROUNDED BY HOTBEDS OF WHITE SUPREMACIST ACTIVITY, STILL-ACTIVE "SUNDOWN TOWNS," AND INFLUENTIAL AREA FASCISTS—
III
INCLUDING THE TRADITIONALIST WORKER PARTY (WHOSE HEAD, SEEN ON PAGE 47 ASSAULTING A BLACK PROTESTOR AT A 2016 TRUMP RALLY, THEN BECAME PR PERSON FOR THE NATIONAL SOCIALIST MOVEMENT).
ON ANY GIVEN DAY, I SPOT MULTIPLE WHITE SUPREMACISTS,
OFTEN IDENTIFIABLE BY SYMBOLS, CODES, AND DOG WHISTLES IN COMBINATION WITH VARIOUS PARAMILITARY CONSUMER PRODUCTS. EVERY SINGLE DAY—
AND I'M ONLY DRIVING BACK AND FORTH TO MY KID'S SCHOOL.

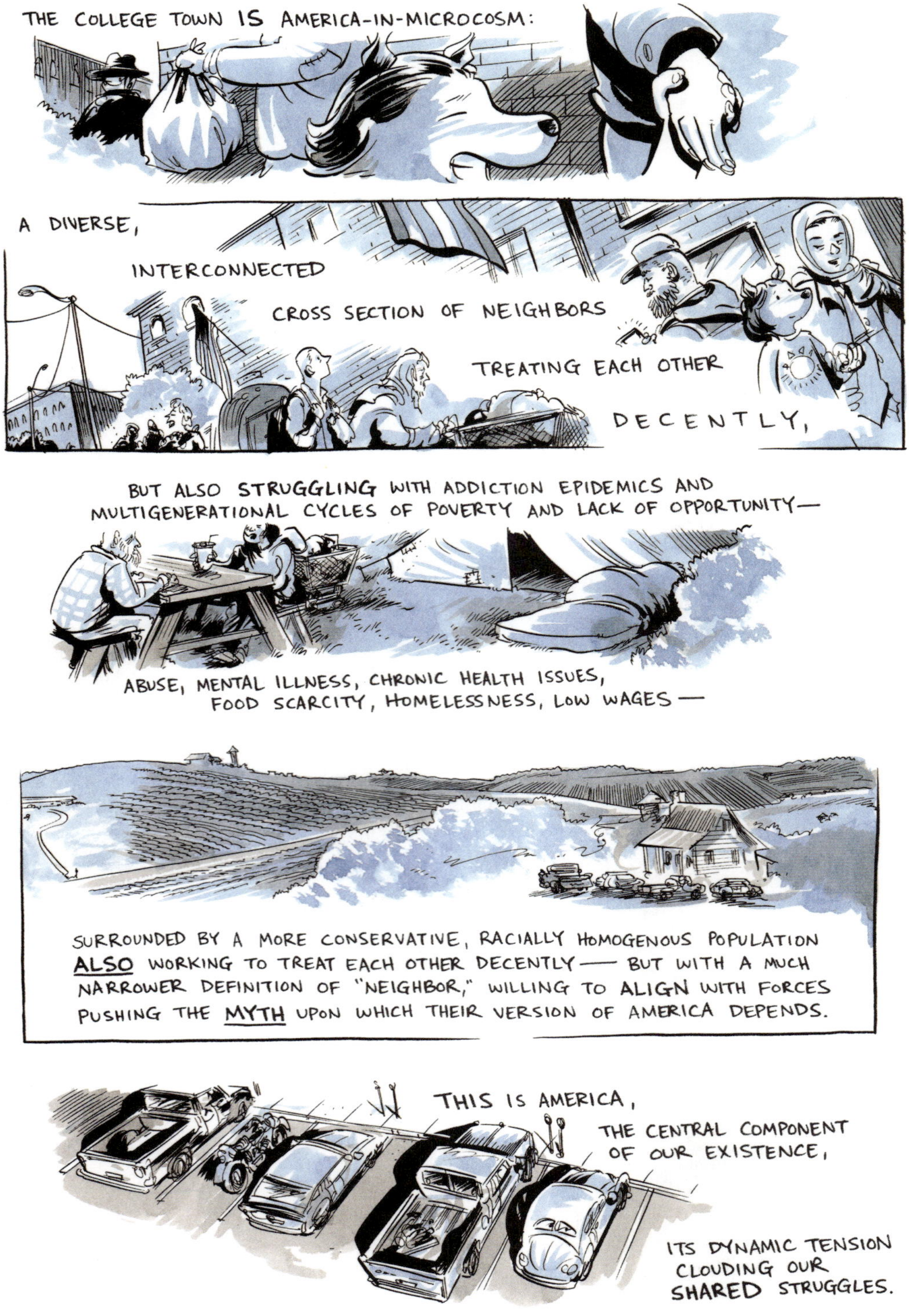
THE COLLEGE TOWN IS AMERICA-IN-MICROCOSM:
A DIVERSE,
INTERCONNECTED
CROSS SECTION OF NEIGHBORS
TREATING EACH OTHER
DECENTLY,
BUT ALSO STRUGGLING WITH ADDICTION EPIDEMICS AND MULTIGENERATIONAL CYCLES OF POVERTY AND LACK OF OPPORTUNITY—
ABUSE, MENTAL ILLNESS, CHRONIC HEALTH ISSUES, FOOD SCARCITY, HOMELESSNESS, LOW WAGES—
SURROUNDED BY A MORE CONSERVATIVE, RACIALLY HOMOGENOUS POPULATION ALSO WORKING TO TREAT EACH OTHER DECENTLY— BUT WITH A MUCH NARROWER DEFINITION OF "NEIGHBOR," WILLING TO ALIGN WITH FORCES PUSHING THE MYTH UPON WHICH THEIR VERSION OF AMERICA DEPENDS.
THIS IS AMERICA,
THE CENTRAL COMPONENT OF OUR EXISTENCE,
ITS DYNAMIC TENSION CLOUDING OUR SHARED STRUGGLES.

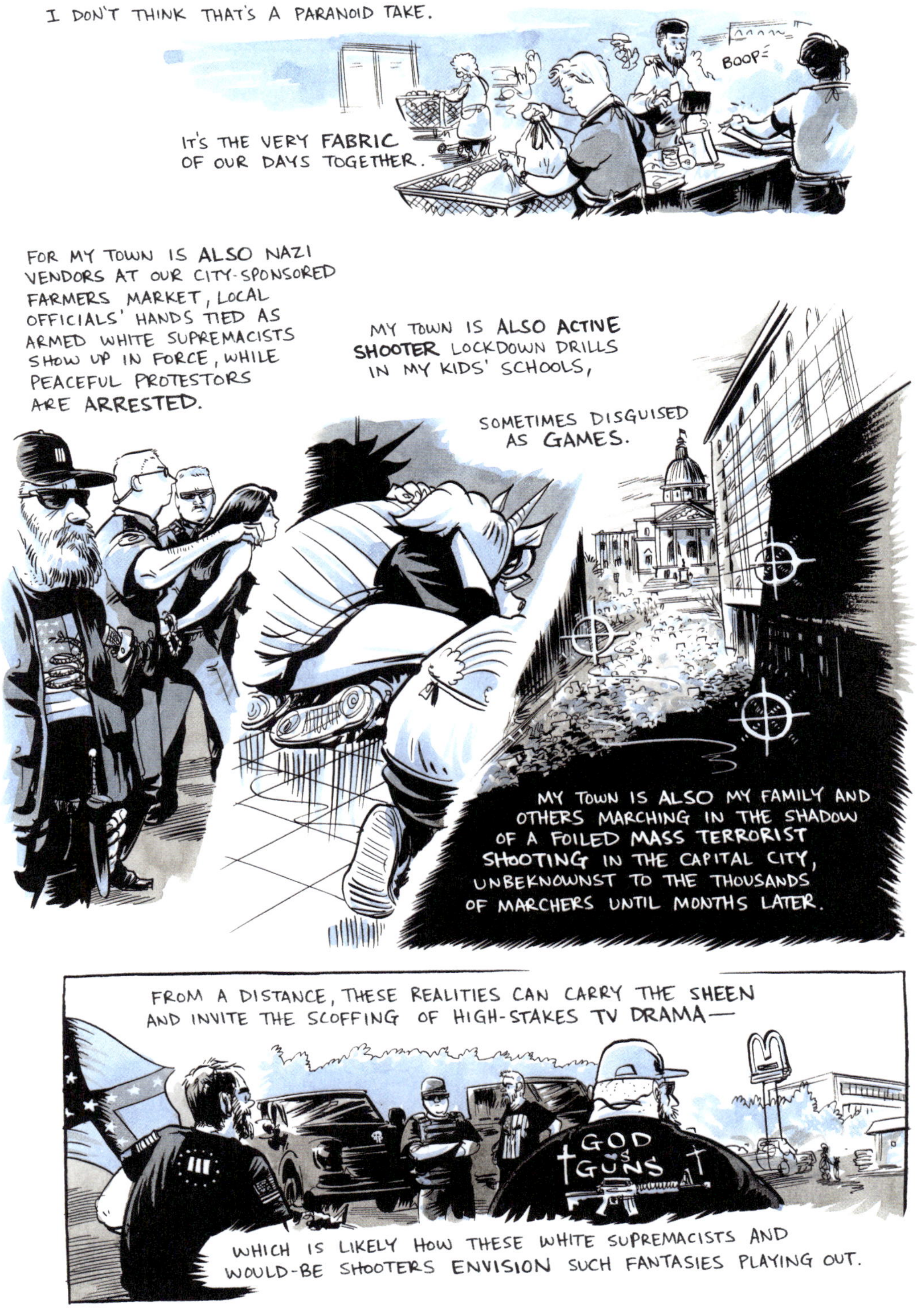
I DON'T THINK THAT'S A PARANOID TAKE.
BOOP
IT'S THE VERY FABRIC OF OUR DAYS TOGETHER.
FOR MY TOWN IS ALSO NAZI VENDORS AT OUR CITY-SPONSORED FARMERS MARKET, LOCAL OFFICIALS' HANDS TIED AS ARMED WHITE SUPREMACISTS SHOW UP IN FORCE, WHILE PEACEFUL PROTESTORS ARE ARRESTED.
MY TOWN IS ALSO ACTIVE SHOOTER LOCKDOWN DRILLS IN MY KIDS' SCHOOLS,
SOMETIMES DISGUISED AS GAMES.
MY TOWN IS ALSO MY FAMILY AND OTHERS MARCHING IN THE SHADOW OF A FOILED MASS TERRORIST SHOOTING IN THE CAPITAL CITY, UNBEKNOWNST TO THE THOUSANDS OF MARCHERS UNTIL MONTHS LATER.
FROM A DISTANCE, THESE REALITIES CAN CARRY THE SHEEN AND INVITE THE SCOFFING OF HIGH-STAKES TV DRAMA—
GOD ♥S GUNS
WHICH IS LIKELY HOW THESE WHITE SUPREMACISTS AND WOULD-BE SHOOTERS ENVISION SUCH FANTASIES PLAYING OUT.

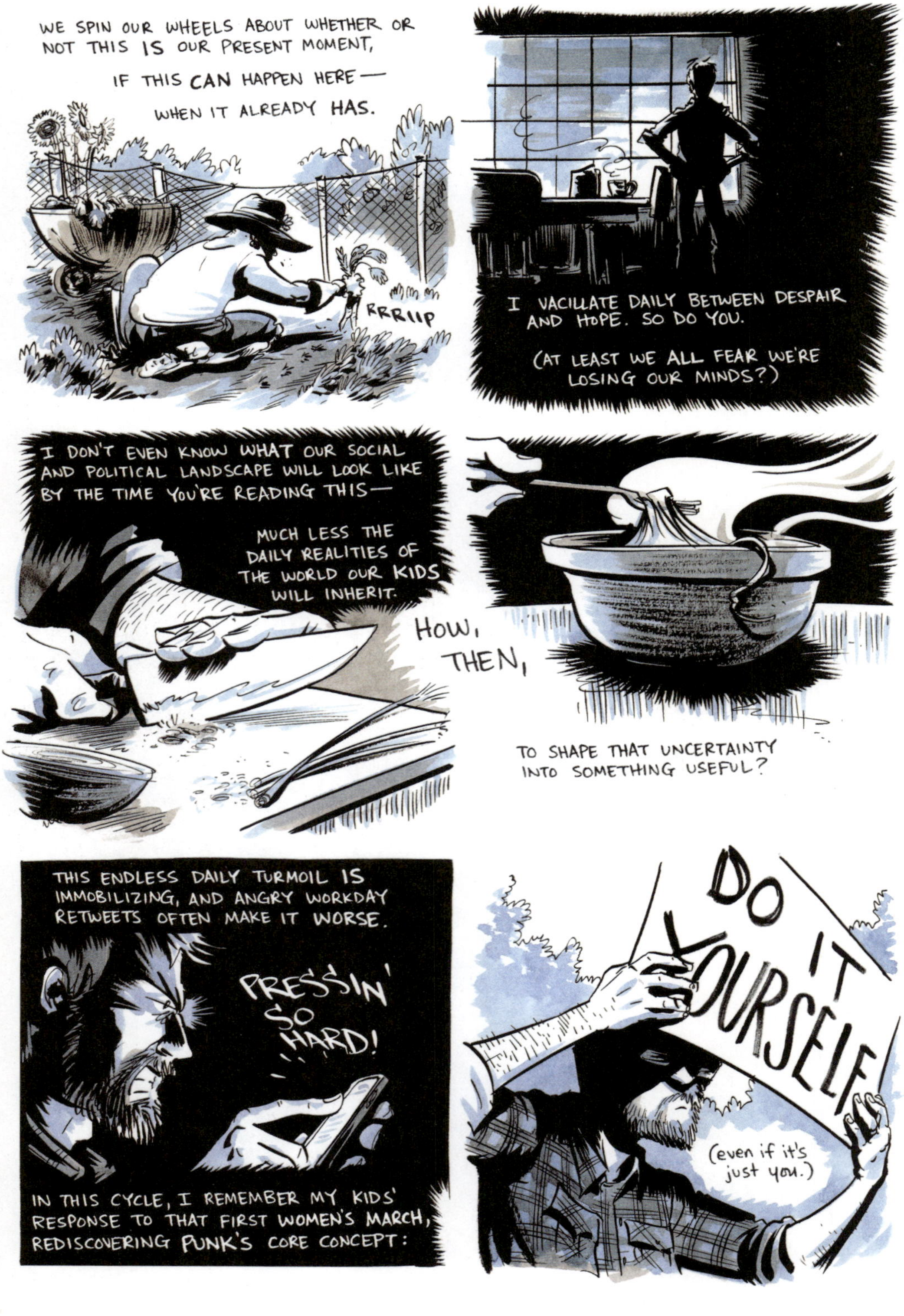
WE SPIN OUR WHEELS ABOUT WHETHER OR NOT THIS IS OUR PRESENT MOMENT,
IF THIS CAN HAPPEN HERE—
WHEN IT ALREADY HAS.
RRRIIP
I VACILLATE DAILY BETWEEN DESPAIR AND HOPE. SO DO YOU.
(AT LEAST WE ALL FEAR WE'RE LOSING OUR MINDS?)
I DON'T EVEN KNOW WHAT OUR SOCIAL AND POLITICAL LANDSCAPE WILL LOOK LIKE BY THE TIME YOU'RE READING THIS—
MUCH LESS THE DAILY REALITIES OF THE WORLD OUR KIDS WILL INHERIT.
HOW, THEN,
TO SHAPE THAT UNCERTAINTY INTO SOMETHING USEFUL?
THIS ENDLESS DAILY TURMOIL IS IMMOBILIZING, AND ANGRY WORKDAY RETWEETS OFTEN MAKE IT WORSE.
PRESSIN' SO HARD!
IN THIS CYCLE, I REMEMBER MY KIDS' RESPONSE TO THAT FIRST WOMEN'S MARCH, REDISCOVERING PUNK'S CORE CONCEPT:
DO IT YOURSELF
(even if it's just you.)

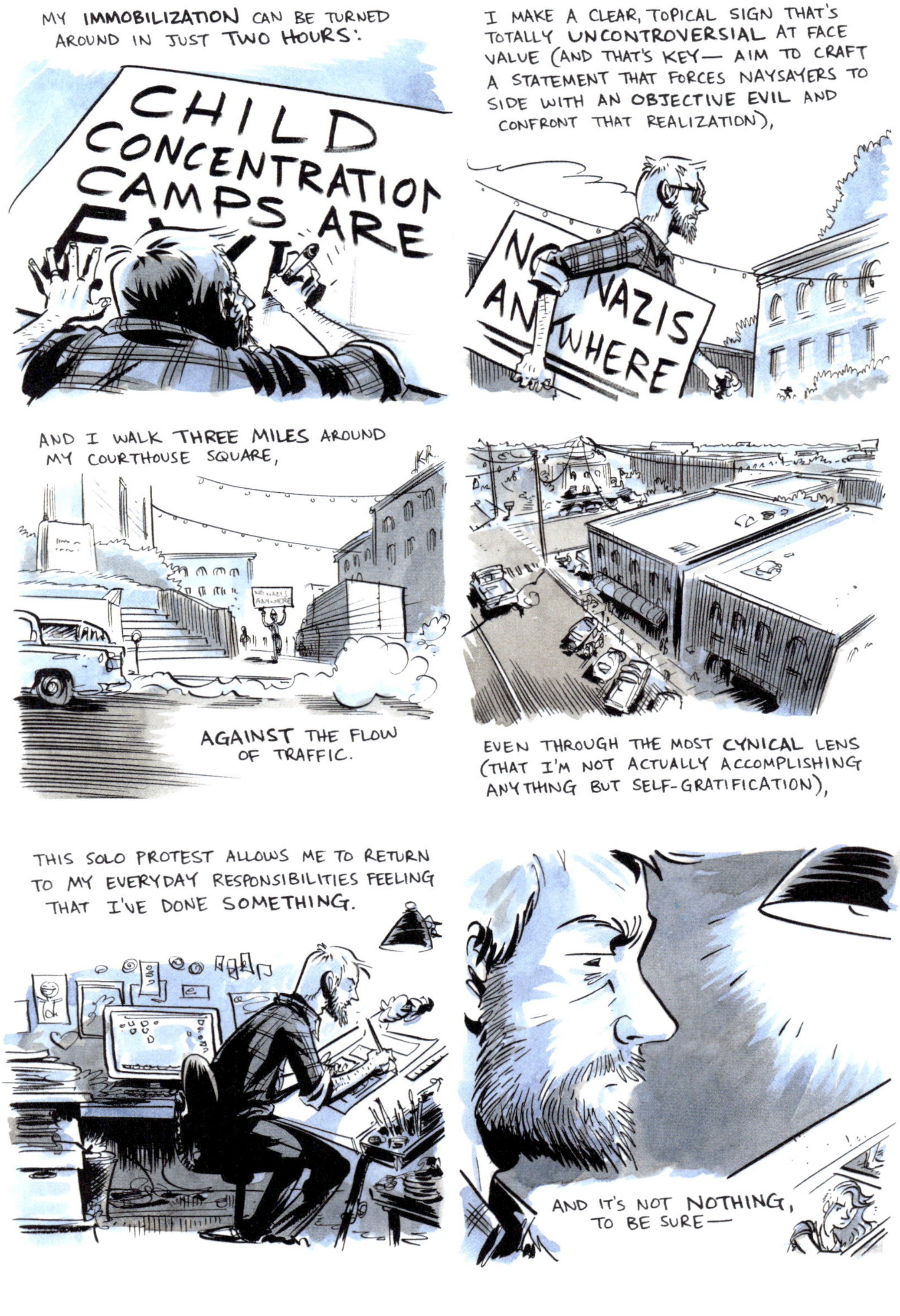

MY IMMOBILIZATION CAN BE TURNED AROUND IN JUST TWO HOURS:
CHILD
CONCENTRATIO
CAMPS ARE
I MAKE A CLEAR, TOPICAL SIGN THAT'S TOTALLY UNCONTROVERSIAL AT FACE VALUE (AND THAT'S KEY— AIM TO CRAFT A STATEMENT THAT FORCES NAYSAYERS TO SIDE WITH AN OBJECTIVE EVIL AND CONFRONT THAT REALIZATION),
NAZIS
AND I WALK THREE MILES AROUND MY COURTHOUSE SQUARE,
AGAINST THE FLOW OF TRAFFIC.
EVEN THROUGH THE MOST CYNICAL LENS (THAT I'M NOT ACTUALLY ACCOMPLISHING ANYTHING BUT SELF-GRATIFICATION),
THIS SOLO PROTEST ALLOWS ME TO RETURN TO MY EVERYDAY RESPONSIBILITIES FEELING THAT I'VE DONE SOMETHING.
AND IT'S NOT NOTHING, TO BE SURE—

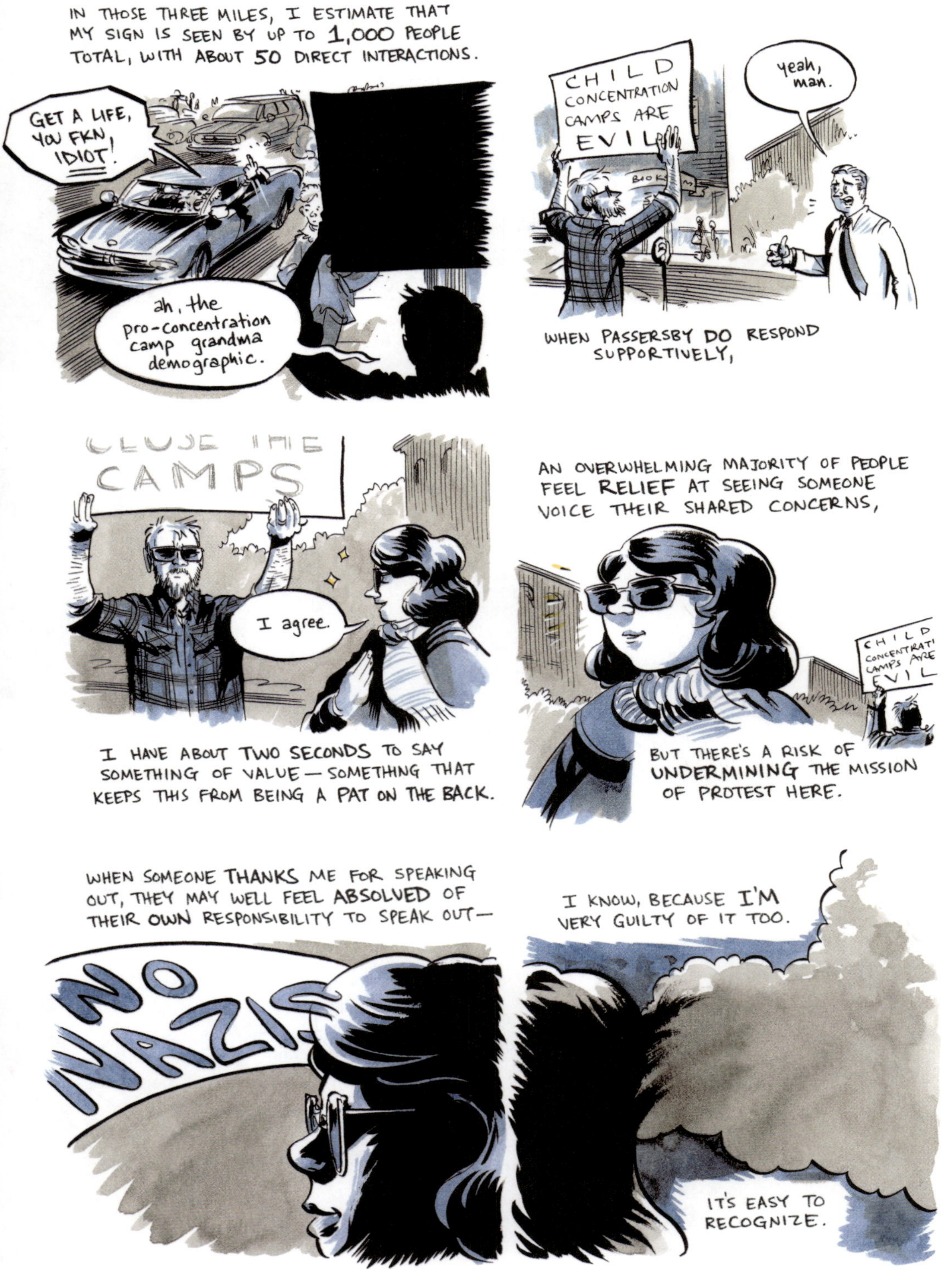
IN THOSE THREE MILES, I ESTIMATE THAT MY SIGN IS SEEN BY UP TO 1,000 PEOPLE TOTAL, WITH ABOUT 50 DIRECT INTERACTIONS.
GET A LIFE, YOU FKN IDIOT!
[redacted]
ah, the pro-concentration camp grandma demographic.
CHILD CONCENTRATION CAMPS ARE EVIL
yeah, man.
WHEN PASSERSBY DO RESPOND SUPPORTIVELY,
CAMPS
I agree.
I HAVE ABOUT TWO SECONDS TO SAY SOMETHING OF VALUE—SOMETHING THAT KEEPS THIS FROM BEING A PAT ON THE BACK.
AN OVERWHELMING MAJORITY OF PEOPLE FEEL RELIEF AT SEEING SOMEONE VOICE THEIR SHARED CONCERNS,
CHILD CONCENTRATION CAMPS ARE EVIL
BUT THERE'S A RISK OF UNDERMINING THE MISSION OF PROTEST HERE.
WHEN SOMEONE THANKS ME FOR SPEAKING OUT, THEY MAY WELL FEEL ABSOLVED OF THEIR OWN RESPONSIBILITY TO SPEAK OUT—
NO NAZIS
I KNOW, BECAUSE I'M VERY GUILTY OF IT TOO.
IT'S EASY TO RECOGNIZE.

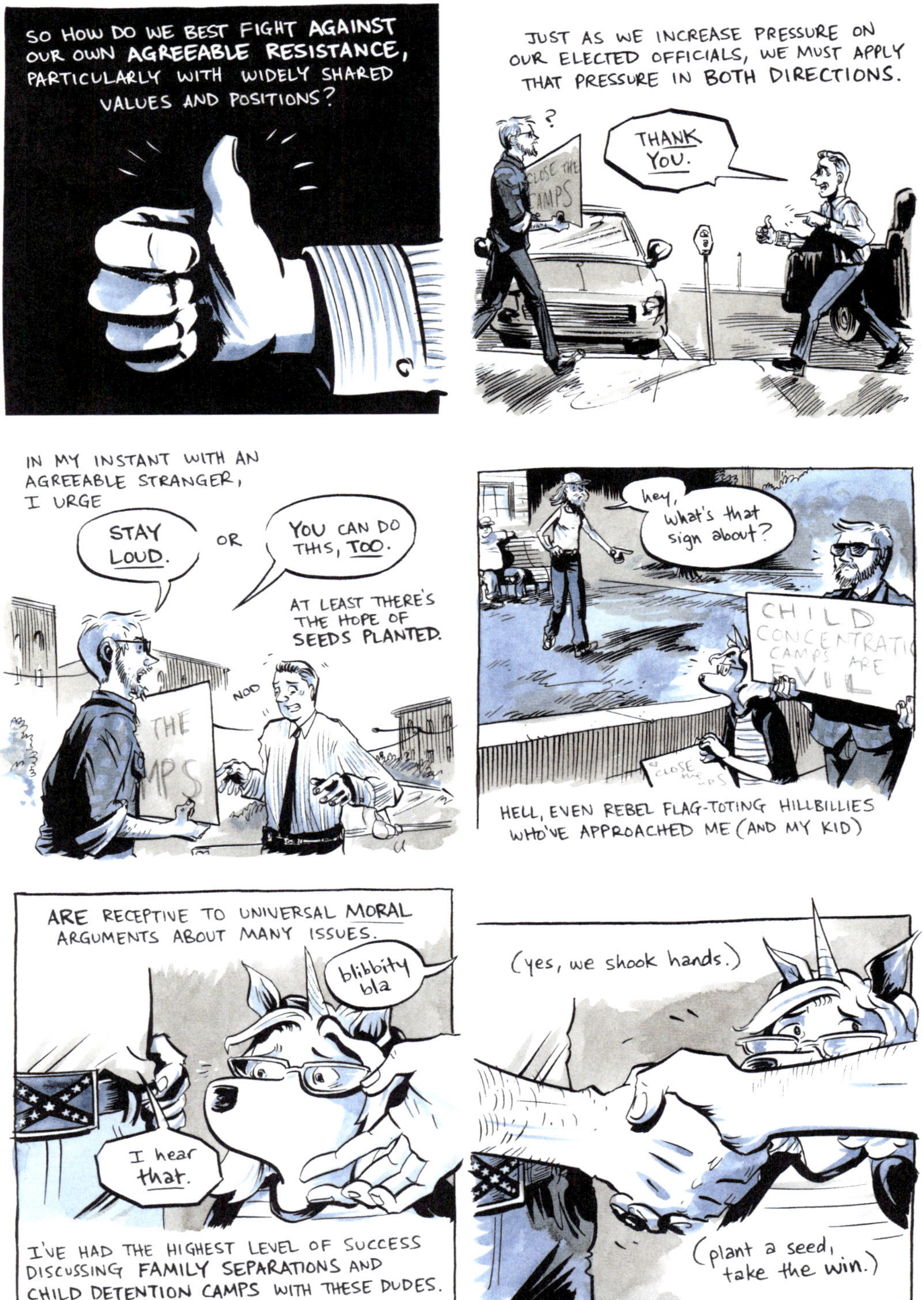

SO HOW DO WE BEST FIGHT AGAINST OUR OWN AGREEABLE RESISTANCE, PARTICULARLY WITH WIDELY SHARED VALUES AND POSITIONS?
JUST AS WE INCREASE PRESSURE ON OUR ELECTED OFFICIALS, WE MUST APPLY THAT PRESSURE IN BOTH DIRECTIONS.
?
CLOSE THE CAMPS
THANK YOU.
IN MY INSTANT WITH AN AGREEABLE STRANGER, I URGE
STAY LOUD.
OR
YOU CAN DO THIS, TOO.
AT LEAST THERE'S THE HOPE OF SEEDS PLANTED.
NOD
hey, what's that sign about?
CHILD CONCENTRATIO CAMPS ARE EVIL
HELL, EVEN REBEL FLAG-TOTING HILLBILLIES WHO'VE APPROACHED ME (AND MY KID)
ARE RECEPTIVE TO UNIVERSAL MORAL ARGUMENTS ABOUT MANY ISSUES.
blibbity bla
I hear that.
I'VE HAD THE HIGHEST LEVEL OF SUCCESS DISCUSSING FAMILY SEPARATIONS AND CHILD DETENTION CAMPS WITH THESE DUDES.
(yes, we shook hands.)
(plant a seed, take the win.)

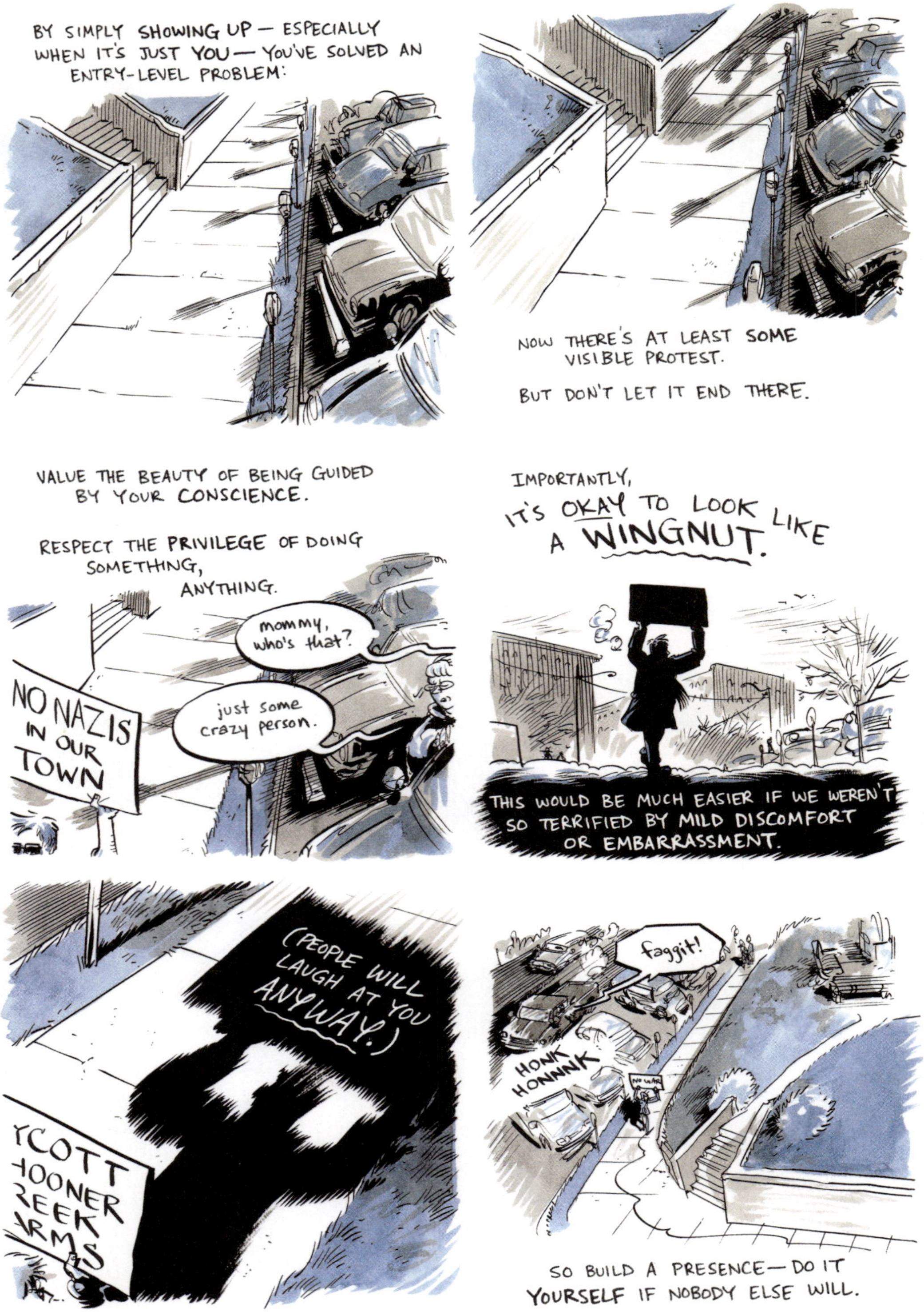
BY SIMPLY SHOWING UP — ESPECIALLY WHEN IT'S JUST YOU — YOU'VE SOLVED AN ENTRY-LEVEL PROBLEM:
NOW THERE'S AT LEAST SOME VISIBLE PROTEST.
BUT DON'T LET IT END THERE.
VALUE THE BEAUTY OF BEING GUIDED BY YOUR CONSCIENCE.
RESPECT THE PRIVILEGE OF DOING SOMETHING, ANYTHING.
NO NAZIS IN OUR TOWN
mommy, who's that?
just some crazy person.
IMPORTANTLY, IT'S OKAY TO LOOK LIKE A WINGNUT.
THIS WOULD BE MUCH EASIER IF WE WEREN'T SO TERRIFIED BY MILD DISCOMFORT OR EMBARRASSMENT.
(PEOPLE WILL LAUGH AT YOU ANYWAY.)
COTT
OONER
REEK
RMS
faggit!
HONK HONNNK
NO WAR
SO BUILD A PRESENCE — DO IT YOURSELF IF NOBODY ELSE WILL.

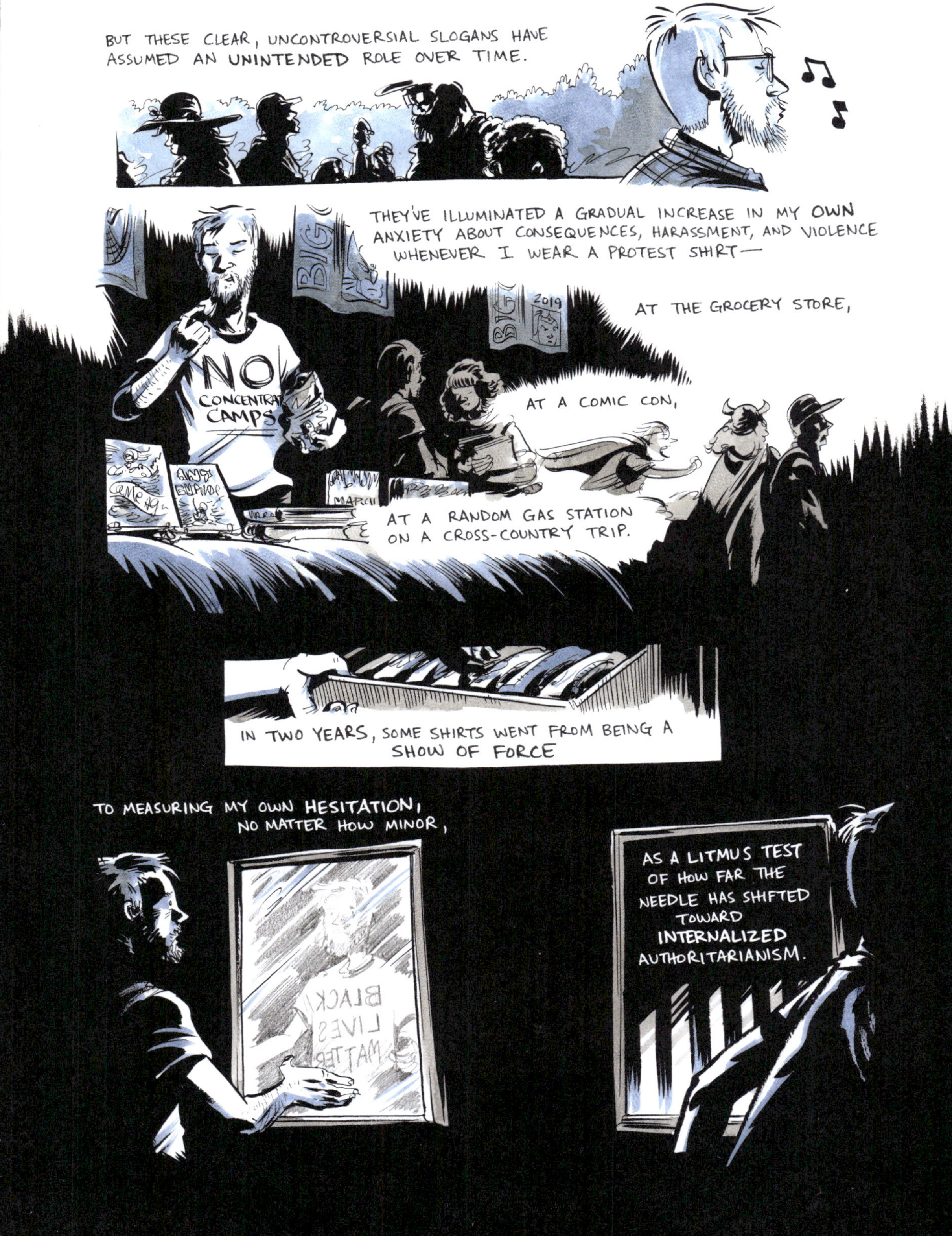
BUT THESE CLEAR, UNCONTROVERSIAL SLOGANS HAVE ASSUMED AN UNINTENDED ROLE OVER TIME.
THEY'VE ILLUMINATED A GRADUAL INCREASE IN MY OWN ANXIETY ABOUT CONSEQUENCES, HARASSMENT, AND VIOLENCE WHENEVER I WEAR A PROTEST SHIRT—
AT THE GROCERY STORE,
NO CONCENTRATION CAMPS
AT A COMIC CON,
AT A RANDOM GAS STATION ON A CROSS-COUNTRY TRIP.
IN TWO YEARS, SOME SHIRTS WENT FROM BEING A SHOW OF FORCE
TO MEASURING MY OWN HESITATION, NO MATTER HOW MINOR,
BLACK LIVES MATTER
AS A LITMUS TEST OF HOW FAR THE NEEDLE HAS SHIFTED TOWARD INTERNALIZED AUTHORITARIANISM.

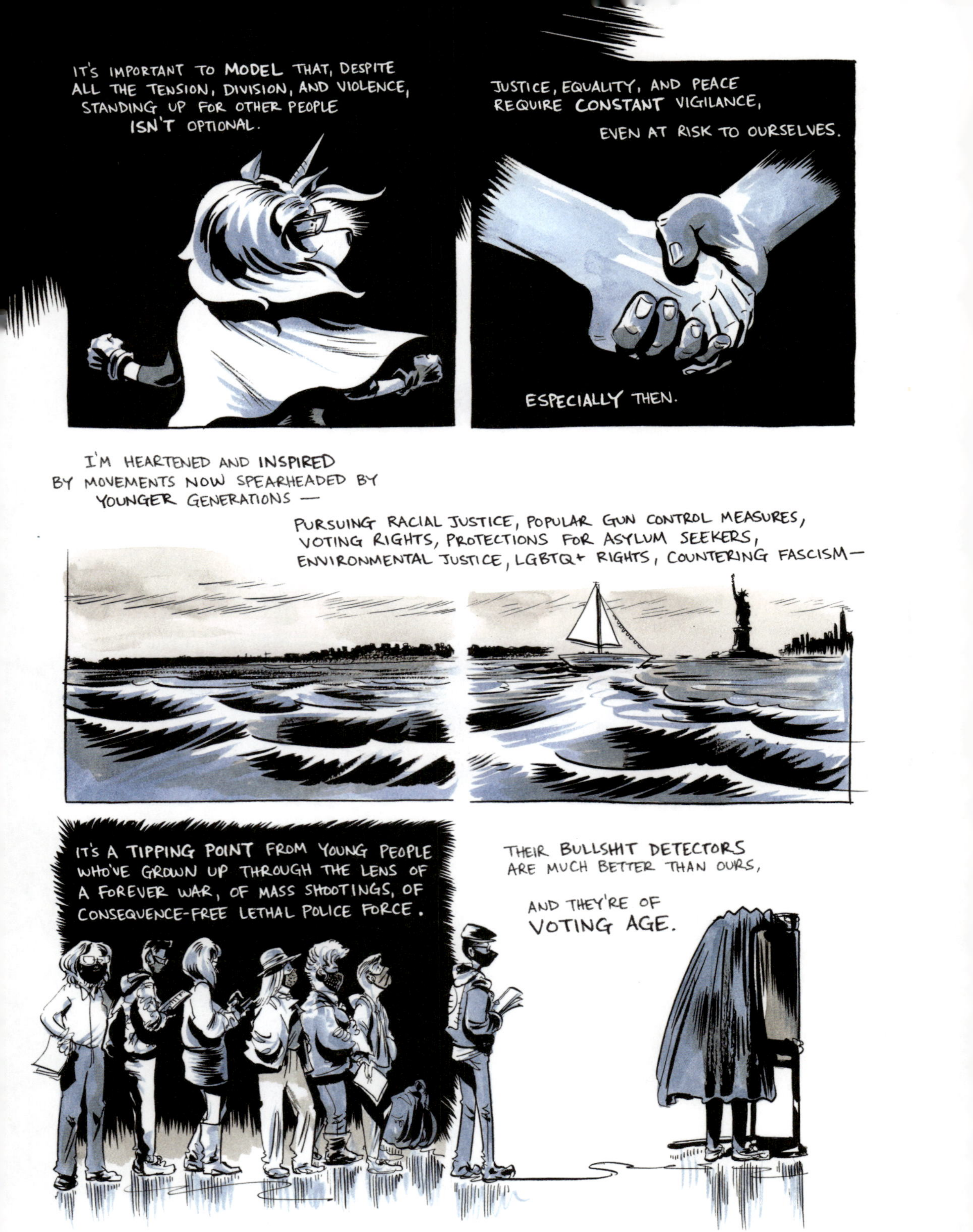
IT'S IMPORTANT TO MODEL THAT, DESPITE ALL THE TENSION, DIVISION, AND VIOLENCE, STANDING UP FOR OTHER PEOPLE ISN'T OPTIONAL.
JUSTICE, EQUALITY, AND PEACE REQUIRE CONSTANT VIGILANCE,
EVEN AT RISK TO OURSELVES.
ESPECIALLY THEN.
I'M HEARTENED AND INSPIRED BY MOVEMENTS NOW SPEARHEADED BY YOUNGER GENERATIONS —
PURSUING RACIAL JUSTICE, POPULAR GUN CONTROL MEASURES, VOTING RIGHTS, PROTECTIONS FOR ASYLUM SEEKERS, ENVIRONMENTAL JUSTICE, LGBTQ+ RIGHTS, COUNTERING FASCISM—
IT'S A TIPPING POINT FROM YOUNG PEOPLE WHO'VE GROWN UP THROUGH THE LENS OF A FOREVER WAR, OF MASS SHOOTINGS, OF CONSEQUENCE-FREE LETHAL POLICE FORCE.
THEIR BULLSHIT DETECTORS ARE MUCH BETTER THAN OURS,
AND THEY'RE OF VOTING AGE.

AS DOWN AS MY WIFE AND I LIKE TO THINK WE ARE,

THERE WILL COME A TIME SOON WHEN WE'RE RIGHTLY CALLED OUT BY OUR KIDS FOR BEING OUT OF TOUCH.

DINOSAURS, FALLING BEHIND OUR KIDS' GENERATION'S CONTINUATION OF THESE IDEAS, JUST AS WE DID.

AND IT'S COMFORTING TO KNOW THAT.

INCREASINGLY, IT'LL BE OUR TURN TO LISTEN AND FOLLOW.

SO WHAT LEVEL OF RISK CAN YOU HANDLE?

WHAT CONSEQUENCES WILL YOU ACCEPT, ACCORDING TO THAT RISK?

DON'T BEAT YOURSELF UP FOR KNOWING YOUR LIMITS.

OUR MOUNTING SOCIAL CHALLENGE:

TO **TRUST** AGAIN,

THAT WE'RE IN THIS **TOGETHER** WITH NEIGHBORS WE'VE NEVER MET,

THAT WE'RE **COVERING** EACH OTHER'S LIMITATIONS,

LEANING ON EACH OTHER'S **HUMANITY**.

IT IS **WE**, TOGETHER,

WHO WILL DETERMINE **WHAT KIND** OF SOCIETY
OUR KIDS GROW INTO, BY WHAT WE **EACH**

CHOOSE TO <u>DO</u>,
OR <u>NOT</u> DO.

A CHOICE IN EVERY
MOMENT.

SO **MAKE IT.**

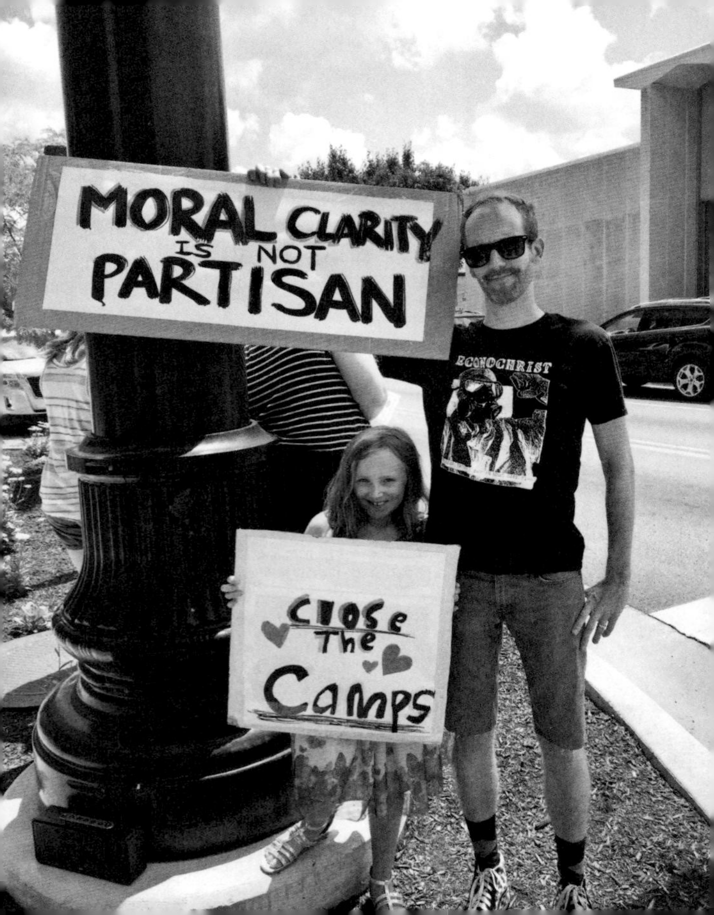
MORAL CLARITY IS NOT PARTISAN
ECONOCHRIST
Close The Camps

THANK YOU:

RACHEL, HARPER, EVERLY.

MY PARENTS AND PEYTON.
MY GRANDPARENTS AND ALL THE BAGGAGE THEY NEVER GOT AROUND TO UNPACKING.

CHARLOTTE, CHARLIE, CHARICE, MAYA, AND EVERYONE AT ABRAMS COMICARTS. CHARLIE OLSEN AND INKWELL MANAGEMENT.

VANESSA DAVIS, MARIA BUSTILLOS, TREVOR ALEXOPOULOS, AND ALL AT POPULA + BRICKHOUSE. MATT BORS, MATT LUBCHANSKY, SARAH MIRK, ELERI HARRIS, AND ALL AT THE NIB.

LEIGH WALTON, CHRIS STAROS, CHRIS ROSS, AND THE TOP SHELF FAMILY.

MIRIAM LIBICKI, MIKE DAWSON, LEELA CORMAN, DARRYL CUNNINGHAM, BEN PASSMORE, SARAH GLIDDEN, DERF BACKDERF, JOEL GILL, SACHA MARDOU.

ERIN TOBEY, CAITLIN McGURK, VAN JENSEN, ANDREW AYDIN, JOHN LEWIS (rest in peace ♡), FURY, SNAKE, KATY NEW, RACHEL HANCOCK, ALL AT BDLC, JONATHAN VANCE, TONIE JOY, ALL IN THE SOOPHIE FAMILY, ANDREA ZOLLO, DEREK FUDESCO, LAURA FLANDERS, ARTICULATE, JARED YATES SEXTON, PAT BLANCHFIELD, JONATHAN GRAY, VINTAGE PHOENIX COMICS, LISA LUCAS, SARAH KENDZIOR, ANDREA CHALUPA, TIMOTHY SNYDER, TINY HAWKS (ART + GUS), BRAD MELTZER, GENE YANG, CHRIS ELIOPOULOS, ELEANOR DAVIS, QIANA WHITTED, JAMES LOEWEN, JOAN DIDION, TA-NEHISI COATES, HASAN KWAME JEFFRIES, IBRAM X. KENDI, LARRY HAMA, WESLEY LOWERY, LAUREN DUCA.

SPECIAL GRATITUDE FOR EVERYONE INVOLVED WITH NO SPACE FOR HATE, BLACK LIVES MATTER BLOOMINGTON, AND EVERYONE SHOWING UP IN THE STREETS.

WE CAN DO THIS.
STAY LOUD, STICK TOGETHER.
♡

NATE POWELL is the first cartoonist ever to win the National Book Award. His work includes civil rights icon John Lewis's historic March trilogy, *Come Again*, *Two Dead*, *Any Empire*, *Swallow Me Whole*, *You Don't Say*, and *The Silence of Our Friends*.

Powell's work has also received the Robert F. Kennedy Book Award, three Eisner Awards, two Ignatz Awards, the Michael L. Printz Award, the Comic-Con International Inkpot Award, a Coretta Scott King Author Award, four YALSA Great Graphic Novels For Teens selections, the Walter Dean Myers Award, and is a two-time finalist for the *Los Angeles Times* Book Prize. He has discussed his work at the United Nations, on MSNBC's *The Rachel Maddow Show*, PBS, CNN, and Free Speech TV. Powell lives in Bloomington, Indiana.

Visit him online at: seemybrotherdance.org

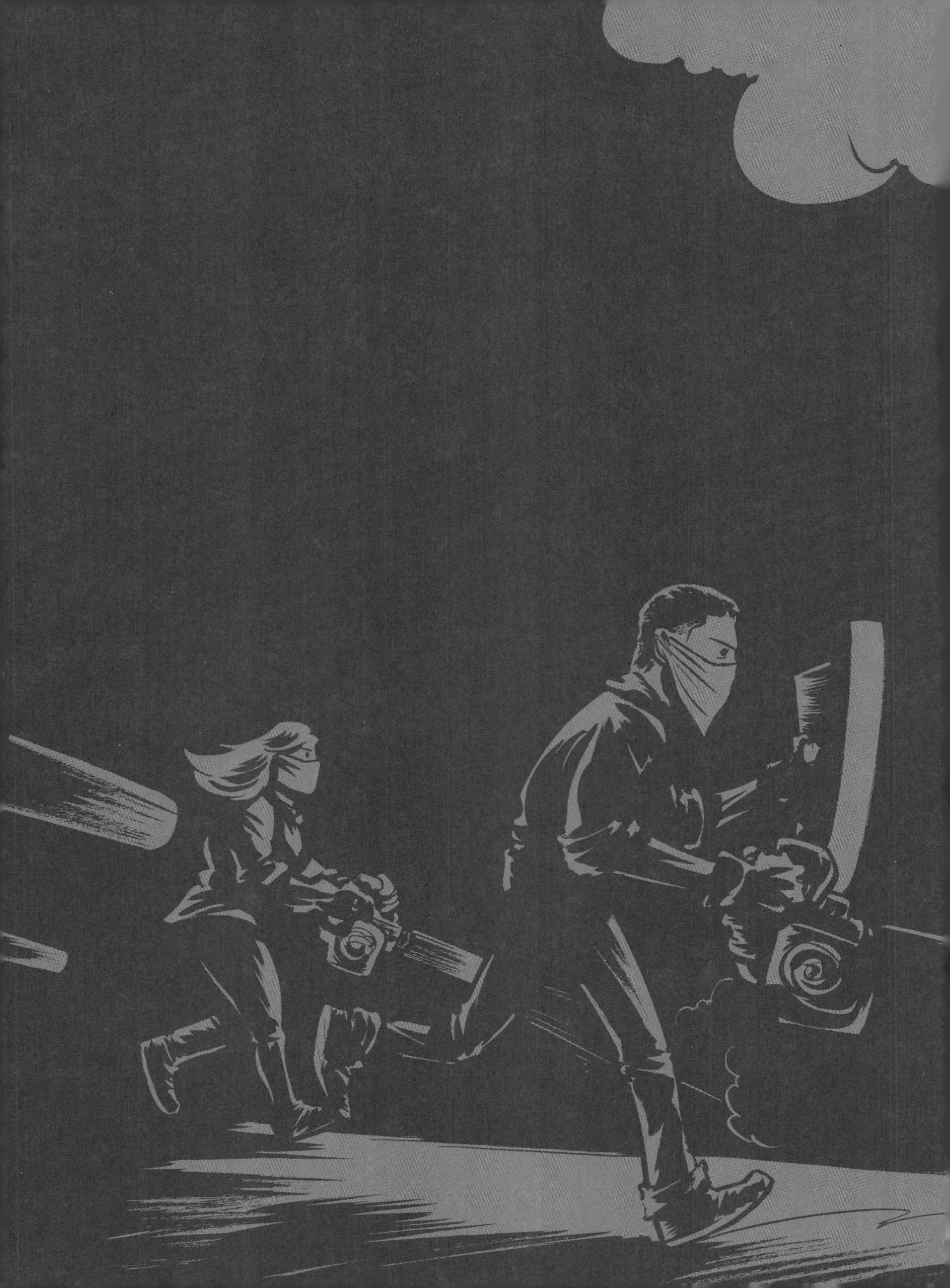